The Internet and Political Protest in Autocracies

Oxford Studies in Digital Politics

Series Editor: Andrew Chadwick, Professor of Political Communication in the Centre for Research in Communication and Culture and the Department of Social Sciences, Loughborough University

The Internet and Political Protest in Autocracies

NILS B. WEIDMANN

and

ESPEN GEELMUYDEN RØD

OXFORD
UNIVERSITY PRESS

OXFORD
UNIVERSITY PRESS

Oxford University Press is a department of the University of Oxford. It furthers
the University's objective of excellence in research, scholarship, and education
by publishing worldwide. Oxford is a registered trade mark of Oxford University
Press in the UK and certain other countries.

Published in the United States of America by Oxford University Press
198 Madison Avenue, New York, NY 10016, United States of America.

© Oxford University Press 2019

Library of Congress Cataloging-in-Publication Data
Names: Weidmann, Nils B., 1976– author. | Rød, Espen Geelmuyden, 1985– author.
Title: The Internet and political protest in autocracies /
Nils B. Weidmann and Espen Geelmuyden Rød.
Description: New York, NY : Oxford University Press, 2019. |
Series: Oxford studies in digital politics |
Includes bibliographical references and index. |
Identifiers: LCCN 2019017492 (print) | LCCN 2019018275 (ebook) |
ISBN 9780190918323 (Updf) | ISBN 9780190918330 (Epub) |
ISBN 9780190918316 (paperback) | ISBN 9780190918309 (hardcover)
Subjects: LCSH: Internet–Political aspects. | Information
technology–Political aspects. | Internet and activism. |
Protest movements. | Political persecution. | Authoritarianism. |
BISAC: POLITICAL SCIENCE / Government / Comparative. |
SOCIAL SCIENCE / General. | LANGUAGE ARTS & DISCIPLINES /
Communication Studies. Classification: LCC HM851 (ebook) |
LCC HM851 .W42596 2019 (print) | DDC 303.48/33–dc23
LC record available at https://lccn.loc.gov/2019017492

Paperback printed by Webcom, Inc., Canada
Hardback printed by Bridgeport National Bindery, Inc., United States of America

Meinem Großvater Martin.
—*NBW*

Til mine foreldre, Wenche og Kåre.
—*EGR*

Contents

Contents

Preface

This book is the product of more than five years of work, and we greatly benefited from the contributions by several people. We started back in 2012 to collect data on political protest, and Lukas Kawerau was part of this effort from the first day. As a self-trained programmer, he created the online coding tool for the Mass Mobilization in Autocracies Database (MMAD), which has now been used for more than five years and has greatly facilitated the work on the database. The coding of the MMAD was later coordinated by Sebastian Hellmeier, who also helped us prepare the first release of the data in 2018. Many people were involved in the creation of the MMAD: In Konstanz, our coders for version 1.0 of the database were Felicia Afriyie, Natacha Bastiat, Marius Bug, Sebastian Heinz, Philipp Hirsch, Theresa Küntzler, Philipp Lutscher, Johann Maier, Nora Schütze, Tinus Steidl, Jonas Stenger, Lea Maria Strassheim, and Johannes Willmann. Several countries in the MENA region were coded by a team at the Department of Political Science, University of Zurich (led by Fabrizio Gilardi and Dumitru Ciocan): Justus Bammelt, Julia Monn, Salimata Sophie Seck, Marwan Serag El Din, Ramona Villiger, and Moritz Wehrli.

Over the years, a large number of people have read and commented on earlier versions of the research presented in this book. The regular meetings of the *European Network of Conflict Research* and the retreats we held with Lars-Erik Cederman and Simon Hug's research groups in Zermatt, Davos, and on the Reichenau peninsula were opportunities for us to get feedback on the project. We also benefited greatly from workshops and seminars at NYU Abu Dhabi, the University of St. Gallen, the University of Geneva, University Pompeu Fabra, the University of Stuttgart, and Uppsala University. We would like to mention in particular Anita Gohdes, who provided detailed and constructive comments on the project on several occasions. Once we developed a rough idea for the book, the help and guidance we received from series editor Andrew Chadwick and Angela Chnapko of Oxford University Press were invaluable to us. Elin Arbin performed a thorough editing of the final manuscript and greatly improved the quality of the text. Lukas Kawerau (again) helped us polish some of the figures for print.

We are extremely grateful to all these people for their contributions and their encouragement along the way. This project was only made possible by a Sofja Kovalevskaja Award for Nils Weidmann from the Alexander von Humboldt Foundation, which was used to fund the research and the creation of the book (2012–2018). Espen gratefully acknowledges funding from the European Research Council (ERC) under the European Union's Horizon 2020 program (grant agreement no. 694640). Finally, we want to thank our families for bearing with us during this project and for sharing the excitement but also the frustration we oftentimes experienced. Espen would like to extend a special thanks to Bine for listening patiently and discussing various theoretical and methodological challenges related to this book over the last years.

1

Introduction

In recent years, a number of dictators have found themselves out of a job as a result of popular uprisings. Zine El Abidine Ben Ali of Tunisia, Hosni Mubarak of Egypt, and Ali Abdullah Saleh of Yemen can all testify to the tremendous political pressure exerted by anti-regime protests. In the aftermath of the Arab Spring, many observers have argued that new Information and Communication Technologies (ICTs), notably the Internet, played a key role in mobilizing the political protests. Egypt reportedly experienced a "Facebook revolution" and Syria a "YouTube uprising" (Khamis, Gold and Vaughn, 2012). The notion that new communication technology promotes peace and democracy is not new, going back at least to the invention of the printing press in the fifteenth century, through to the introduction of telegraph and the mass media revolution (Diamond, 2010).

While the idea that the Internet is a "liberation technology" has existed since its commercialization in the 1990s, one could argue that the Arab Spring popularized the assumption that ICTs ease mobilization in authoritarian regimes by increasing the flow of information and reducing organizational costs. This optimism was reflected in Hillary Clinton's (2010) "Remarks on Internet Freedom," where she claimed that despite increasing government control of the Internet, "viral videos and blog posts are becoming the samizdat[1] of our day." Similarly, in 2011 *Time* magazine named Wael Ghonim, an Internet activist who used Facebook to mobilize people for protest during the Arab Spring, one of the 100 most influential people in the world, because "he quickly grasped that social media, notably Facebook, were emerging as the most powerful communication tools to mobilize and develop ideas" (El-Baradei, 2011b).

At first glance, the assumption that the Internet can lead to political change—particularly in autocracies—is certainly plausible. In authoritarian regimes, from

1

Russia under Vladimir Putin and Zimbabwe under Robert Mugabe to China under Xi Jinping, civil liberties are usually severely restricted, which significantly limits political participation among the general public. Hence, open political dissent in the form of mass protest is not a regular occurrence in dictatorships, and typically happens much less frequently than in democracies. For example, according to the Cross-National Time-Series dataset (Banks, 2011), in 2010 there were twenty-six protest incidents in democratic regimes compared to only nine in autocracies, which means the average rate of protest in democracies was almost twice as high as that of autocratic regimes (0.31 vs. 0.17). However, when mass protest does occur under autocratic rule, it can have much more severe consequences. In fact, research has shown that mass uprisings is a common way dictatorships end (Geddes, Wright and Frantz, 2018), and that protests are one of the most important triggers of transitions from autocratic to democratic rule (Rød, Knutsen and Hegre, 2017). Thus, if information communicated over the Internet makes people more critical of autocratic rulers and allows opposition activists to mobilize political protests, the introduction and expansion of this technology may have far-reaching political consequences. In fact, if the technology leads to increased political protests, it can indirectly contribute to political reforms and regime transitions, but also to the escalation of political violence and the outbreak of civil war.

However, the "liberation technology" perspective is not void of criticism. Broadly publicized events such as Edward Snowden's revelations about large-scale government interference in digital communication and the recent scandal about the consulting firm Cambridge Analytica have prompted scholars and pundits to focus increasingly on the pernicious use of communication technology. Particularly in autocratic environments, digital communication channels provide new and powerful opportunities for government propaganda and surveillance (Morozov, 2011; Rød and Weidmann, 2015). Gunitsky (2015, p. 46), for example, describes how the Bahraini government mobilized people to identify protesters by posting pictures on Facebook: "The pictures were then marked off with a red checkmark as individuals were identified and arrested." Not surprisingly, it was soon recognized that the Internet is neither inherently good nor bad, and that it sometimes can be used as "liberation technology," while serving as "repression technology" in other cases (Tucker et al., 2017).

Now that we know that Internet technology sometimes benefits political leaders and sometimes benefits activists, how can we advance the scientific debate about the impact of ICT on political mobilization? In order to do so, there are a number of challenges we need to overcome. First, as discussed, we should not expect the effects of communication technology to be deterministic, where technology either drives popular mobilization against autocracy or allows authoritarian regimes to control and repress the population (Deibert and Ro-hozinski, 2010; Shirky, 2011). Thus, one of the main challenges for researchers studying the political impacts of information technology is to identify the conditions under which this technology helps protesters mobilize vs. when it benefits autocratic governments in their repressive efforts. Gaining insight on this topic requires comprehensive theoretical development as well as innovative empirical work.

A second challenge in the current literature on Internet and protest is the lack of attention given to traditional means of control in autocratic regimes. Even if modern communication technology can potentially benefit opposition activists, autocratic governments have a number of means available to counter threats to their rule. In fact, the prevention of popular mobilization is a frequent and ongoing challenge for leaders such as Kim Jong-un, Muammar Gaddafi, and Alexander Lukashenko (Svolik, 2012). Unlike in democratic systems, autocratic governments have few constraints through political institutions, which allows them to fend off political opposition by legislative and judicial means, and oftentimes also violent repression. These conventional means of autocratic politics continue to be used in the digital age. Hence, if we study the effect of technology on mobilization, we need to factor traditional means of repression in dictatorships into the equation. Coercion and violence are pervasive in autocracies and enable autocratic leaders to counter the new threats to their rule arising from technological development.

A third challenge is how to determine whether there is a causal effect of Internet technology. Was information communicated via digital channels really responsible for triggering protest? In other words, if protesters had not had access to the Internet, would protest have failed to emerge? Much work in the current literature on the Internet and protest is unable to answer this question, since the empirical focus is exclusively on cases where protests actually occurred (Walgrave et al., 2011; Hussain and Howard, 2013; Breuer, Landman and Farquhar, 2015; Theocharis et al., 2015). Thus, while this research allows us to study the use of ICT by protesters during episodes of contention, it cannot tell us whether this technology was indeed causal for protest emergence in the first place. As Lynch (2011, p. 302) concludes in his analysis of the Arab Spring, "[w]hile protestors effectively used social media in their struggles, it is surprisingly difficult to demonstrate rigorously that these new media directly caused any of the outcomes with which they have been associated."

The fourth and final challenge—which is by no means specific to the topic of this book and applies to much work in the social sciences—is the tension between rich and detailed micro-level research and aggregated macro-level studies. The former typically analyze protests in particular cases, such as the protests in Cairo in 2011 (Tufekci and Wilson, 2012; Hassanpour, 2014), while the latter compare countries with respect to their respective ICT penetration and protest frequency (Brancati, 2014; Ruijgrok, 2017; Stein, 2017). Case analyses can tell us much about the dynamics of particular protests but are difficult to generalize to other contexts. It is often unclear whether a particular observed effect of technology applies elsewhere in a similar fashion. Comparative macro-level studies are much more powerful in this regard, but are at the same time lacking when it comes to the validity of their findings. For example, if we find that countries with high rates of Internet penetration exhibit higher rates of protest, it is difficult to conclude that Internet-based communication is responsible for this, since we do not know whether the activists who organized the protests actually had Internet access.

In summary, the four challenges we have presented suggest two general directions in which we need to advance the current literature on communication technology and protest: We need better theory to understand if and how the Internet contributes to political mobilization, and also determine the circumstances under which it does the opposite and prevents protest. At the same time, however, we need to improve the empirical analysis of how the Internet affects popular mobilization, to provide us with more reliable and nuanced insights into the dynamics of protest and the potential digital drivers behind it. This book does both: It presents a theoretical framework to understand better how digital communication technology affects protest, and introduces new data and analysis to examine this relationship empirically.

Main Argument of the Book

The main argument we make in this book is based on the assertion that the relationship between Internet technology and protest in autocracies is fundamentally multifaceted. While much of the literature has focused on protest as a whole, we argue that the temporal dynamics of protest has been neglected. More precisely, our argument is that *starting* a protest is a challenge that is different from *sustaining* ongoing popular mobilization. We claim that while Internet technology is an important resource for mobilization, it is not particularly powerful in the beginning. However, once narratives, pictures, and videos about ongoing unrest are widely circulated online, the technology can make a big difference.

Following this logic, we introduce a more nuanced treatment of political protest by differentiating between the different phases of protest, both in the theoretical framework and in our empirical analysis. Essentially, the central claim in this book is that Internet technology affects protest in important ways, but that its effect varies depending on the stage of the protest. In line with most of the relevant literature, our initial focus is on the emergence of protest. In other words, we investigate whether higher Internet penetration increases the occurrence of public mobilization against the government. In explaining how the Internet affects political mobilization in autocracies, we distinguish between long-term and short-term effects. In autocracies, most infrastructure—and telecommunication networks in particular—is introduced and maintained by governmental actors, and we therefore assume that governments generally maintain a high level of control over the Internet. In Belarus, for example, Internet access is provided through the national telecommunications provider Beltelecom, which belongs entirely to the government (Crabtree and Weidmann, 2018). This means that the government controls not only who can obtain access to the Internet, but also to some extent the content that can be communicated over digital channels. Hence, in the long term, autocratic governments will use this technology in their favor to keep the level of dissent low. This is why, counter to optimistic beliefs in the Internet's power for political transformation, we argue that the Internet should reduce levels of mobilization and that well-connected places should have fewer instances of protest.

At the same time, however, starting a protest involves different challenges for the people involved compared to situations where protest has just recently occurred. Hence, unlike much of the existing literature, our theoretical framework is not narrowly focused on the occurrence of new protest, but also covers the persistence of protest over time and its spatial diffusion to other cities in the same country. In these situations, a short-term effect of Internet technology can kick in. Information about ongoing protest can spread quickly over digital channels, which is difficult for governments to stop or contain. Consider the example of the activist Wael Ghonim, who was one of the leading figures in the Arab Spring protests in Egypt. One of his big contributions to the uprising against Mubarak was to inspire increased protest participation by publishing material about ongoing unrest on Facebook, which supposedly led to sustained protest in Cairo. As discussed, governments may well enjoy long-term control over Internet communications, but have only limited capabilities to respond quickly and swiftly to ongoing mobilization and its repercussions in the digital realm. For that reason, we expect Internet technology to strengthen and sustain ongoing protest, making it last longer and spread to other locations.

The distinction between the different phases of protest and the different effects the Internet can have in each of them is central to our book. By arguing that the Internet reduces the occurrence of protest in general, but fosters ongoing protest efforts once they have started, we push the debate about ICT and political mobilization to a new level. Our book not only highlights that different stages of protest entail different challenges for opposition activists, but also demonstrates there is no simple answer to the question of whether the Internet contributes to political "liberation" or rather fuels repression. In fact, the book shows that both "cyber-optimists"—people regarding digital communication technology as politically transformative—and "cyber-pessimists"—people believing that ICT empowers malicious political leaders—are right: It simply depends on the stage of the political protest we are looking at.

Another important theoretical consideration is the fact that the emergence of protest and the influence that digital technology exerts over it occur in the context of authoritarian political systems. A key omission in the past literature on ICT and autocratic politics is the lack of attention to how the use of digital technology by governments relates to other, more conventional means of political control that these governments have at their disposal. Unlike their democratic counterparts, autocratic governments are not bound by strong institutions, which is why they can resort to repressive and sometimes violent ways to fend off political opposition. When we consider the impact of digital technology on political mobilization, we need to do so taking into account how these modern forms of political influence interact with existing means of autocratic control.

Our distinction between short- and long-term effects of governmental influence helps us understand how control of digital technology operates together with conventional means of autocratic repression. As we have argued, the asymmetrically high level of control over the Internet allows autocratic governments to keep levels of dissent low in the long run, which reduces the frequency of popular protest. This advantage means that other, more traditional tactics of autocratic control may no longer be as important as they were previously. One of the most important traditional means to prevent anti-regime mobilization are restrictions of the freedom of association; in some autocratic countries such as China and Saudi Arabia, it is illegal to form political parties or other political organizations. Alternatively, prior registration and approval by the government is required for new associations, which gives the government full control over the emergence of formal organizations.

In particular in recent years, however, many autocracies have loosened these restrictions. This pattern is perhaps particularly apparent in many of the former one-party states in Africa, but the post–Cold War era has seen a global pattern of political liberalization. Why? Our theoretical argument suggests that one of the reasons for this could be that autocratic governments can increasingly rely on modern, digital tools to influence and control the population. In other words, modern ICT can *substitute* traditional repressive tactics that autocratic governments have relied on in the past. From this argument, we expect that the protest-reducing effect of the Internet is particularly pronounced in those autocracies that rely to a lesser extent on traditional means of repression. In other words, we argue that there is a shift in repressive tactics from conventional to digital ones, which is one of the questions we pursue in our empirical analysis.

However, since liberalization inevitably enables the political organization of opposition, it can amplify the continuation of protest when combined with Internet technology. Hence, the distinction among phases of protest also helps us gain theoretical traction when considering how the authoritarian context shapes the political effects of ICT.

While governmental influence over the Internet gives autocratic leaders an advantage in the long run, how does autocratic repression affect the short-term dynamics of ongoing protest? As we have argued, the introduction of fast and pervasive digital communication has made it more difficult for leaders to contain the further escalation of protest once it has started, and political protest in the digital age may be more likely to persist and grow. Yet, as the Internet helps protesters keep popular mobilization high, it can also quickly spread news about government repression and violence. Here, the Internet can serve as an amplifier of a violent governmental response to political opposition; once protesters know that autocratic leaders are determined to crush dissent, they may be discouraged from joining an ongoing protest.

Summarizing our argument about the interrelationship between digital communication technology and conventional means of repression, there are long- and short-term effects. In the long run, the advent of digital communication technology has given autocratic leaders new ways to manipulate and control the population, which has reduced the need for traditional and sometimes costly repressive tactics. Still, this does not mean that these tactics are about to disappear. In fact, violent responses to political protest continue to occur regularly, and police interference with anti-regime protests remains the norm rather than the exception. In these instances, in the short run, the Internet can exacerbate the protest-dampening effect of government violence by signaling to potential protesters that participation carries significant risks.

New Data and Analysis to Study the Internet and Protest

Testing the main argument of the book while attempting to resolve the methodological challenges we have identified requires us to devise a new research design for the study of digital communication technology and its impact on political protest. The approach we present in this book is distinctive in a number of ways.

A DISAGGREGATED, CROSS-NATIONAL RESEARCH DESIGN

As we have described, the empirical study of political protest has almost exclusively relied on macro-level comparisons of different countries, or on detailed micro-level studies of individual cases. In the analyses we present in this book, we aim to combine the strengths of both approaches. To do so, we employ a disaggregated research design in which we study the relationship between Internet technology and protest at the level of individual cities, but at the same time across a large sample of autocratic countries. Specifically, we analyze how a city's Internet penetration relates to its level of protest activity. This design helps us overcome several limitations of existing work. Most important, national-level studies typically compare aggregate numbers of Internet users in different countries with the countries' overall levels of protest. By drawing exclusively on national-level data and indicators, these studies cannot ascertain whether protest actually occurs in areas of particularly high or low Internet coverage.

In contrast, our empirical analysis includes fine-grained data on Internet penetration and political protest at the level of cities, which allows us to relate local levels of ICT coverage to local levels of protest—if the Internet really affects people's motives and opportunities to take to the streets, this level of analytical resolution should be much better suited to capture this effect. In particular, it allows us to study different stages of protest, which is a key innovation of our main argument. Separating protest occurrence from protest persistence and diffusion gives us better theoretical leverage, but at the same time requires the use of data and methods that can capture these dynamics. This is what we are able to do by using disaggregated data and a multi-level statistical model to analyze them.

This fine-grained resolution is relevant not only to study how access to the Internet is related to political mobilization, but also to find out how conventional, violent means of government repression interfere with this process. As we have argued in the previous section, the Internet can serve to disseminate information about a violent governmental response to protest, thus sending a signal to potential protesters that can deter them from taking action. The highly dynamic process of opposition activism and government responses is extremely difficult to observe in a macro-level analysis. In our approach, however, we can easily distinguish protest that was violently repressed from those instances that were not, and test how the Internet contributes to a potentially deterring effect of violent repression on future protest. We can also study whether this signaling effect travels from one city to another; in other words, whether repression in one city deters protest elsewhere.

At the same time, it is of key importance that we implement our fine-grained city-level analysis not just for a single case, but across a set of more than sixty autocracies. This addresses the shortcomings of existing single-case analyses, which make it difficult to draw conclusions that go beyond the countries or protest episodes that were examined. The effects of digital technology on political mobilization we estimate in our analysis, in contrast, are averages across a large sample of countries, and therefore reflect insights from many different autocracies. Moreover, the inclusion of many different countries is a key feature that allows us to analyze the interrelationship of digital mobilization and conventional means of autocratic repression. As we have argued, new communication technology can provide autocratic governments with new opportunities for monitoring and influencing their citizens, which could reduce their need to rely on conventional repressive methods. To study this relationship empirically, we compare the effect of the Internet across autocratic regimes that differ with respect to the restrictions they impose on the freedom of association. In our cross-national analysis, we therefore analyze how the Internet's effect on protest varies depending on the freedom of association (or rather, the lack thereof) in a given country, something that is greatly facilitated by the multi-level research framework we employ.

A NEW DATABASE OF POLITICAL PROTEST IN AUTOCRACIES

The cross-national, disaggregated analysis we present in this book obviously requires data on the occurrence of political protest. We need data that are broad in coverage, but at the same sufficiently fine-grained to capture political protest at the level of individual cities. For that reason, we created a new database on protest in autocracies, the Mass Mobilization in Autocracies Database (MMAD). In the first version of the MMAD, which is the one used for this book, the database lists more than 14,000 incidents of political protest across a set of more than sixty autocratic countries, covering the period 2003–2012. The coding of these incidents is based on more than 26,000 reports. Our database is regularly updated to include more recent years; for more details on updates and data releases, see https://mmadatabase.org. Following recent conventions in the development of event data, it records each incident with the precise date and the location (city) where it occurred. In addition, the database provides several useful variables for each protest event that are necessary for our analysis, but also for many other empirical studies on protest in autocracies. For example, we code the protest issue and the involved actors, as well as the number of participants. The database also includes information on whether violence was used by the protest participants or the government, the latter allowing us to analyze the deterring effect of violent repression communicated over the Internet.

Similar to many efforts in this field of study, the database is coded from news reports. Combining automatic preselection of source material based on machine learning methods with a final coding step performed by humans, we are able to cover considerable amounts of source material, but at the same time achieve a high quality of the final dataset. Nevertheless, there are known limitations of media-based event data, some of which we try to address with a novel coding approach for our database. In contrast to other event coding projects, the MMAD provides users not only with information about the final list of protest events, but also about the individual news reports that constitute the basis for the coding of a given protest event. This way, we can address some of the limitations of media-based event datasets, but also make the coding of the final events more transparent and replicable.

NEW MICRO-LEVEL DATA ON INTERNET PENETRATION AND DEVELOPMENT

The need for fine-grained data at the local level does not only apply to the outcome we study (protest), but also to the degree of Internet penetration and other variables we include in our analysis. Hence, the book introduces different new types of measurement that allow us to compute these variables. Most important, our research design necessitates the use of city-level Internet penetration estimates. While national-level estimates can be obtained from different organizations such as the International Telecommunications Union, these numbers are not suitable for our analysis. Since there are oftentimes considerable differences in the extent to which different regions in a country have access to the Internet, we need subnational estimates for the degree of Internet penetration at the level of cities. This is why we resort to a different measurement method, developed in collaboration with computer scientists: By observing the amount of Internet traffic that originates from particular places, we can identify those cities in our sample that have a large population of Internet users, that is, high Internet penetration. This estimation based on data traffic flows is one of the first applications of so-called network measurement data in the social sciences.

We use yet another estimation approach to calculate the level of development for the cities in our sample. This information is key for our analysis, since development can affect both the degree of ICT penetration, but also the emergence of political unrest. Again, we face a major problem of data availability, since city-level estimates of economic development are not available from conventional sources. Therefore, we make use of remote sensing techniques, which rely on satellite observations of the earth. In particular, existing research has shown that night light emissions can serve as a way to approximate the level of development, not just at the level of entire countries, but also at local levels such as cities or villages. Overall, the availability of new and fine-grained data makes it possible for this book to employ a multi-level analysis that examines the relationship of ICT and political protest at unprecedented levels of detail and from new angles.

An Interdisciplinary Perspective

A book with a focus like ours is a truly interdisciplinary undertaking. We approach our research question mainly from a political science perspective, rooted in the field of comparative authoritarianism. This field of research is concerned with autocratic regimes and their strategies for gaining and consolidating power, both within the ruling elite and between the regime and its citizens. Another political science field that is closely related to this book deals with transitions from autocracy to democracy and the particular conditions that facilitate or prevent it. The topic also intersects with a number of other disciplines in the social sciences and beyond. The study of social movements and political protest has traditionally been the domain of (political) sociologists, who have made few attempts to apply their insights beyond democratic countries, however. Still, classic theories of resource mobilization and political opportunity structures are highly relevant for our research question. Due to the book's partial focus on violent repression, we also draw on literature on political conflict and violence, in particular the protest-repression dynamics between regimes and opposition activists. Finally, the field that has produced most of the work on the Internet and its political effects is (political) communication studies. Here, we find a large amount of research illustrating how digital channels have been used by protesters to mobilize, but also how governments have become more skilled in monitoring citizens, censoring content, and spreading political propaganda via digital means. All of these fields of research are highly relevant for the theoretical part of this book. Methodologically, we rely on recent progress in the development and processing of spatial data, which traditionally has been the domain of computational geography and related disciplines. We further benefit from expertise in computer science, particularly the field of communication networks, to better understand how the Internet works and how we can use data collected online to derive estimates of local Internet penetration for the cities in our sample.

Plan of the Book

We start our analysis of the Internet and political protest with an overview of the relevant literature in Chapter 2. Using the familiar triad of motives, mobilization, and opportunities to structure our review, we integrate classic theories of protest mobilization with innovations in communication introduced by the Internet. Our review centers on the opposition movements as the crucial actors that can benefit from new ICTs, even though governments can also use this technology against them. Our main theoretical framework in Chapter 3 builds on this review, but changes the focus to governments. We argue that governments enjoy a disproportionate level of control over the Internet compared to the general public. This gives them a political advantage in the long run, but limits their power to contain the short-term escalation of political mobilization among protesters. This distinction requires us to study three different protest phases: occurrence (onset), continuation (persistence), and spread to new locations (spatial diffusion).

Chapter 4 introduces one of the main data sources for this book, the new Mass Mobilization in Autocracies Database (MMAD) of protest events. We review existing event coding approaches and explain the hybrid coding approach used for the MMAD, which combines computer-based text classification and human coding. Most important, the chapter lays out our report-level coding approach, which opens up a number of new research opportunities the data can be used for. In Chapter 5, we develop a research design that allows us to test the relationship between Internet penetration and anti-regime protest at the local level. A core part of our empirical strategy is the use of multi-level regression models that are able to incorporate the nested structure of our data (cities located in different countries). They can tell us about the local effect of Internet penetration on protest at the city level, but also how this effect varies across different national contexts.

The following four chapters present the core empirical contributions of this book. In Chapter 6, we investigate how Internet penetration affects the occurrence of protest in general. Chapter 7 narrows the analysis down to cities that have experienced protest before and examines whether Internet penetration can lead to renewed protest at these locations (persistence of protest). Chapter 8 is closely related to the previous one and examines how the Internet contributes to the spread of protest to other cities in the same country (spatial diffusion). Finally, Chapter 9 studies variation in the Internet's effect on protest occurrence, persistence, and diffusion across different national contexts. In particular, we examine how the political effects of communication technology interact with existing, traditional means of autocratic control, namely restrictions on the freedom of association. In the conclusion in Chapter 10, we summarize the insights of our research and discuss implications for policy.

2

Political Mobilization in Autocracies in the Digital Age

We started the introductory chapter by describing the debate between scholars believing that the Internet fosters peace and democracy, and those pointing to the various ways in which nefarious regimes can use it to control the population. Before we attempt to solve this debate in the remainder of this book, we must first understand how Internet technology is related to political outcomes such as mobilization and protest. The overarching question of how modern ICT affects politics has received a lot of attention over the decade (for a comprehensive overview, see Chadwick and Howard, 2009). The bulk of this literature covers democratic systems, where scholars have examined, for example, how the Internet affects political participation (Boulianne, 2009, 2015), changes political communication (Chadwick, 2017), or improves democratic governance (Kakabadse, Kakabadse and Kouzmin, 2003).

In democracies, Internet communication occurs in environments characterized by relatively low state intervention and regulation, and where a free flow of public information and debate—both online or offline—is generally possible and desired (see for example Merkel, 2004). This is typically very different in autocratic regimes, which we focus on in this book. Autocracies are regimes that, unlike democracies, do not fill executive and legislative offices through contested elections (Przeworski et al., 2000). Throughout this book, we therefore consider political systems autocratic if the government came to—or holds on to—power using means other than competitive and fair elections (Geddes, Wright and Frantz, 2014a).[2] Historical examples of such autocratic power seizures include Augusto Pinochet's bloody coup in Chile in 1973, Fidel Castro's insurgency in Cuba in 1959, the Iranian revolution in 1979, and Hugo Chávez's consolidation of power during his presidency in Venezuela. These historical examples of power seizures differ starkly from the free and fair elections that determine the change or continuation of democratic governments in countries such as Norway, India, and Chile today.

Autocratic regimes limit the freedoms of their citizens in various ways. Most importantly for our purpose, most autocracies firmly restrict the freedom of speech and keep a tight grip on the domestic mass media. In these information-sparse contexts, we expect the political effects of Internet technology to be much more profound, or at least fundamentally different, compared to democratic environments. This is why the main research question in this book is whether Internet technology—with its ability to rapidly disseminate information—has an influence on political mobilization in autocracies. In order to set the stage for the remainder of the book, this chapter surveys different theoretical mechanisms linking the Internet to political mobilization—or the absence thereof—in autocratic contexts. More precisely, in our review we explore how political opposition in autocracies can benefit from or be suppressed by Internet communication. In line with the classic literature on political protest, we use the well-known framework of *motives*, resource *mobilization*, and political *opportunities* to structure our review. This framework sketches out the different analytical perspectives through which we later examine the relationship between Internet technology and mobilization in more detail. We introduce the general logic of this theoretical framework in the next section, then apply it to the technological innovations introduced by the Internet and their impact on mobilization.

Motives, Mobilization, and Opportunities

Social science research has a long tradition of explaining the emergence of social movements—particularly political protest. This literature has three distinct explanatory foci that have emerged over the course of several decades of research. According to Kriesi (2011), early models of social unrest emphasized individual motives as main explanations. Simply put, the assumption was that people mobilize in protest because of grievances over a real and/or perceived unjust state of affairs. For example, this thinking is clearly represented in Gurr's (1970) theory of relative deprivation, where a systematic socioeconomic disadvantage of certain groups is assumed to be the driving force behind collective mobilization.

These classic models put the main emphasis on individuals and their motives while ignoring the collective nature of protest. In other words, while individuals clearly need a reason to protest, these models do not explain how individuals manage to join together to collectively advance their goals. This is why a second generation of explanations for protest focused primarily on obstacles to collective mobilization and how movements were able to overcome them (see, e.g.,

McCarthy and Zald, 1977). The literature on "resource mobilization" emphasizes the capacity of a social movement or organization to acquire resources and mobilize people to accomplish its goals.[3] In doing so, an organization faces two obstacles. First, there are practical challenges in coordinating people for a collective effort: Activists need to inform others and coordinate with them on the precise action to be taken. This is where an existing network or an organizational structure can help. Second, even if this challenge can be overcome, it may not be easy to motivate people to participate: The contribution individuals make to the movement is costly, but if successful, the outcome often also benefits those individuals who did not participate. For example, joining a protest requires time and effort and is potentially dangerous if protesters face repression from the regime. However, if the protest is successful and the autocratic government is replaced with a democratic one, everyone—including those who did not protest—will benefit from regime change. Therefore, individually rational people will "free ride" on the efforts of others without incurring the costs. In a nutshell, this is the collective action problem stated by Olson (1965) that needs to be overcome for successful political mobilization.

A third generation of explanations for protest focuses on the context in which protest movements operate. These "political opportunity" theories argue that rather than individual motives or resources and strategies of mobilization, protest is best explained by the political environment in which it is used (Meyer, 2004). More precisely, political protest is more likely to be a feasible and useful tactic for achieving a particular goal in some political environments than in others. Political opportunities that can be conducive to protest include structural factors (international system, national institutions, existing political organizations) and events (previous protests, coups, elections). For example, Tilly (1978) argues that protest occurrence and the openness of the political environment have an inverted-U relationship: If the political context allows for different, institutionalized channels through which citizens can affect political outcomes (e.g., voting in democratic elections), collective mobilization for protest is often unnecessary and the frequency of protest should be low. The same is expected to hold in politically repressive contexts, where authorities actively prevent collective mobilization, in particular by restricting political organization (Davenport, 2007b; Hencken Ritter and Conrad, 2016). Regimes in the middle, that is, those that are not pure democracies or pure autocracies, should experience the highest levels of unrest since institutions are ineffective and political organization is allowed.

The distinction between *motives* for protest, the *mobilization of participants*, and the *political context* in which protest is used gives us a useful framework for the following discussion. Although the vast majority of work on social movements and political protest so far has focused on democratic environments, some examine autocratic contexts, particularly the question of how the Internet shapes protest dynamics in these regimes. We acknowledge, however, that autocratic contexts differ fundamentally from democratic ones in several respects. Due to the exclusion of a large share of the population from political decision-making and a lower level of government responsiveness, citizens in autocratic countries will typically have higher levels of individual grievances and dissatisfaction. However, these motives often do not translate directly into collective action because autocratic countries significantly limit opportunities for citizens to form groups and act collectively by using repression. According to Kuran (1989), who studied the French Revolution of 1789, the Russian Revolution of 1917, and the Iranian Revolution of 1978–1979, this is why revolutions in autocracies tend to be rare and unanticipated. In short, individual motives for protest will be greater and mobilization and political opportunities will be fewer in autocracies compared to democracies.

How does the advent of modern communication technology impact motives for protest, the mobilization of participants, and political opportunities? Before we return to a detailed discussion of the implications of new technology for these theoretical arguments, let us first take a closer look at the technological changes introduced by the Internet in general.

Technological Change and Why It Matters for Politics

As discussed in Chapter 1, pundits have argued that protest in closed, autocratic environments has been crucially driven by the availability of new communication technology, particularly the Internet. To understand this view, it is necessary to first discuss the technical innovations the advent of the Internet has brought with it. From an engineering point of view, the Internet is a global network of computers that exchange encoded, electronic, computer-readable data. This information can be accessed, stored, transmitted, and manipulated from computers and hand-held devices. The Internet's physical infrastructure can be used for a variety of network services. One of the earliest and still most important of these is the World Wide Web, a system of websites that publish, disseminate, and, as of recently, jointly produce information (Kurose and Ross, 2013). During the first generation of the Internet, the production and dissemination of web content was unidirectional, where the operators of web servers created and published content that could then be accessed by the users (or web "clients"). With the introduction of social media in the age of Web 2.0, this has changed. Nowadays, in addition to simply receiving information, each Internet user can provide and share content, which essentially has turned what was once a unidirectional communication channel into a bidirectional one.

Generally speaking, the Internet has introduced three innovations that offer advantages over "old" technologies such as newspapers, telephones, radios, and television (Weidmann, 2015). First, the pervasiveness of (digitally transmitted) information has increased massively. In particular, the *speed* and *availability* of information offered by ICTs is unprecedented. Information can now be sent and received from almost any part of the globe instantly, for example in the form of news articles on web pages, e-mails, tweets, Facebook posts, WhatsApp messages, or Internet-based calls. This has fundamental implications for the spread of information. For example, major political events—such as coups, uprisings, and terrorist attacks—can be followed "live" by users of digital technology. Moreover, the fact that ICT coverage has expanded massively over the past 10–15 years means that many more people have access to information and communication than before, and in many countries digitally transmitted information is an integral part of everyday life.

A second innovation is the *nature of the information* that can be transmitted using digital technology. Newspapers are limited to text and images, while ordinary phone technology and radio transmission is limited to audio. The new digital technology can be used to transmit any type of content, including text, images, audio, and video. As a consequence, communication is not only faster and more easily available, it is also in many ways more comprehensive, which can have implications for the impact of information. For example, videos from war zones in Syria provide a more visceral representation than text or audio descriptions alone. The videos of bombs exploding in the Turkish parliament during the 2016 coup attempt and President Erdoğan's supporters putting up resistance in the streets had a similar effect. For better or worse, videos like this are now readily available to anyone with Internet access.

Third, the *type of network* used to spread information is also changing. Traditionally, communication technology relied on two types of networks: broadcast and peer-to-peer networks. Broadcast networks allow a central node to distribute information to a large number of receivers, for example via TV or radio. In this type of network, the direction of the information flow is fixed (from the sender to receivers). By contrast, peer-to-peer networks, such as telephone networks, allow communication between two or more nodes, where the direction of the information flow is not fixed. Both conventional broadcast and peer-to-peer networks are susceptible to government interference. In a broadcast network, governments only need to secure control over the central broadcasting node, for example a TV or radio station. It is no surprise that autocratic governments historically have been keen to control these broadcasting networks and use them for their own propaganda (Boas 2006). Classic examples of this include the totalitarian regimes in the Soviet Union under Stalin and in Germany under Hitler (Friedrich and Brzezinski, 1965). But control over the press is still a key component of autocratic rule today, with the strictest control in countries such as North Korea, Cuba, and Iran (Freedom House, 2016c). Peer-to-peer networks are more difficult to control due to their decentralized nature. However, since most of these services are offered by national providers (e.g., telecommunications providers), autocratic regimes can obtain direct access to the infrastructure and restrict access for political reasons as they deem necessary.

Today, however, the Internet as a communication network no longer follows the broadcast and peer-to-peer network prototypes. Internet technology can implement both types of communication: For example, a news website is the modern equivalent of a broadcasting station, while e-mail and instant messaging are examples of peer-to-peer communication over the Internet. In addition, however, the Internet enables a hybrid type of communication, where users essentially become information broadcasters themselves. In the Web 2.0, users can distribute information (e.g., tweets or Facebook posts) that reaches a large number of people. This new type of information network blurs the distinction between information providers and information consumers, enabling ordinary citizens to reach potentially large audiences. In addition, Internet infrastructure no longer follows national boundaries. Quite the opposite, many companies offering broadcast services (such as news websites) or social media services operate in countries outside those where most of their users reside. This limits the influence of authoritarian governments when it comes to controlling the flow of information on the Internet.

In short, due to its supranational structure, large bandwidth, and speed, the Internet enables a faster and more pervasive exchange of information in a network structure that has become more difficult for governments to control. In the following, we take a closer look at how these technological changes and innovations can affect political mobilization.

Protest in Autocracies in the Age of the Internet

How can the Internet help opposition movements organize for protest? Or does the technology empower the state, ultimately leading to more propaganda and surveillance? In this section, we identify different theoretical arguments about the relationship between Internet communication and political protest. Our discussion follows the theoretical framework described above, which explains protest as a result of three factors: the grievances and motives individuals have for protest, the ability of a movement to mobilize its supporters, and the political opportunities that dictate whether protest is a feasible and useful tactic to advance a political goal.

In our discussion of the theoretical mechanisms, we rely on three stylized actors that may use Internet technology to achieve their goals: On the government side, we have the autocratic *regime*, consisting of the group of individuals who control leadership selection and policy-making (e.g., a specific ethnic group, high-ranked military officers, or party members). The regime's main motivation is to stay in power (Bueno de Mesquita et al., 2003; Geddes, 1999), and popular dissent organized by the opposition poses a potential threat. On the opposition side, we distinguish between two types of actors: *Activists* are individuals who advocate for a political cause, usually against the government. To pursue this cause, these activists attempt to mobilize *potential dissenters* in the population. The participation of a significant share of the population is necessary for the activists to be successful in their aims.

THE INTERNET AND INDIVIDUALS' MOTIVES FOR PROTEST

The first part of our discussion links the availability of digital communication technology to potential dissenters' grievances against the regime, hence falling under the first determinant of protest according to our framework of motives, mobilization, and opportunity. Here, some argue that digital communication expands citizens' perspective on politics in their own country and makes them more critical of the regime.

In his account of the Arab Spring in Egypt, Mohamed El-Baradei argues that the Internet played a key role for the protests in Egypt because it gave young Egyptians an idea "of the freedoms and opportunities they lack" (El-Baradei, 2011a). New information about other countries that is transmitted through decentralized networks with little government intervention gives people under semi- or non-democratic rule an idea of how different their lives would be in a democracy. In other words, Internet connectivity increases international (communication) linkage (Levitsky and Way, 2006), which facilitates learning about social and political realities abroad. Comparison to other more wealthy and liberal countries can fuel grievances, increasing demands on authoritarian governments and motivating anti-regime protests. Existing research has uncovered some evidence of this effect. In a field experiment, Bailard (2012) shows that in non-democracies, exposure to online information makes citizens more in favor of democratic norms and practices. This echoes findings from cross-national research, which shows that increased Internet use leads to greater commitment to democratic governance (Nisbet, Stoycheff and Pearce, 2012).

Perhaps more important, the Internet allows for improved communication between the citizens of a country. Better, richer communication conveys a more detailed picture of ongoing events and practices by the government, which may aid domestic mobilization. Once more people become aware of grievances they share with a large number of their compatriots, the more likely it is that mass uprisings will take place. These grievances are usually related to long-term political and economic development, such as growing limitations on political freedoms or economic downturns. Identifying shared grievances is what Little (2016) calls "political coordination" between citizens. Internet-based communication can also lead to grievances and outrage in the short term, triggered by events such as election fraud or repression by the police. One of the most prominent examples is the spread of the story about the Tunisian fruit vendor who set himself on fire following police harassment, arguably sparking the Arab Spring in the process (Fisher, 2011).

While this suggests that digital communication makes citizens more dissatisfied with the regime, other arguments say exactly the opposite, namely that the Internet reduces individual motives for protest. One reason for this is that one of the main uses of the Internet is entertainment. Services such as YouTube, Netflix, and Steam supplement existing sources of entertainment provided by television and radio, and social media can be used to connect with friends and exchange gossip rather than discuss politics. The result is an abundance of online video games, movies, and pornography that can distract and pacify the population, and thus reduce their need to engage politically. According to Morozov (2011, ch. 3), this leads to a significant depolitization of online communication, and constitutes one of the main arguments against the "liberating" effect of the Internet. Existing research seems to support this reasoning. In democracies, reduced levels of political participation and engagement have partly been attributed to increased media options (Prior, 2005). In a study on the German Democratic Republic, Kern and Hainmueller (2009) found that the availability of Western TV in certain regions of the country led to a measurable increase in political satisfaction, rather than the expected opposite effect. These results support the notion that TV can serve as "opiate of the masses" and therefore decrease political dissent and mobilization. A similar effect could apply to modern online communication technology as well.

At the same time, however, governments can use online communication in more sinister ways. One is to use Internet technology for propaganda purposes, as exemplified by the increase in "fake news." The spreading of regime-friendly information online takes a number of forms. First, state-controlled news outlets propagate their articles on the Internet. For example, the television network "Russia Today" not only broadcasts via cable and satellite, it also publishes news on the official website, broadcasts via YouTube, and is present on a range of social media platforms. Second, regime officials often use social media to actively influence public opinion. Morozov (2011) describes how former Venezuelan president Hugo Chávez, after some initial reservation, became an ardent user of

Twitter to advance his political agenda. Today, most dictators and regime insiders have private social media accounts that are used to mobilize support (Barbera and Zeitzoff, 2018). Third, in many countries, regimes employ web commentators to spread pro-regime messages and actively "combat" regime criticism. In China, for example, propaganda units known as the "50 Cent Party" mount coordinated campaigns to vilify high-profile government critics (King, Pan and Roberts, 2017). In Sudan, the government-funded "Cyber Jihadist Unit" both monitors and actively plants misleading information online (Freedom House, 2017). Similar tactics are also used in Bahrain, Ethiopia, Russia, and Zambia. Specially employed web commentators can lend even more credibility to the information because official (government-controlled) sources are considered untrustworthy. Therefore, a blog or social media comment praising a government policy can be more convincing compared to a similar editorial in a national newspaper. On the other hand, this can generate distrust in information obtained on the Internet, as it is difficult to determine whether it is true or false. This in turn can decrease the likelihood of individuals acting on information, for example by mobilizing political protest based on reported government corruption or other abuses of power.

The unintentional depoliticizing effect of online entertainment and the strategic use of online propaganda to prevent protest are difficult to distinguish in practice. However, what matters here is that both the intentional and unintentional mechanisms are thought to have an appeasing effect on citizens' political motives for protest, in contrast to the above arguments that predict the opposite. In the next section, we turn to the second factor in our theoretical framework and look at how the Internet can help activists mobilize for protest.

DIGITAL MOBILIZATION FOR PROTEST

Traditionally, mobilizing political opposition in non-democratic regimes has faced significant obstacles, restrictions on political organization being a cornerstone of autocratic rule. In the digital age, modern communication technology is assumed to be able to undermine autocratic rule by rendering restrictions on political organization less effective. Before the introduction of the Internet, restrictions on the right to organize could effectively curb the coordination of large groups. But in today's information environment, the features of online communication allow activists to circumvent these limitations and reach a broader audience. In other words, Internet technology can provide a new and alternative channel of political organization that facilitates the coordination of anti-regime protests in places where political organization is tightly controlled. This is perhaps the most frequently discussed argument for the advantage of the Internet for opposition movements in both academic and popular discourse. During the

Arab Spring, online coordination was frequently referred to as a driving force of the uprisings. For example, Egypt reportedly experienced a "Facebook revolution" and Syria a "YouTube uprising" (Khamis, Gold and Vaughn, 2012). Numerous other anti-regime protests organized using new technology have also been mentioned, including spontaneous mobilizations in Kazakhstan in 2009 and 2010, unrest surrounding elections in Iran in 2009 and Russia in 2011–2012, and anti-regime protests in Ethiopia in 2015 organized under the hashtag #OromoProtests (Freedom House, 2011, 2012, 2016d).

How exactly does online mobilization work? One explanation focuses on the intentional use of the Internet for planning protest; another emphasizes the spontaneous protest "bandwagon effect" triggered by spreading news online. These explanations are laid out in more detail below.

Instead of using formal organizations as vehicles for coordination, activists can utilize Internet technology to interact with other like-minded people online, for example through blogs, e-mail newsletters, and social media platforms. In this way, Internet technology enables activists to spread information about planned events widely without relying on an existing organizational structure. Potential activists may seek out information themselves (e.g., by visiting a website or subscribing to an e-mail newsletter) or be exposed to information by accident (e.g., on a social media platform) (Bimber et al., 2005). In this way, Internet technology can be a tool for activists to provide information for "tactical coordination" (Little, 2016), including when and where anti-regime protests are taking place, or what material protesters should bring (e.g., placards, identifiable clothing). In fact, Internet technology makes the recipient group's size and geographic radius irrelevant in terms of organizational costs, since digital information can be multiplied and distributed at no effort or expense. As underlined by Lupia and Sin (2003, 320), "political campaigns, for example, use electronic communications to motivate supporters and organize simultaneous public rallies in multiple and spatially dispersed places." This implies that Internet technology can be used to spread protest from one location to others. But even if, as Bennett, Breunig and Givens (2008) argue, the use of digital media means that social movements have less dense ties with their members, at the same time it makes individual-level networks between the members much denser, which may ultimately be necessary for successful mobilization.

While the above discussion highlights the intentional use of Internet technology to mobilize and coordinate supporters of a movement, earlier work on collective action has argued that increased density of information alone can lead to protest escalation. Research has revealed a relationship between wired communication (telephones) and protest incidents (Ten Eyck, 2001), and the effect of modern ICT is likely even stronger. Shirky (2008) explores a series of coordination problems when many people act together, and argues that ICT can dramatically decrease transaction costs, thus making spontaneous coordinated efforts more likely to occur. In the context of political protest, this means that ICT should not only make the emergence of these protests more likely, but also increase their escalation and persistence. High turnout signals the true preferences of a certain share of the population and their willingness to participate, as well as the likelihood that a movement will succeed, and can therefore draw in more participants (Granovetter, 1978; Kuran, 1989; Lohmann, 1994).

In sum, the above-described mechanisms show how Internet communication allows activists to successfully mobilize large numbers of protesters. This can be done by intentionally using Internet channels for protest coordination, but also by Internet technology successfully disseminating information that makes spontaneous mobilization more likely. The gist of these explanations is that digital connectivity facilitates resource mobilization for movements, and should therefore lead to more protest.

However, this perspective assumes that activists can navigate freely on the Internet, at least to some extent. This may not necessarily be the case, as autocratic regimes control and censor online content by selectively blocking specific websites and search results. In many ways, online censorship is therefore similar to censorship of traditional media: It limits information about events and content that the autocratic regime deems subversive. The most prominent example of online censorship is China, where the autocratic regime infamously allows government criticism, but censors expressions of collective action (King, Pan and Roberts, 2013). However, this practice is not unique to China. In many countries, the World Wide Web has been replaced by a country-specific Wide Web, tailored to the government's wishes (Deibert, Rohozinski and Zittrain, 2008, 31). The censored content is usually political, but in some countries social content is restricted as well. In Saudi Arabia, for example, censoring of social content is used to promote "a single religious creed" (OpenNet Initiative, 2009, 5). This type of compartmentalization happens not only in countries in which the state runs the telecommunication agencies (e.g., Belarus, Cuba, Ethiopia), but also where the autocratic regime can put pressure on domestic or international private companies. For example, after the 2014 coup in Thailand the new military leadership ordered the Norwegian telecommunications company Telenor to censor online content (Winsnes, 2014). However, Internet censorship does not need to be complete (all unsanctioned content is unavailable) or constant (certain websites are permanently unavailable) to have an effect. A simple signal of government presence on the Web can be an important deterrent. A blocked page, for example, makes users aware of the fact that they are attempting to access content the government does not approve of, and that this behavior is being monitored (Rød and Weidmann, 2015, 341). In fact, temporary blocking can be used strategically in times of political uncertainty. During elections in Venezuela in 2010, for example, Internet users with connections hosted by state-owned telecommunications firm CANTV were blocked from blogs and news sites sympathetic to the opposition (Freedom House, 2011). Similar events were reported in Uzbekistan in the run-up to the presidential election in 2007 (BBC, 2007).

In this section, we have discussed how Internet technology can facilitate resource mobilization and lead to political protest. However, this expectation is challenged by the observation that in many cases activists cannot use online services without government interference. Online censorship and the selective disabling of Internet services make it possible for autocratic governments to intercept and prevent digital mobilization attempts, although these interventions are unlikely to be so pervasive as to fully prevent activists from using the Internet. We now turn to the last factor of our theoretical framework—how political opportunity structures can change as a result of digital communication technology.

THE INTERNET AND POLITICAL OPPORTUNITIES

Finally, in addition to affecting motives and resources for mobilization, Internet technology can affect the feasibility of protest by shaping political opportunities in autocracies. One way digital communication can do this is to affect governance. In democratic countries, accountability and responsiveness are key features of good governance. Elected governments are expected to cater to the needs of the population, since they otherwise face legal or electoral consequences (Putnam, 1993; Powell, 2000). Consequently, one would assume that non-democratic regimes, absent these incentives, would generally be unresponsive to the population. While it is true that accountability is generally lower (Bardhan, 2002), the absence of democracy does not lead to a general lack of accountability and responsiveness. On the contrary, research has shown that under certain conditions, non-democratic regimes are highly responsive to popular demands (Tsai, 2007; Evans, 2012).

Digital channels can be key for communicating demands to the government and triggering policy change, which is why the Internet has been referred to as "accountability technology" (Diamond, 2010). In fact, some autocratic governments intentionally rely on the Internet to collect feedback from the population and allow them to voice their demands. Online platforms (e.g., e-governance initiatives, social media, and blogs) improve communication between the population and the autocratic regime. This communication can even be public, which means that it can be followed by the public and thereby signal the government's responsiveness. Research on China, for example, shows that government officials seem to be equally receptive to citizens' demands whether they are received via the Internet or conventional institutional channels (Meng, Pan and Yang, 2017). Provincial administrations have even set up forums specifically for the purpose of recording citizens' complaints, which are then addressed either privately or may even receive a publicly visible response from the administration (Chen, Pan and Xu, 2016). Yet other studies argue that these low-level complaints can be used by the government to monitor the lower levels of the state bureaucracy, while at the same time avoiding demands for larger political change (Lorentzen, 2014). In sum, the accountability technology arguments show how Internet technology can be used to facilitate information exchange between activists/potential dissenters and the autocratic regime. By doing so, the technology can improve governance and give people a higher degree of political influence, which makes mobilizing potential dissenters for political protest a less compelling option for activists.

At the same time, however, Internet technology can be used by governments for repression, which should also reduce opportunities for protest. Online surveillance makes it easier for autocratic regimes to identify and track activists and potential dissenters. Repressing activists who are known for engaging in online activities is likely to send a signal of government surveillance and policing to potential dissenters, which in turn can encourage self-censorship (Rød and Weidmann, 2015). Examples of punitive action taken against online activists abound. In Saudi Arabia, Freedom House, (2011, 290) reports that "dozens if not hundreds of alleged extremists have been arrested after apparently drawing the authorities' attention through activity on online forums." In 2016, a Saudi court found an activist guilty of spreading atheism using Twitter and sentenced the activist to 10 years in prison and 2,000 lashes (Freedom House, 2016d, 8). Activists are frequently tried under broadly defined laws aimed at preventing the spread of terrorism and extremism. In Ethiopia, a blogger was sentenced to 18 years in prison for terrorist activity after publishing an article promoting political freedom (Freedom House, 2012, 7). Often, however, activists are not tried in courts, but are intimidated, assaulted, tortured, killed, or made to disappear. In many countries, activists and potential dissenters are frequently harassed by regime security agents. In Cuba, for example, the blogger Angel Santiesteban was subjected to torture in detention (Freedom House, 2016d, 255).

Whether it improves governance and responsiveness or gives governments a better way to spy on its citizens, the above discussion shows that the use of digital communication technology by regimes reduces opportunities for protest. For the factors discussed above—motives and mobilization—it is difficult to make a prediction regarding whether Internet technology facilitates or suppresses protest. When it comes to political opportunities, however, the expectation is clearer: Digital communication technology should give the government the upper hand in avoiding or repressing public dissent, an argument we will develop further in the next chapter.

Conclusion

Modern information and communication technology has changed social and political life profoundly. Many assume that these changes are particularly pronounced in autocratic political systems, where media and communication have traditionally been severely restricted. Using a theoretical framework of motives, mobilization, and political opportunities, we have reviewed different mechanisms with regard to how Internet technology relates to political protest. Motive-based mechanisms emphasize how increased information exchange affects individuals' satisfaction or dissatisfaction with a regime, and thus may provide an impetus for joining a protest. Explanations that focus on the mobilizing potential of digital ICT describe how these technologies enable opposition movements to mobilize participants and coordinate their actions. Last, explanations related to political opportunities posit that the political context set by an autocratic government determines how Internet technology affects political mobilization.

In our discussion, the distinction between motives, mobilization, and opportunities mainly serves as a heuristic device to structure our review of the different theoretical mechanisms. Rather than complementing existing work, it overlaps with similar efforts proposed in the literature. For example, Aday et al. (2010) present a more fine-grained distinction between individual transformation, intergroup relations, collective action, regime policies, and external attention to explain how new communication technology can trigger political mobilization in non-democratic contexts. Similarly, Lynch (2011) discusses four ways in which new media can be used to challenge autocratic regimes: by fostering collective action, limiting repression, affecting external support, and loosening control of the public sphere. Similar to these existing contributions, we recognize that the use and effects of ICT may be fundamentally different in autocratic countries compared to democracies, which demands a refined theoretical discussion and empirical analysis. Moreover, the introduction of the Internet affects different actors and power constellations in different and potentially opposing ways, which makes it difficult to attribute a clear effect to it. These are central issues we return to in the next chapter.

3

Internet Technology and
Political Protest

As we saw in the previous chapter, there are many different mechanisms that may explain how Internet technology can facilitate or dampen political protest in dictatorships. Despite our attempt to develop a tripartite framework of motives, resource mobilization, and political opportunities, it is difficult to derive theoretical expectations regarding whether modern ICT fosters anti-regime protests by increasing the flow of information and undermining restrictions on formal organization (as cyber-optimists believe) or whether it empowers autocratic governments and suppresses public dissent (the cyber-pessimists' view).

Why exactly is this so? The complexity of the debate stems from at least four issues. First, and most importantly, different political actors benefit from Internet technology, and they do so in different ways. While opposition activists may become much more effective in their attempts to mobilize, these efforts can be monitored and counteracted by autocratic governments. Contrast this with other types of new technology (for example, military drones) that are used primarily by one side and are thus much more likely to have a predictable effect on violent contention. Second, the Internet now encompasses a multitude of technologies and services that are continually changing, and innovations are being introduced at a high speed.[4] These can be used in different ways—sometimes benefiting, sometimes hindering popular mobilization. In one sense, the continuously changing technology is similar to an arms race in which an innovation temporarily gives one actor the upper hand, prompting a counter-innovation from another actor. Third, even if we assume that the Internet mainly serves as a vehicle for information exchange (an overly simplistic view), more information alone does not necessarily foster or inhibit the emergence of protest. Rather, it depends on the type of information, as well as the sender and receiver: Information about a protest that led to policy concessions may trigger more protest elsewhere, but may have the exact opposite effect if it was met with violent force by the government. Finally, we cannot derive clear theoretical expectations regarding the effect of Internet technology on mobilization without taking into account alternative strategies of authoritarian control, such as restrictions on citizens' rights and violent repression. Although some of these strategies may become less or more effective as a result of ICT introduction, they nonetheless continue to be fundamental parts of everyday authoritarian politics.

Because of these theoretical complications, it is impossible to attribute a uniquely positive or negative effect to Internet technology on political protest. As a number of scholars have pointed out, the frequently invoked dichotomous debate between optimists and pessimists is overly stylized and simplistic. But how, then, should we proceed? The most common response to the complex relationship between Internet technology and political protest is that it varies from case to case. For example, the use of Internet-based communication may have helped protesters in Cairo to mobilize and escalate the protest quickly (Hussain and Howard, 2013), while government censoring of collective action attempts helps prevent protest in China (King, Pan and Roberts, 2013). Essentially, this approach entails that we explore the effect of Internet technology on protesters and governments on a case-by-case basis and conduct separate empirical analyses for each. This strategy is helpful for acquiring in-depth expert knowledge on the dynamics of one or a few cases over a short time period. However, case analysis alone cannot tell us anything about why the Internet sometimes empowers activists and other times autocrats. In other words, it makes it difficult to refine a theory so that it explains the different observed outcomes.

Such a theoretical refinement is our goal in this book. We set out to identify the theoretical conditions that lead to a protest-facilitating effect of the Internet, and those that do the opposite. Hence, we aim to (at least partly) resolve the debate about the transformational or repressive use of the Internet by developing an overarching theoretical argument rather than by restricting the theoretical scope to single cases. In this chapter, we lay several theoretical foundations for this task. Most important, we provide a theoretical perspective with regard to the role of the autocratic government. After all, Internet technology is usually introduced by governments themselves, who are aware of its opportunities as well as its potential political risks. These governments possess established means of controlling the population. Hence, governments do not face the threat of revolution as helpless actors; rather, they have a variety of tools available that they can use to counter revolutionary movements. This chapter introduces the basic problem of Internet technology and political protest through the eyes of an autocratic government—considerations that will later be refined in the empirical chapters of the book. Before we enter this discussion, however, we set the theoretical and empirical scope of the technology in question, the Internet.

Our review in the previous chapter showed that the Internet encompasses a number of technologies and services. Using the Internet, we can transmit e-mail messages, browse news websites, and post messages to social media platforms. These services differ in the extent to which they affect political dynamics, with many being likely to have no effect at all. A detailed analysis of different services (such as specific social media platforms) would not only require a refined theoretical discussion of its effects on political dynamics, but also a corresponding empirical analysis. Some researchers have started to look at such specific services (see, e.g., Steinert-Threlkeld, 2017), but our approach here is different. We assume that the Internet generally leads to new (and possibly improved) information flows between people, which can be monitored by governments. If these new information flows affect protest dynamics, we should see empirical variation in protest activity depending on the level of Internet penetration in that society. Hence, our theoretical and empirical approach does not differentiate between the type of information that is exchanged via the Internet or the respective service that is used to disseminate it.

In the next sections we outline two key considerations we use to unpack the relationship between Internet technology and political protest in autocracies. First, we discuss the relative advantage autocratic regimes enjoy over opposition activists when it comes to using the technology in their favor. Since the political leadership chooses when and where to introduce and expand the technology and has an overwhelming resource advantage for shaping the online environment once it is established, communication technology should play into the hands of autocrats over the long run. Second, we discuss the role of conventional tools of popular control in the digital age. After outlining these considerations, we tie them to three phases of protest, namely their occurrence, continuation, and spread.

Asymmetrical Control of the Internet

Most of the literature on the Internet, social media, and political mobilization studies the problem from the perspective of opposition activists and the benefits and challenges that arise from the new technology. Does the Internet as a communication channel help activists mobilize potential dissenters? Or does it allow governments to spy on them and interfere with their efforts? Existing accounts generally pay little attention to the question of how Internet technology is introduced in a country in the first place (but see Boas, 2006; Rød and Weidmann, 2015). If, as discussed in the previous chapter, Internet technology potentially empowers opposition activists and fuels popular mobilization, it is necessary to ask why autocratic regimes adopt it in the first place.

In today's world, being connected to the Internet and expanding access at the domestic level is necessary for a number of reasons. As economists have long recognized, the Internet enhances economic growth, both nationally and at the local level (Litan and Rivlin, 2001). Digital connectivity is essential for transnational businesses to support product development and manage supply chains. At the local level, Internet connectivity boosts the local economy and creates new economic opportunities (Crandall and Jackson, 2001). At the same time, digital channels can improve governance and public goods provision, as discussed in the previous chapter. Overall, there are clearly a number of economic and political reasons for autocratic governments to innovate in the realm of Internet technology.

In light of these considerable advantages, the potential political risks of modern communication technology pose what Göbel (2012) calls the autocratic "innovation dilemma": Failing to adopt technological innovation such as digital communication technology helps an autocratic government avoid the risks associated with it, but at the same time means forgoing tremendous economic opportunities—and the consolidating effect these could have on autocratic power. For this reason, many autocratic governments opt for a controlled strategy of Internet expansion that manages the political risks it entails while still making it possible to benefit from the economic and political advantages. This course of action should come as no surprise; most students of autocracy recognize that non-democratic regimes continuously monitor the potential threats to their rule (Geddes, 1999; Svolik, 2012).

The tight level of authority an autocratic government has over national-level telecommunications makes it possible to introduce and expand the technology in a controlled way (Deibert and Rohozinski, 2010). In fact, in most autocratic countries, Internet service is provided by state-owned telecommunications companies (Boas, 2006). One of these countries is Belarus, where state-owned telecom provider Beltelecom administers Internet services (Crabtree and Weidmann, 2018). If multiple providers exist, as in Egypt for example, the provision of Internet services is heavily regulated and often subject to intervention (Dainotti et al., 2014).

Given the high level of control that autocratic governments exert over Internet expansion and communication flows, their strategy for containing political risks is twofold. The first part focuses on how regimes implement and expand Internet technology. As Weidmann et al. (2016) argue, governments can strategically limit access to particular geographic areas. If political opposition is expected to arise from particular regions of the country, Internet expansion to these areas can be delayed or withheld entirely. Prominent examples illustrate how autocratic regimes strategically delay implementation and expansion until they have acquired the tools to control the new technology. In Saudi Arabia, for example, the government developed sophisticated control mechanisms before the Internet was allowed. Specifically, this was done by restricting access to non-Saudi hosted websites through a government-controlled gateway (Deibert, Rohozinski and Zittrain, 2008; Kalathil and Boas, 2003). Similarly, Freedom House (2012, 1) reports that the Ethiopian government stalled the expansion of Internet services while they implemented one of the most extensive filtering regimes in Africa. Conversely, expansion of the technology is expected to be more likely in regions with a low risk of revolt and where it can bolster support for the regime. Note that this strategy is only applicable if political dissent is geographically delineated, and when cutting off these regions does not incur other economic costs. This strategy is therefore rather limited, since major cities are usually economic strongholds and the places where political opposition is most widespread.

This is why many autocratic governments also resort to a second strategy, which is to control communication on the Internet as much as possible, and at the same time use these channels in their favor (Morozov, 2011; Tucker et al., 2017). As discussed in the previous chapter, these methods include improving governance using online tools, removing content that is critical of the regime, and using online propaganda to boost the government's image. Here, it is sufficient to say that the resource advantage autocratic regimes enjoy over opposition activists makes Internet control highly asymmetrical, with the government at an advantage. In other words, despite the Internet being a global network (Goldsmith and Wu, 2006), the state and the influence it exerts over the Internet still matter to a great extent. What does this mean for the Internet's effect on protest and protest dynamics?

To understand this, we need to distinguish between long- and short-term effects of Internet control. As mentioned above, by "control" we mean the government's ability to critically influence what is communicated on the Internet and how information is used. Establishing and maintaining Internet control is fundamentally a long-term strategy. It requires building platforms for e-governance and information exchange between governments and citizens. Furthermore, the national Internet must be centralized in such a way that interference is possible at a small number of central nodes. It often requires sophisticated technical filtering or blocking infrastructure, China's "Great Firewall" being a case in point. Highly skilled technical personnel and professional producers of propaganda are essential. Once this infrastructure is in place, governments can use the Internet to mitigate political risks, maintain the upper hand, and reduce dissent among citizens over the long run.

However, this does not mean that Internet control by autocratic governments is perfect in the sense that it completely eliminates all political threats. In fact, unexpected events and miscalculations by the regime can lead to these long-term strategies failing, resulting in political protests. Once protests occur, Internet technology can play into the hands of opposition activists. Much research points to the importance of the speed with which digital communication travels during ongoing protests (Breuer, Landman and Farquhar, 2015; Tufekci and Wilson, 2012). Once protest starts and information dissemination gains momentum, the long-term strategies of control described above are presumably ineffective. In these situations, governments sometimes opt for a complete shutdown of the national Internet (Gohdes, 2015), as President Mubarak of Egypt did in January 2011. However, this measure involves high costs because it affects the population and the economy as a whole. In addition, research has shown that the effectiveness of shutdowns is limited (Hassanpour, 2014). Thus, in the vast majority of cases, the Internet continues to be available to activists for motivating and co-ordinating potential protesters, and thus fuels ongoing protests in the short run (Kuran, 1989; Little, 2016). Hence, the short-term, protest-facilitating effect may very well be different from the long-term, protest-suppressing one.

Online Activism and Offline Repression

Asymmetrical control of the Internet is only one of two important considerations that we need to discuss when theorizing about the impact of Internet penetration on the emergence of protest. The second consideration is the use of conventional authoritarian control tools that continue to be available in the age of the Internet. In other words, even if the Internet empowers opposition activists, we cannot conclude that protest mobilization is more likely to be successful, since autocratic governments can counter these threats with conventional means of repression. Again, we distinguish between long-term and short-term measures that governments employ.

Autocratic countries implement a number of policies to fend off challengers in the long run. While some countries have strong restrictions on citizens' rights and individual freedoms, others are relatively tolerant even though they do not have fair and equal political competition (Levitsky and Way, 2010). Consequently, the impact of digital communication technology may differ depending on what political environment it is used in. Even though repression always has been, and remains, an inherent part of autocratic rule (Svolik, 2012), recent decades have seen the emergence of more and more so-called hybrid regimes where the strict control of the population has shifted toward less repressive governance. This more liberal approach to authoritarian politics has in many ways amplified the political risks for autocratic regimes (Hegre et al., 2001; Levitsky and Way, 2010). Does the introduction and expansion of the Internet contribute to increasing these risks, or does it allow governments to mitigate them?

In this book, we focus in particular on restrictions on the freedom of association, because this is where the Internet can potentially make a great difference by allowing movements to bypass these restrictions. An important trend in the development away from repressive authoritarian politics has been that overall restrictions on the freedom of association in autocracies have decreased over time. In practice, this means that citizens face fewer obstacles to form parties and political associations, and hence have more influence on politics. Consistent with our theory of the Internet as being asymmetrically controlled by the government and therefore advantageous to governmental interests in the long run, digital channels can serve as a tool to regain some of the control that autocratic governments lose when they grant citizens more political freedom. In essence, this means that if Internet penetration helps governments fend off political mobilization, this effect should be particularly strong in environments where governments have fewer traditional means in place to control the population—in other words, places where freedom of association is high.

However, the Internet can also affect short-term measures employed by the government in the context of ongoing political protest. A classic question in sociology and political science is how violent government response affects subsequent protest levels (Davenport, 2007a; Earl, 2011). For studying how digital communication technology affects the dynamics of protest, we consider how the informational advantage of the Internet interacts with governments' violent repression of protesters. Better communication flows is key: The Internet is used to spread information not only about ongoing protest, but also about repression of previous protests. This can trigger a backlash: Enraged by government violence, more and more citizens may turn against the government elsewhere. On the other hand, by making violent government actions more widely known among the population, future protest can potentially be deterred by raising the stakes of participation, thus amplifying the effect of protest repression beyond the case where it is actually applied.

In summary, our above discussion has revealed two important insights that are central to the remainder of the book and the analyses presented. First, we need to recognize that Internet technology does not magically appear out of the blue, but is strategically introduced, expanded, and utilized by autocratic regimes. Second, the advent of digital communication technology and its impact on protest mobilization needs to be examined together with traditional means of autocratic repression. Control of Internet-based communication channels is sometimes used in place of these traditional means, and in conjunction with them in others. In the next section, our discussion turns to different protest phases. Above, we argued that governments have the upper hand when it comes to the introduction and expansion of the Internet. This may give them an advantage for using this technology in the long run, even though Internet communication can still contribute to the short-term escalation of protest. Hence, it is important that we analyze the effect of Internet communication on the occurrence, continuation, and spread of protest.

Different Phases of Protest

One of the main contributions of this book is the theoretical and empirical distinction between different phases of protest. Starting a new wave of protest involves very different challenges for political activists compared to sustaining and growing a movement that has already started, and modern communication technology should have very different effects depending on the protest phase it is used in. In this section, we introduce the three stages of protest that constitute the focus of this book: the occurrence of protest in general, its continuation, and its diffusion across a country. We briefly define these three stages and summarize the theoretical expectations that guide our empirical analyses in the following chapters. Each empirical chapter includes a refined theoretical discussion of the general reflections we have presented in this and the previous chapter.

PROTEST OCCURRENCE

The most obvious (and probably most frequently studied) question when it comes to the Internet and political mobilization is whether the former contributes to an increase in the *occurrence* of protest. Does Internet technology lead to more or less protest in those locations where it is available? In the previous chapter, we identified three broad conditions for protest: motives, resource mobilization, and political opportunities. If governments have an advantage over the opposition in the long term because they control the expansion of the national Internet and information communicated online, this will affect the three conditions as follows. First, individual motives for protest are expected to decrease, since pro-regime propaganda and entertainment make people less critical of the regime. Second, regimes will presumably censor attempts by opposition activists to mobilize, though absolute control is probably not feasible. Third, governments will likely shape the national Internet infrastructure in their favor, potentially using it to improve governance, but also to ramp up surveillance and repression.

Overall, then, we assume that in the long term, Internet technology plays into the hands of governments when it comes to preventing public dissent in the first place. We will provide a more detailed theoretical background and test this hypothesis in Chapter 6, where our core focus is on the relationship between Internet penetration and protest occurrence. In line with our above argument, however, we also need to examine how this long-term relationship is affected by conventional tools of repression. In Chapter 9, we address this question and analyze how the effect of Internet penetration on protest occurrence varies depending on whether conventional restrictions on freedom of association are enforced by the government.

PROTEST PERSISTENCE

If activists are successful and protest occurs despite the efforts of the government to prevent it, the effect of the Internet is likely to play out differently. Since people have been protesting, grievances must be present, mobilization attempts have been successful, and political opportunities must be such that protest could emerge. In this situation, does the Internet contribute to the *persistence* (or continuation) of protest? Here, the government can no longer rely on its long-term strategy to prevent unrest. Once protest hits, there is a race between activists trying to sustain it and governments trying to contain it. As argued above, under these circumstances the effect of digital communication is likely to play into the hands of protesters. During an ongoing episode of protest, it is difficult to completely limit the rapid flow of news via digital channels. This can lead to national protest surges, but also a rise in international attention, which exacerbates this effect even further.

In sum, we expect that the effect of Internet connectivity on protest depends on the phase of the protest: While governmental attempts to control and shape the Internet generally lead to a lower occurrence of protest, the opposite should apply once protest has started. Here, higher connectivity presumably leads to a higher likelihood of protest being sustained and possibly even escalated. In short, if we were to use the labels from the overly simplistic debate that has shaped much discussion on this topic, both "cyber-optimists" and "cyber-pessimists" may be right: Governments can use digital communication to prevent emerging public dissent. However, once protest has started, activists can use the Internet to keep protest going and possibly increase its impact.

Our analysis in this book incorporates the basic distinction between the start of a new protest (as in Chapter 6) and the continuation of an ongoing one. In Chapter 7, we analyze episodes of ongoing protest in order to find out how the Internet contributes to the continuation of protest at a given location. By examining locations that have recently experienced protest, we are able to study whether higher Internet penetration indeed leads to renewed protest, as our theoretical considerations suggest. We also follow up on the issue of the effects of digital mobilization in conjunction with traditional means of government repression in a two-part analysis. First, we examine in Chapter 7 how violent government response during an ongoing campaign affects the protest-enhancing effect of the Internet. Second, in Chapter 9 we analyze how this effect plays out across different authoritarian countries, depending on the restrictions on political organizations that are in place.

PROTEST DIFFUSION

While protest persistence refers to the continuation of protest in the city where it started, a related phenomenon we study is the *diffusion* of protest to other cities in the same country. In Chapter 8, we explore whether the flow of information between locations facilitated by the Internet contributes to the occurrence of protest in new locations once people have successfully mobilized elsewhere. In line with our expectation that digital communication generally dampens the likelihood of protest occurrence but can strengthen ongoing campaigns once they have started, we also expect that it contributes to the geographical diffusion of protest across a country. This, again, is due to the government's ability to adjust and control online communication in the long run and the difficulty involved in containing the spread of information as events unfold. In line with this reasoning, we expect that if Internet penetration in cities with protest is high, this will make it more likely that protest will break out elsewhere in response.

We also examine how the effect of the Internet on protest diffusion interacts with traditional means of public repression and control employed by the government. In the short run, governments can violently repress ongoing episodes of protest, which may reduce—or even reverse—the facilitating effect of the Internet. In Chapter 9, we study how the effect of digital communication on diffusion is related to the political environment it occurs in by testing how the Internet's diffusion-enhancing effect interacts with alternative strategies the government employs to restrict freedom of association.

Conclusion

In this chapter, we have laid out our general theoretical considerations regarding the effect of Internet penetration on protest occurrence and dynamics. Our discussion and theory are guided by two gaps in the existing literature. First, we argue that governments have an advantage in digital communication due to the fact that Internet implementation and expansion occur under the auspices of the government. Autocratic regimes can therefore employ a number of strategies to control Internet communication and shape it in their favor. This should lead to a dampening effect of Internet penetration on protest mobilization in the long run, which is what we analyze in Chapter 6. At the same time, however, control over information disseminated using Internet technology is much more difficult during ongoing protest episodes. This is why we expect that once protest has started, better communication channels such as those provided by the Internet can contribute to the persistence of protest (Chapter 7) or its diffusion to other places in the same country (Chapter 8).

The second issue we address is how digital channels and their potential effect on mobilization interacts with conventional measures autocrats use to keep citizens in check. We consider short-term governmental responses such as violent repression of protest and expect these to significantly reduce the effect that digital communication has on protest persistence and diffusion. This is a question we can only study during ongoing episodes of protest, which is why we amend the analyses in Chapters 7 and 8 accordingly. In addition to these violent responses to mobilization, autocratic governments can also implement long-term strategies to prevent public unrest, such as restricting the freedom of association. Autocracies vary greatly in the extent to which they do this, and we need to study how the potentially mobilizing effect of the Internet interacts with this strategy. In Chapter 9, we therefore repeat our main analyses of protest occurrence, persistence, and diffusion across different national contexts.

In the following chapters, we carry out our empirical investigations of how Internet technology affects the dynamics of protest in autocracies. Importantly, our theoretical discussion calls for an empirical analysis at the *local* level. In line with our theory, Internet access should exacerbate, or suppress, protest in locations where it is available. For example, Internet expansion in a given city should primarily influence protest behavior in that city, but not necessarily elsewhere. This constitutes a considerable problem when using national-level data on Internet penetration and anti-regime protests, as many empirical studies do: We cannot be sure that Internet technology is actually available and being used at the locations where protests emerge (or fail to emerge). In order to address this challenge, we present a disaggregated analysis at the city level.

A fine-grained analysis like this, however, faces several challenges, particularly when it comes to the availability of data. Essentially, we need to measure protest, Internet penetration, and several other variables at the city level. Before turning to our empirical analysis, the following chapters introduce the necessary data and methods step by step. In Chapter 4, we present a coding effort—the Mass Mobilization in Autocracies Database (MMAD)—that produces city-level event data on protest for a global sample of autocracies. Chapter 5 describes a research design for our disaggregated study that is able to capture the determinants of political protest at different analytical levels. This allows us to examine variation in Internet penetration and protest at the city level, but also variation between different countries and over time. The data and the research design are then used in Chapter 6 to analyze how local Internet penetration affects protest occurrence, before turning to analyses on the continuation and diffusion of protest in Chapters 7 and 8, respectively. Finally, in Chapter 9, we analyze how institutional context shapes the effect of Internet technology on political protest in autocracies.

4

Coding Protest Events in Autocracies

In this chapter, we begin our empirical investigation into the effect of Internet penetration on political protest. Clearly, our analysis is not the first of its kind. As discussed in the first chapter of this book, previous work has typically fallen into one of two categories. The first type of study has a relatively narrow geographic and temporal scope and usually focuses on individual protest episodes, such as the Tahrir Square protests in Egypt in 2011 (Tufekci and Wilson, 2012) or the Arab Spring as a whole (Hussain and Howard, 2013). While this approach can reveal interesting insights for a particular case, it is difficult to generalize these results. The second type of study analyzes protest by comparing different countries and time periods (Brancati, 2014; Ruijgrok, 2017). These studies, however, typically work with aggregated, country-level indicators such as annual protest counts, which is why they cannot capture patterns *within* these countries. For this reason, we use a combination of both approaches. We study the relationship between Internet access and protest occurrence for a global sample of autocracies, but also analyze variation between their major cities for each case. This allows us to examine how the density of the Internet in particular places affects protest, but also how this effect varies across different national contexts. This disaggregated analysis obviously requires fine-grained data, not only for the outcome in question (protest), but also for the degree of Internet penetration as well as other variables in the analysis. In this chapter, we focus on the former before introducing our research design in the next chapter. We introduce a new dataset on protest in autocracies—the Mass Mobilization in Autocracies Database (MMAD)— which contains information on individual protest incidents, including dates and locations. For access to the data, please visit https://mmadatabase.org/. The data collection is based on information from media reports that identify instances of protest. The use of information from the media raises issues regarding the selectivity and accuracy of the reported information. Therefore, we briefly review existing data collection approaches to political protest before describing how our new coding effort deals with these challenges.

Existing Data on Political Protest

Political protest has been a frequently studied topic in the social sciences for decades, particularly in political science and sociology. For that reason, there are a number of data collections on protest at the national and local levels. Almost all of these collections are based on information reported in the media, from which a structured list of protest events was created. We can distinguish between *human-coded* datasets, where information from other sources is extracted entirely by humans, and *automatic* coding, where computer-based text analysis is used for this task. Human coding, while producing high-quality content and being extremely flexible in terms of the type of information that can be extracted, is very costly and time-consuming. Automated coding is good for categorizing news articles into various topics of interest or extracting actors from known actor lists ("actor dictionaries"), but may have shortcomings when it comes to the precision of the extracted information from the text (e.g., the number of fatalities or the date of the incident). We briefly review existing human- and computer-coded datasets before introducing the hybrid approach used for the MMAD, which combines the two approaches at different stages of the coding process.

HUMAN CODING

When it comes to the study of protest in non-democratic environments, most of the large-N analyses on mass mobilization and regime stability utilize data from the *Cross-National Time-Series dataset* (Banks, 2011). It contains count variables of domestic disturbances (riots, anti-government demonstrations) at the country-year level from 1815 until today. The dataset is unique with regard to its extensive spatial and temporal information and is widely used. However, the highly aggregated nature of the data makes micro-level analysis—such as the one presented in this book—impossible. The events are derived exclusively from a single newspaper, the *New York Times*, which can lead to gaps in reporting compared to collections that draw from multiple sources (Hendrix and Salehyan, 2015).

Currently, there are a number of available datasets that contain both spatially and temporally disaggregated information on collective action events. These datasets are coded by humans who extract event-level information from media reports. An early dataset of this kind is Francisco's (2006) *European Protest and*

Coercion Data, a collection of daily, city-level information about protests. Due to the focus on European states and the 1980–1995 period, however, the dataset includes almost exclusively democratic states, and is thus of limited use to students of autocracy. Recently, a number of data projects have emerged on collective action and violence in civil wars. One of these efforts is the *Geo-referenced Event Dataset* created by the Uppsala Conflict Data Program (Sundberg and Melander, 2013). The *Armed Conflict Location and Event Data* project (Raleigh et al., 2010) and the *Social Conflict in Africa Database* (Salehyan et al., 2012) have a slightly broader focus with regard to the type of action recorded and also include large-scale protests and riots. Finally, the recently released *Mass Mobilization* dataset contains geolocated protest events from 162 countries (Clark and Regan, 2016). The level of detail and scope of these datasets is unprecedented and enables a host of interesting research questions to be pursued. However, because their main focus is on more violent forms of collective action, or because their scope and coverage is limited, these datasets may not be an optimal choice for our study on Internet and protest in autocratic regimes.

AUTOMATIC CODING

Rather than relying on human coding, some researchers use computer-based methods to code protests from primary and secondary sources. Automated event coders such as the *Kansas Event Data System* (Schrodt and Gerner, 1994), *TABARI* (Schrodt, 2001), and the *VRA Reader* (King and Lowe, 2003) have been used for a number of data collection efforts on contentious politics. These projects are typically much more extensive regarding the type of events they cover and the sources they can process because automation makes the coding very resource-efficient. One of these machine-coded databases is *The World Handbook of Politics IV* (Jenkins et al., 2012), which contains more than 250,000 observations on 40 event forms between 1990 and 2004. Although tests show that machine coding is comparable to human coding if the same coding conventions are used (King and Lowe, 2003; Mikhaylov, Laver and Benoit, 2012; Ruggeri, Gizelis and Dorussen, 2012), the data generated by these collection efforts still have a number of downsides. For one, machine-coded datasets require an a priori specification of relevant actors in the form of actor dictionaries—pre-specified lists of politicians, groups, or organizations involved in the events coded. This means that every news report using alternative names, or no names at all, will not be coded. Most important, traditional machine-coded event datasets do not provide spatial event coordinates, and are thus unsuitable for studying subnational protest dynamics.

A more recent machine-coded event dataset, the *Global Data on Events, Location, and Tone* database (GDELT, Leetaru, 2018), does add spatial coordinates to events. It contains more than 200 million geo-referenced events from 1979 to 2012, divided into 20 main categories with 26 subcategories for "protest." Despite this seeming advantage, GDELT has some data quality issues which make it a less than ideal choice for certain analyses. As Hammond and Weidmann (2014) show, the automatic geo-referencing used in GDELT is often inaccurate and possibly even biased, which can lead to completely different findings compared to human-coded datasets. The *Integrated Crisis Early Warning System* event dataset (O'Brien, 2010) uses a similar coding approach to GDELT and earlier machine-coded data in the sense that each event consists of a particular action, the source actor of this action, and the target. As with all actor dictionary-based systems, it requires the prior specification of all involved actors and actions in the form of dictionaries, which constrains the coding to known and clearly identifiable entities.

Because of the drawbacks of fully automated coding with respect to the types of actions that can be captured and its poor precision in extracting information, the MMAD project presented here uses a combination of automation and human coders to extract events from news reports. The coding procedure differs markedly from existing projects in a number of ways, however. In the next section, we identify common problems in the coding of data from media reports and show how the MMAD addresses these.

Coding Protest Events from Media Reports

As described above, a typical event coding process turns the source material into a standardized list of protest events, each of which has a set of attributes (e.g., the number of protesters, location, issue, etc.). While this process sounds straightforward and easy to implement, a number of potential problems can arise in doing so, particularly those relating to source selection, report selection, and information extraction and aggregation. We first introduce these problems before discussing the solutions developed for the MMAD.

The source material for event coding consists of "reports" (or "articles") covering political developments in the countries of interest. Typically, these reports come from news outlets such as newspapers, magazines, or news agencies, but can also stem from international or non-governmental organizations operating on the ground. Öberg and Sollenberg (2011) provide an excellent overview of the process by which actual events are reported by news outlets and eventually reach the consumer, which we do not discuss in detail here. The number of available media sources is considerable, and limited resources typically require coders to include only some of them. Thus, the *source selection problem* refers to the challenge of having to select a limited number of sources for a coding project. This selection will of course vary with the scope of the project: For example, if we are interested in coding protest in a single country, we may be best served by relying on local newspapers, as they are likely to provide the best coverage of these events.

However, the use of local sources can be problematic when coding protests *across* countries, which is the aim of our MMAD project. First, the availability of news stories can differ widely between countries. While some countries have excellent and regular local newspaper coverage, in others coverage may be spotty. This can lead to widely differing numbers of protest events that can be recorded, simply because there are few (or no) sources reporting them in the first place. Ultimately, this makes it difficult to compare codings across countries, since we do not know whether a low number of protest events is the result of little actual protest activity, or a consequence of low reporting. A second, practical problem in using local sources is language. Whether done by humans or computers, the processing of language requires language-specific skills or software. In a large cross-national project, however, it is simply not feasible to analyze sources in many different languages. For these reasons, the standard approach for most cross-national event coding projects—including MMAD—is to rely on international, English sources only. Yet this restriction does not fully solve the source selection problem, as there are still a large variety of English-language news sources to choose from that need to be narrowed further. Below, we return to this problem and describe our strategy for solving it.

Even with a fixed set of sources from which to draw protest data, we cannot proceed straight to the coding of events. This is because it is difficult to select relevant reports from the respective sources, that is, those that actually cover political protest. In many cases, database searches are limited to simple keywords and return news reports containing terms such as "protest" or "riot." The resulting set of reports is usually very large, since many of the search terms do not unambiguously refer to political protest. Only few of these articles are relevant for the coding of political protest—for MMAD, their proportion is less than 5 percent. Thus, the second problem we face when coding protest events from news sources is the *report selection problem*—in other words, the problem of choosing articles that are relevant for the coding of political protest. In order to reduce the large number of irrelevant reports, MMAD uses an automated approach based on computational text analysis and machine learning. We describe this approach below.

Given a set of relevant articles, a (human or machine) coder then faces the task of creating a standardized list of protest events from them. This final stage of the coding process poses additional challenges: The third problem of event coding is the *information extraction problem*, which refers to the identification of those parts of a news report that contain information about the key variables of interest. For example, the sentence "A group of 300 people rallied in Bishkek on December 4 to protest the ban of the ruling party" contains information about the date, location, number of protesters, and the issue of the protest, all of which should eventually be recorded in the protest database. The coder's task is to identify these pieces of information, convert them into the format used by the database, and enter them in the correct field in the coding form.

Beyond information extraction, a final and fourth problem remains to be solved. During ongoing episodes of protest, it is rarely the case that only a single source reports about a particular protest event. Quite the opposite, we frequently receive reports about a particular protest event from multiple sources, and sometimes even multiple reports from the same source. These different reports often contain conflicting information, for example, about the number of protesters or the level of violence. How do we turn this information into a single entry in our final database? In order to do this, we need to solve the problem of aggregating multiple reports into a single event coding, that is, the *aggregation problem*. To build on the above example of different sources reporting different numbers of participants: Should we consider one of the sources to be more trustworthy, and thus prefer its estimate over others? In a scenario where multiple sources agree on the number of participants, the reported number is probably more reliable compared to a situation where the estimates differ widely across sources. Existing event coding projects are largely opaque when it comes to this problem. If anything, we know the number of reports a particular event is derived from, but not how the information was eventually aggregated into the final coding for this event. For MMAD, we developed a revised coding process that attempts to resolve this issue.

In sum, when creating an event database from news sources, there are four problems we need to address: (i) source selection, (ii) report selection, (iii) information extraction, and (iv) information aggregation. When researchers devise solutions to these problems, they need to balance several requirements for their event database:

- **Completeness** of coverage, or the degree to which the dataset includes the events of interest
- **Feasibility**, or the extent to which the coding effort can be completed with the available resources
- **Transparency and reliability**, or the degree to which the coding process can be understood and replicated by others, with similar results.

The first two requirements are at odds with one another. While coverage is certainly never complete in the sense that we can never record all events that fit our coding criteria, the selection of the sources (the first problem) and/or relevant articles from these sources (the second problem) have a considerable impact on the number of events we fail to record. As mentioned, relying on local sources can in some cases improve the completeness of our dataset, but it fails to satisfy the second requirement in that the effort quickly becomes unfeasible. This is similar for the selection of reports. If we fail to drop news articles that are irrelevant for our coding, the volume of articles to be processed would require an amount of manual labor that quickly exceeds the limits of a typical research project. Similarly, the third requirement, transparency and reliability, can conflict with feasibility. In order to make it possible to understand why an event was coded with particular attributes, the coding decisions should ideally be documented in detail, along with the respective parts of the original report they were derived from (the third problem). In particular, coders would have to document how they integrated potentially conflicting information from different sources into single events (the fourth problem). Due to feasibility reasons, this is hardly ever possible. Still, we can improve on existing event coding approaches by implementing a number of innovations for event coding, which we describe in the following sections.

SOURCE SELECTION

Above, we discussed the problem of selecting media sources for event coding. Since media outlets cater to different audiences and have varying geographic scope, the choice of an outlet matters tremendously for how many protests we "see" (Jenkins and Maher, 2016). To some extent, the problem can be addressed by relying on news *agencies* rather than newspapers. News agencies produce media content for a large number of outlets in different countries, which is why they are typically much broader and inclusive in their coverage as compared to national or local media. Moreover, the fact that these agencies are much bigger in size makes it possible for them to have reporters in many different locations around the globe, which increases scope and depth of coverage. Still, even if we rely solely on English-language news agencies, we will unavoidably have some bias in coverage, as these agencies typically cater to audiences in Western countries and primarily report on events that are of some interest to them. The choice of sources is especially important in projects spanning the non-democratic regions of the world, where media coverage by Western media is often sparse. Nam (2006) illustrates the problem by comparing protest data on South Korea and Burma collected in KINDS—a local news database—and LexisNexis. Unsurprisingly, the results show a significant increase in data comprehensiveness using the local news database. However, as discussed, for larger coding projects the use of local news databases is often unfeasible due to cost, language, and time constraints.

In order to gauge the extent of the source selection problem and to select a good combination of sources for MMAD, we performed an extensive trial coding. The trial coding was performed on Kyrgyzstan for the period of October 2004 through June 2005 searching *all English-language sources* in LexisNexis, restricting the search to articles from that country and using a broad set of search terms.[5] This is the same search string that was later used during the active coding phase, though with a more limited number of news sources. Kyrgyzstan is a suitable sample candidate for two main reasons. First, it is a relatively liberalized autocracy where—despite its US military base and strategic location near Afghanistan, China, and Russia—we expect limited coverage in Western media. Second, in March 2005 there was a mass uprising that forced Askar Akayev, president since independence, to flee the country. We therefore expect Kyrgyzstan to be the center of attention in late March 2005 with coverage up until then to be limited, allowing us to determine coverage by different sources both for periods of calm and unrest. All news reports were screened for events that fit the MMAD definition of mass mobilization events. The resulting data consisted of 602 event reports from 73 unique sources, which together describe 193 protest events in the nine-month period.[6]

The trial coding reveals a number of interesting patterns. We examined the news sources that identify the largest number of events: the Associated Press (AP), the Agence France-Presse (AFP), and BBC Monitoring. While we would assume that Western news agencies cover similar events, this is not necessarily so. According to Figure 4.1 (left panel), the AP covers the smallest number of events, and many events captured by the AFP are not recorded by the AP. Individually, the AP and AFP cover only 25 percent and 39 percent of all recorded events, respectively. Both the AP and AFP together only identify less than half of all events we obtain when examining all sources. This suggests that relying on large news agencies alone leads to the omission of a significant number of events, which is why we need other sources to achieve higher coverage. Figure 4.1 (left panel) shows that including BBC Monitoring boosts coverage dramatically. BBC Monitoring is a service provided by the BBC that translates and aggregates news from a large number of local news sources worldwide (BBC, 2017). For this reason, it provides much more detailed coverage of events that typically do not make it into the international news. BBC Monitoring alone provides coverage of 56 percent of recorded protest incidents. At the same time, however, the overlap between the agencies is only partial, which means that omitting even one of them would make us lose a considerable number of events.

Figure 4.1 (right panel) shows the combined coverage of our three sources (AP, AFP, and BBC World Monitoring). Together, they cover around 84 percent of all events reported during the coding period. Overall, this is a good result, in

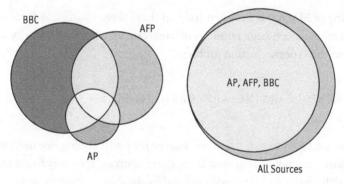

Figure 4.1 Coverage of protest events by different sources

particular since the number of articles from these three sources alone is quite small relative to the total number of articles from all sources: In the nine-month period of the trial coding, searching all sources returns 2,711 hits, while restricting the search to the AP, the AFP, and BBC Monitoring reduces the number to 1,023. In other words, 84 percent of the events come from 38 percent of the material. About 59 percent (1,606 of 2,711) of the reports using all sources are from March 2005 while 53 percent of all event reports were published the week leading up to the March 24 storming of the presidential palace. In comparison, 48 percent (495 of 1,023) of the reports searching AP, AFP, and BBC Monitoring are dated March 2005, while 29 percent of event reports using these sources were reported in the week leading up to March 24. This indicates that the coverage is more balanced using AP, AFP, and BBC Monitoring compared to using the complete set of sources.

While it is clearly difficult to make strong general claims regarding the source selection problem from a single case, we believe that the results from our trial coding can provide some guidance regarding the selection of sources for MMAD. In general, we cannot expect to obtain a complete set of events using media sources alone (Jenkins and Maher, 2016). Rather, we need to accept the fact that gaps in the data will remain, although our results indicate that certain strategies help to minimize these gaps. For the three sources we examined in detail, there is a high trade-off between the number of source materials (articles) and the amount of coverage. This trade-off is likely even higher in countries with better coverage by Western media, for example Egypt and Iran. For countries outside the international spotlight, the inclusion of BBC Monitoring leads to much better coverage of protest events that are not picked up by international media, as in Kyrgyzstan. In short, the use of international news agencies such as the AP and AFP combined with local reports provided by BBC Monitoring seems to strike a balance between coverage and feasibility for our coding project. Thus, the coding of MMAD is based entirely on these three sources. Still, simple key-word searches return large numbers of irrelevant articles, which is why we need to address the report selection problem.

A MACHINE LEARNING APPROACH TO FILTERING NEWS REPORTS

Now that we have chosen the news sources for event coding, we need to select articles covering political protest from these sources. One way to do this is by using article topics and categories defined by database providers, as for example LexisNexis. However, such an approach does not satisfy scientific standards of transparency and replicability. Opaque and non-replicable methods are used to assign these tags, which makes it difficult to assess whether they can produce a reasonably complete selection of articles. Consequently, these proprietary meth-ods were avoided and simple keyword searches were used (in combination with the respective country names) to retrieve the relevant articles for a given coun-try. These terms had to be kept rather general in order to avoid losing too many relevant articles due to too-narrow criteria. For the MMAD, articles were re-trieved by searching for *protest, demonstration, rally, campaign, riot,* or *picket.* Not surprisingly, the number of false positives (selected articles that do *not* cover political protest) in the simple keyword search is extremely high. In the first cod-ing phase for the MMAD project, we performed an extensive human coding of roughly 250,000 articles from our three sources, covering 19 autocratic coun-tries from different regions of the world to avoid regional biases. Figure 4.2 shows the distribution of relevant and irrelevant articles across these countries in this initial set.

Overall, the proportion of relevant articles obtained through a simple key-word search is only around 2 percent. In other words, a huge share of the work by human coders would involve sifting through articles that ultimately provide no information on political protest and are thus irrelevant for the project. This suggests that a coding process based entirely on human coding would not be feasible for the entire set of around 70 countries in the MMAD. Therefore, a ma-chine learning approach was developed to eliminate a large share of the irrelevant articles, while keeping most of the relevant ones. For this task, the application of computer-assisted text classification seems reasonable, since the task is not to extract individual pieces of information from a news report (which, as dis-cussed, is fraught with problems), but rather to assess the general relevance of the article based on the presence of certain terms and combinations of terms. Using a *supervised* machine learning approach, the 250,000 articles from the first coding phase were used as a training set in which the computer "learned" how to detect relevant articles covering instances of political protest. Once this

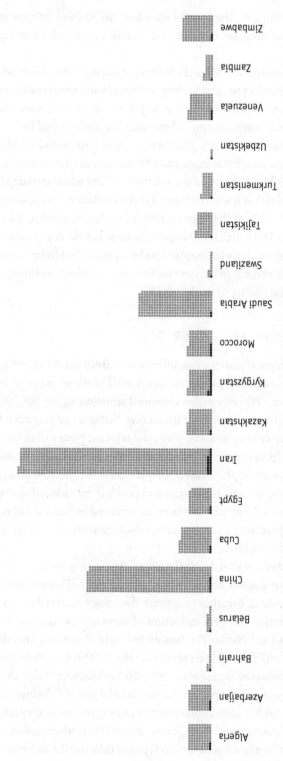

Figure 4.2 Share of articles describing political mass protest from the first coding phase (modified based on Croicu and Weidmann, 2015). The black squares correspond to the number of articles for each country that describe mass protest (and are thus "relevant" for the coding), the gray squares represent the number of irrelevant articles that do not describe mass protest.

learning process is complete, the trained classifier can be used on new articles to determine whether they are relevant and should be passed on to humans for coding.

The classifier designed for MMAD follows standard approaches in automated text coding and relies on a set of frequent words and word combinations. Since the distribution of irrelevant and relevant articles is extremely skewed (only 2 percent are relevant), existing off-the-shelf algorithms had to be modified (Croicu and Weidmann, 2015). The final result of Croicu and Weidmann's effort is a classifier that eliminates more than 60 percent of all irrelevant articles while retaining around 90 percent of the relevant articles when evaluated "out-of-sample" on countries that it was not trained on (for detailed results, see Croicu and Weidmann, 2015). Given the large number of irrelevant articles, this trade-off seems acceptable. Thus, articles obtained through simple keyword searches were pre-filtered using machine learning before being passed on to human coders for the final step of the coding. In the next section, we describe how this final step is implemented for the coding of the MMAD.

SEPARATING EVENTS AND REPORTS

An event coding process translates raw information from media reports into a simplified, usually numeric representation of events that allows for large-N analyses of the coded cases.[7] We refer to this source information as "reports." Reports rarely come in a form that is convenient for coding. Instead, two steps need to be performed during the coding process: First, the relevant pieces of information need to be extracted from the report—for example, information about the location and time of an incident, the issue of a protest, and the number and type of participants. This is the information extraction problem introduced above. Second, once the relevant information has been determined across a set of reports, it needs to be aggregated into a set of events, which constitute the final dataset. This is the aggregation problem.

Figure 4.3 provides a stylized illustration of the coding process. For now, consider only the two dashed boxes on the left and right. The left box shows a set of two reports, which together constitute the source material for a coding project. For example, this can be a collection of news articles obtained from a news archive such as LexisNexis. The box on the right shows the final dataset, which in our case is a set of individual events. Usually, data projects do not specify how exactly they get from the source material to the final dataset. While almost all datasets specify the type of information that needs to be available before an event is coded, the fact that both information extraction and aggregation are performed by the coder without precise guidelines leaves us with two problems: First, we do not know the precise formulation of certain types of information in a report. For

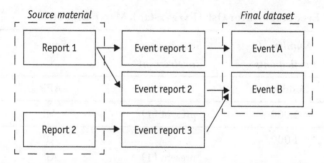

Figure 4.3 Reports, event reports, and events (from Weidmann and Rød, 2015). Reports can contain information about multiple events, thus generating multiple event reports (report 1 and event reports 1 and 2). Events, on the other hand, can be based on different event reports (event B and event reports 2 and 3).

example, was the location reported as a precise city, or as a village outside a city? What was the precise label the news report used for a group of protesters? Without transparent coding rules, it is essentially up to the coder to map a particular piece of information in a report to the corresponding entity (i.e., a location or group) and thus create the data the dataset is based on. A similar but perhaps even more severe problem arises when the coder aggregates different pieces of information. For example, if two reports are about the same event, but mention different numbers of protesters, which one is used in the final coding? How do we know that multiple sources, rather than one source, were used to code the event? So far, existing coding projects (human or automatic) have not tackled this problem directly, which can lead to serious problems (Jenkins and Maher, 2016).

In order to remedy these problems, we propose separating information extraction and aggregation into two steps. Essentially, the idea is to introduce an intermediate type of output from the coding process, called an "event report." As the name suggests, an event report is an individual statement of an event derived from a news report. It contains fields for all the relevant information needed to eventually code an event. Thus, an event report is the output of the information extraction step that serves as input for the aggregation step to generate the final list of events. Figure 4.3 illustrates this. From the source reports (left) we extract a set of event reports (center), which are later aggregated into the events that constitute the final dataset (right). While many reports will only contain information about a single event (for example, report 2 generates only one event report, no. 3), this procedure is able to deal with more complex reports: Report 1 mentions two events, which result in event reports 1 and 2. Once we have generated the set of event reports, we need to aggregate them to obtain the final dataset. Again, many events will be based on only one event report, as is the case

Table 4.1 **Event reports for Osh (Kyrgyzstan), March 21, 2005**

Number of participants	Security force involvement	Source
hundreds		AFP
2,000	present (1)	AP
1,000		AP
	present (1)	AP
	present (1)	BBC Monitoring
1,000	not present (0)	BBC Monitoring
several thousand		BBC Monitoring
3,000	physical intervention (2)	BBC Monitoring
200		BBC Monitoring

for event A in Figure 4.3. However, in cases where there are multiple event reports for one event, the coder will have to aggregate them into a single event. Since the extracted information is provided in a standardized form in the event record, this process can largely be automated, thus making it extremely cheap and transparent. We will provide an example of this below.

How does this procedure solve the problems discussed above? First, it makes the information extraction step much more transparent. By using the event report(s) that an event is based on, a user can find out, for example, what phrase in the report was used to pinpoint the location of an event. This applies to other types of information as well, such as the number and type of protesters or the issue of the protest. Also, the user has full information about, and can even control, the aggregation process. For example, it is possible to change the way that participant numbers from the event reports are aggregated into a single number, or even to weigh information by source. Last, the event records can serve as training data for automatic text coding of event data. To date, these routines perform information extraction and aggregation in a single step, similar to human coding. This leads to exactly the same concerns described above, particularly regarding information aggregation. In contrast, using the intermediate stage of event reports for training computational classifiers can support new efforts to automate information extraction and the aggregation of these reports, and thus improve the transparency of automated coding techniques.

A short example from the "Tulip Revolution" in Kyrgyzstan helps to illustrate this. Table 4.1 displays nine event reports with divergent information on

Table 4.2 **Alternative event codings for Osh (March 21, 2005), according to two different aggregation rules**

Aggregation rule	Number of participants	Security force involvement
average(#part), mode(sec. force inv.)	1,440	present (1)
max(#part), max(sec. force inv.)	3,000	physical intervention (2)

two variables included in the MMAD: the number of participants and the level of security force involvement (ordinal, values in parentheses).[8] The last column displays the news source. All of the event reports in Table 4.1 took place in the city of Osh on March 21, 2005. It is immediately apparent that the information in the event reports diverges both across reports from the same source and across sources: the number of participants differs in all three reports from the AP and all five reports from BBC Monitoring. Also, the estimate given by the AFP (hundreds) is very different from the AP estimates (1,000 and 2,000) and three of the BBC Monitoring estimates (1,000, several thousand, and 3,000). In addition, there are two reports without participant number estimates. There is similar uncertainty regarding security force involvement in the protest. In fact, the information ranges from not present (0) to physical intervention (2). Four event reports indicate the presence or intervention of security forces, four do not mention security force involvement at all, and one asserts that forces were absent. Without transparent guidelines, it is not clear how different coders would have aggregated these event reports in a conventional event dataset.

Once we have extracted these event reports from the selected news reports, we need to aggregate them to the level of individual events. Table 4.2 shows this for our above example. For the sake of illustration, we employ two alternative aggregation rules. The first uses the *average* number of participants across all news reports (1,440) and the *most frequent value* for security force involvement (present, 1).[9] However, users who prefer other aggregations can do so easily, as the second line shows. Here, we use the *maximum* reported number of protesters (3,000), and the *maximum* level of security force involvement (physical intervention, 2). Of course, other aggregation rules are possible and can easily be applied by the user. For instance, one could compute confidence intervals around the aggregated numbers. In addition, one can focus on other variables in the aggregation process. For example, one could give preference to more recent reports by using the date and time a report was released (not shown in the table).

In short, our procedure adds a new type of output to the coding process: the list of event reports. For the MMAD, these event reports are distributed alongside the finished list of events, which allows users to explicitly incorporate any uncertainty in the news reports into their analyses (Cook and Weidmann, 2019) or to study patterns of higher or lower reporting (Hellmeier, Weidmann and Rød, 2018). However, before generating a final set of protest events, the different reports need to be aggregated, as demonstrated in the example above. Before introducing the design of our analysis in the next chapter, we briefly describe the scope and variables contained in the MMAD and give a few examples of protest episodes covered in our data.

The Mass Mobilization in Autocracies Database

In this section, we give a short overview of the database, starting with its scope: autocratic regimes.

DEFINING AUTOCRACY

How can we tell democracies and autocracies apart? Political scientists agree that, at a minimum, democracies must fill executive and legislative offices through competitive elections (Przeworski et al., 2000). Beyond this, however, there are different definitions, some arguing that the distinction between democracy and autocracy is gradual (Diamond, 2002; Freedom House, 2015; Marshall, Gurr and Jaggers, 2014), while some conceive of them as distinct categories (Przeworski et al., 2000; Cheibub, Gandhi and Vreeland, 2010; Hadenius and Teorell, 2007). We follow one of the most popular latter approaches: The *Autocratic Regime Data* by Geddes, Wright and Frantz (2014a) considers a regime to be autocratic if the government came to power either (i) by using means other than a direct, reasonably fair competitive election, or (ii) through a competitive election but changed the rules while in office to prevent future elections from being competitive.

Regimes of the first type seize power through military coups or popular uprisings, for example. An example of the second type of regime is Hugo Chávez's presidency in Venezuela, where a democratically elected government prevented future elections from being competitive. This, of course, raises the question: Under which circumstances does an election fail to meet a reasonable level of fairness and competitiveness? According to Geddes, Wright and Frantz (2014a), this is the case if large opposition parties are not allowed to participate, there is extensive repression of opposition leaders or supporters, or vote fraud alters the outcome of the election (see Geddes, Wright and Frantz, 2014b, ch. 6 for details). Importantly—and this is where the definition deviates from many others—this excludes cases where no government exists or the government does not control the territory (e.g., Somalia since the end of Siad Barre's regime in 1991) and countries occupied by a foreign power (e.g., Iraq from 2003 to 2005, after the US-led invasion).

The Geddes, Wright and Frantz (2014a) regime classification identifies countries as autocracies for certain time periods. In other words, countries that used to be democratic can later become autocracies (such as Peru in 1992), but autocracies can also drop out of the autocratic sample by transitioning to democracy (such as Portugal in 1974 and Mexico in 2000). Our coding project and the analysis follow this definition and include those countries that are considered autocratic during the relevant time periods. In its initial version used for this book, the dataset covers the years 2003–2012, although more recent years will be added in the future. The MMAD includes data from 70 different countries, whereby some are covered only for a certain part of the coding period. The appendix shows the corresponding list of countries/time periods included in the dataset.

POLITICAL PROTEST

Having defined the type of political regime to be included in the MMAD, we now need to take a closer look at political protest, the object of study of this book. The public discourse about protest in autocratic countries is often dominated by more recent events such as mass protests in the Middle East during the Arab Spring or the anti-regime demonstrations against President Nicolas Maduro in Venezuela. However, these dramatic events conceal the fact that political protest occurs much more frequently, although often on a smaller scale. So, what constitutes political protest? In short, we focus on overt events that (i) are directed against the government, (ii) involve a large number of people, (iii) take place in a public space, and (iv) do not explicitly aim to use violence. Let us take a closer look at the four elements of this definition.

Anti-regime. Political protests can be directed at different political actors or institutions. In this book, we will deal with the most frequent and—for our purpose—most relevant type of protests: those that address the government ("anti-regime").[10] If successful, this type of protest can seriously destabilize and even topple autocratic regimes. In its typical form, anti-regime protest is associated with maximalist demands such as replacing the government, but this does not apply in all cases. In fact, we frequently see anti-regime mass protests with much more specific demands, such as lower wages for public officials, the release of arrested opposition members, or the reversal of commodity price increases. As a consequence, these demands are not necessarily directed toward the domestic central government; rather, they can address regional or even local governments and governmental institutions.

A large number of people.   By definition, political protest is a collective endeavor by a large number of people. In this book, we therefore analyze protest events involving at least 25 people. This excludes a number of dissident activities carried out by single individuals or small groups. The power of large numbers of participants derives from the fact that large protests are more visible and are thus more likely to attract the attention of national and international audiences, and therefore also the government. While more powerful, larger protests are also more difficult to coordinate, which is one of the reasons why modern communication technology is believed to have a potentially strong impact here..

A public gathering.   Protest is a public activity. This means that it excludes acts of dissent that are carried out in private, such as "blackouts" where activists turn off the electricity in their homes, or when activists display flags or paint their homes in political protest (Schock, 2005). These activities take many forms and are carried out frequently, but are less likely to receive attention and thus have a smaller impact.

No systematic use of armed force.   It is also important to distinguish protest from other, more violent forms of political contest, such as civil war. While both are similar in the sense that a political opposition confronts a government outside of regular political channels, civil wars by their nature are characterized by the systematic use of military force on both sides (Gleditsch et al., 2002). This is not the case for protest, which does not necessarily rely on armed force. Hence, our definition excludes armed dissent such as terrorist attacks and rebel violence. Importantly, however, we do not exclude events based on the level of violence; protests can turn violent, and can be violently repressed by the autocratic government.

By focusing on these four main criteria, we leave out others such as the level of organization. Protests differ in the extent to which they rely on existing political organizations, or rather emerge as spontaneous instances of collective action. In reality, however, many protests involve both organized groups and unorganized citizens, which is why we do not exclude one or the other. The MMAD contains variables for the date, location, actors, number of participants, and level of violence by participants and by security forces. The full list of variables included in the database is available in the appendix of this book and in the codebook that accompanies the dataset. A key feature of the database is the geo-referencing of protests to particular cities. During the coding process, coders assign the corresponding location based on the GeoNames database (http://www.geonames.org), a free gazetteer of geographic entities around the globe. This way, each event report is assigned a unique city from GeoNames, which later helps us to identify corresponding reports from other sources about the same city and on the same date.

SOME EXAMPLES

The following three short examples help to illustrate the information contained in the MMAD: (i) the events leading up to the Tulip Revolution in Kyrgyzstan in 2005, (ii) the anti-regime protests before, during, and after the Iranian presidential elections in 2009, and (iii) the Arab Spring uprisings and their aftermath in Egypt in 2011. For these illustrations, reports in the MMAD were aggregated to events based on their reference to the same day and the same city. The examples highlight the spatial and temporal precision of the data, which is key for the disaggregated analysis of protest behavior we present in the remainder of this book.

Kyrgyzstan 2005   In the period after it gained independence from the Soviet Union, Kyrgyzstan was often hailed for its relatively liberal political environment (Anderson, 1999). Multiparty elections and economic reform created a stark contrast to the closed autocratic regimes in the neighboring states (e.g., Turkmenistan, Uzbekistan). In 1996, however, President Askar Akayev increased his power through constitutional amendments. Moreover, in the period following these changes, fraudulent election practices and persecution of political rivals ensured that Akayev and his loyalists remained in power (Freedom House, 2002). After the Tulip Revolution ousted Akayev in 2005, Kurmanbek Bakiyev came to power and maintained the nepotistic rule of his predecessor. Five year later, in 2010, Bakiyev was ousted in a new uprising after the killing of dozens of protesters led to a popular backlash. Since the ouster of Bakiyev, there has been little stability in Kyrgyzstan, as predatory elites rotate between being in office and being the opposition (Freedom House, 2016b).

Figure 4.4 maps the events leading up to the Tulip Revolution in Kyrgyzstan (Radnitz, 2006). The popular uprising is commonly referred to as one of the "Color Revolutions," a term used to describe successful non-violent mobilization against authoritarian regimes following disputed elections (Chenoweth and Stephan, 2011; Beissinger, 2007; Bunce and Wolchik, 2006; Way, 2008). Similar uprisings also overthrew incumbents in Serbia ("Bulldozer Revolution," 2000), Georgia ("Rose Revolution," 2003), and Ukraine ("Orange Revolution," 2004–2005). Like the other "Color Revolutions," the uprising in Kyrgyzstan

Figure 4.4 The Tulip Revolution (2005). January: 3 protests, 1 location. February: 26 protests, 16 locations. March: 78 protests, 24 locations.

was the result of stolen elections (Tucker, 2007). In February 2005, parliamentary elections marred by election fraud removed a number of influential local elites from power. As a result, these elites mobilized anti-government protests across the country (Temirkulov, 2010; Lewis, 2008). On March 24, demonstrators stormed the presidential palace and forced sitting President Akayev to flee the country.

On the maps, the black dots are anti-government demonstrations. The size of the dots corresponds to the number of events in each location. The left map shows that there was little activity in January, with protests restricted to the capital (Bishkek). In February (middle map), fraudulent parliamentary elections led to widespread protests. The MMAD records protests in 16 different cities in February. However, the number of events in each location was relatively low, peaking at four in Bokombayevskoye and Kochkor. In March (right map), political violence escalated as protesters stormed and occupied government buildings throughout the country (24 cities in total). The southern capitals of Osh and Jalal-Abad were the epicenters of protest (Temirkulov, 2008) with 12 and 17 recorded anti-government demonstrations, respectively. In fact, protests only spread to Bishkek after security forces raided an occupied building in Jalal-Abad and killed several protesters. Prominent opposition politicians, such as former prime minister Kurmanbek Bakiyev and founding member of the Fatherland Movement (Ata-Jurt) Roza Otunbayeva, joined the Bishkek protests and led the overthrow of president Akayev.

Iran 2009   Since the overthrow of Shah Mohammad Reza Pahlavi in 1979, Iran has been governed by religious leaders. The Supreme Leader Ali Khameini is the highest authority in the country, with the power to appoint and dismiss highly ranked members of the government, the judiciary, and the military. The office of Supreme Leader is not subjected to popular elections, and power has only been passed once in the 37 years since the regime was established when the first Supreme Leader, Ruhollah Khomeini, died in 1989. However, Iran holds presidential and legislative elections. Candidates for elected political offices must

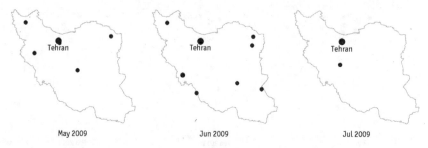

Figure 4.5 Iranian presidential election protests (2009). May: 8 protests, 6 locations.
June: 20 protests, 8 locations. July: 8 protests, 2 locations.

be approved by the Supreme Leader and other religious leaders (the Guardian
Council and the Assembly of Experts). This approval ensures that no candidate
can fundamentally oppose the regime, yet candidates commonly campaign under conservative or reformist agendas, and the resulting elections have brought
about some policy implications. For example, under the period of reformist
rule by Mohammad Khatami, restrictions on freedom of expression and gender
separation were relaxed (Freedom House, 2010).

The 2009 presidential elections pitted the conservative incumbent Mah-
moud Ahmadinejad against reformist opposition candidate Mir-Hossein Mousavi.
The pre-election phase was perceived to be rigged in favor of Ahmadinejad, in
particular by attempting to control communication via cell phones and the Internet (CNN, 2009). Observers have argued that the election fraud was part
of a larger crackdown on the reformists by the religious leadership (Freedom
House, 2010). Official election results published on June 12, 2009 proclaimed
victory for Ahmadinejad, with 62 percent of the votes against Mousavi's 34
percent. The announcement of the results sparked large-scale protests that
quickly turned violent. The protest movement, claimed to be the largest since
the Iranian Revolution, is often referred to as the Green Movement. Green
was originally the color of Mousavi's campaign and became a symbol of the
resistance against the incumbent administration. A number of studies have
identified Twitter as a catalyst of the protests (Grossman, 2009; Morozov,
2009).

Figure 4.5 maps the MMAD events from May to July 2009 in Iran. Before the
election in May (left map), the number of protests was quite low: eight events in
six cities. In June (middle map), the month of the election, anti-regime protests
spread, occurring in eight cities and totaling 20 events, with more than half
of these (12) occurring in Tehran. Moreover, many protests featured violence
from both protesters and government security forces. In July (right map), the
protests subsided, and the data record eight events in two cities. This also marks
a shift in the tactics employed by the Green Movement, who started boycotting

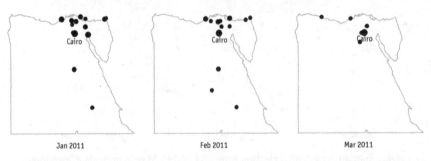

Figure 4.6 Egyptian uprising (2011). January: 35 protests, 14 locations. February: 38 protests, 14 locations. March: 19 protests, 7 locations.

goods, scribbling anti-regime slogans on banknotes, and marking properties of militiamen with the color green (Wright, 2009).

Egypt 2011   After the overthrow of King Fuad in 1952, Egypt was governed by military officers. Hosni Mubarak, the fourth officer in a row to become president of the republic, ruled for 30 years (1981–2011). Following a brief period of civilian rule after Mubarak's resignation, military officers regained power in 2013. Since then, repression of political activities and persecution of opposition have increased. For example, the victors of the 2012 election—the Muslim Brotherhood—were declared a terrorist organization shortly after the coup. Similar action has also been taken against non-religious political rivals (Freedom House, 2016a).

In early January 2011, protests calling for regime change in Tunisia quickly spread to Egypt. A few weeks later, the ousting of Tunisian president Ben Ali intensified hopes of a successful overthrow in Egypt. The Egyptian protests were launched under an umbrella of grievances related to corruption, power abuse, unemployment, and fraudulent elections. Moreover, a number of observers have highlighted the role of social media for protest mobilization in Egypt (Lotan et al., 2011; Khondker, 2011), while others have downplayed its importance (Anderson, 2011). On January 25—the so-called Day of Revolt—thousands of people took to the streets in cities across the country. Protests persisted over the next weeks, prompting the government to impose a curfew and increase military presence in Cairo. In addition, political reforms were promised. On February 10, protests intensified once more when Mubarak stated his intent to stay in office. However, the day after it was announced that he had resigned from his post as president. During the upheavals, hundreds of people were killed and thousands were injured.

Figure 4.6 plots the events in Egypt from January to March 2011. In January (left map), 35 protests in 14 different locations are recorded in the MMAD. Thirty-one of these protests occurred on or after the "Day of Revolt" (January

25). Nine of the protests occurred in Cairo, five in Suez, and four in Alexandria. In February (middle map), the number of recorded protests and locations is very similar to January. However, protests in Cairo intensified. In total, 17 protests were recorded in the capital in February. After the overthrow of Mubarak, the number of protests subsided to about half. In March (right map), the MMAD records 19 protests in seven different locations, with most of these (13) occurring in Cairo.

Conclusion

We began this chapter with a review of the two main approaches for event coding: traditional coding by humans and computer-based automated coding through natural language processing. Each of them has its downsides: Human coding is resource-intense and potentially less reliable, while automated coding is less precise and (at present) unable to capture the detailed information on protests that scholars require for their analysis. Regardless of whether we use human or automated coding, there are four challenges we need to overcome: the problem of selecting sources, the problem of selecting relevant reports from these sources, the problem of extracting information from the selected reports, and the problem of aggregating different reports to individual events.

The chapter described in detail how the MMAD project addresses these challenges: A set of three news agencies were selected as sources, since together they cover 84 percent of all events reported. Articles from these sources were filtered using a machine learning classifier that separates relevant from irrelevant articles. The articles classified as relevant were then processed by human coders. During the coding process, the coders extracted reported information on specific characteristics of the protest incidents from each article that covers a political protest. Rather than aggregating these different reports about a single event, the database retains the individual reports. Not only does this make the event coding process much more transparent and lead to a more comprehensive database for this book, it also allows for a number of new applications of the data. For example, Cook and Weidmann (2019) show that the use of report-level data leads to better and more accurate results in quantitative analyses of protest compared to the use of event-level data. Hellmeier, Weidmann and Rød (2018) used the MMAD to study patterns of media attention, which they measure as the number of reports per event. Thus, the more complex coding procedure and more involved use of the dataset add considerable scientific value.

5

From Event Reports to
Protest Analysis

In this chapter, we describe the core elements of our research design. As elaborated in Chapter 3, the aim of this book is to determine how Internet penetration relates to anti-regime protest in autocratic regimes. In particular, we study how it influences the different phases of protest, including occurrence, persistence over time, and diffusion across space. We are also interested in how this relationship is affected by regime institutions and violent repression by the autocratic government. But how do we get from event reports in the MMAD to a statistical analysis that tells us about the effect of digital communication on protest dynamics? As described, we take a disaggregated approach in which our main variables are measured at the city level. This allows us to study the effect of Internet penetration on protest within countries, but also across different countries. The chapter starts with an overview of current research approaches in our field, before presenting a multilevel research design that combines a subnational perspective with a cross-national one. We describe our spatial and temporal units of analysis as well as the most important variables and our modeling approach. Importantly, since we need detailed data at the city level, we present novel ways of measuring some of our main variables remotely, for example by using observations of Internet traffic or night light emissions captured by satellites. This chapter presents the main elements of our research design, which we build on in the different empirical sections of this book.

Basic Considerations

We begin this chapter with a list of requirements for our research design. Most of this is in line with current standards in political science, and therefore does not need much elaboration. Our central research question is how Internet use by activists and autocratic governments affects patterns of protest in autocracies. The question implies that we seek to identify a causal relationship and determine whether this relationship plays out differently under certain conditions. Most empirical research of causal effects in our field is comparative: Scholars examine how variation in a certain independent (or treatment) variable leads to variation in an outcome by comparing different cases or instances of the causal process in question. Variation in the independent variable can be due to intentional or unintentional manipulation, as is the case in experimental research, or can occur naturally outside the analyst's control, as in observational research. The comparative aspect, that is, the comparison of units with different values of the independent variable, is essential here, as it is necessary to assess whether a variable has any implications for the outcome we are interested in.

There is a considerable amount of qualitative work on protest, particularly on episodes of large-scale unrest such as the uprisings in Egypt in 2011 (Holmes, 2012) and Kyrgyzstan in 2005 (Radnitz, 2006). The main aim of these studies is to provide in-depth descriptions of single cases and to develop theory, but they do not attempt to make strong causal claims. An exception are studies that use causal process tracing, which is the analysis of different stages of a theorized process and the assessment of causal effects (Collier, 2011; Beach and Pedersen, 2013). It is difficult to make strong causal claims within a process tracing framework, however, since it only involves hypothesizing about counterfactual outcomes rather than observing them in comparable cases. While we value the insights that this work has revealed, we prefer to examine causal effects by means of comparison and therefore opt for a comparative design.

Comparative designs can take a variety of forms, ranging from qualitative or quantitative comparisons of few cases to analyses covering large samples. Typically, this distinction carries a trade-off between depth and breadth: Small-N studies are able to produce rich evidence on particular cases that is typically unattainable with larger samples. For example, the studies by Bunce and Wolchik (2006), Beissinger (2007), and Way (2008) compare the Color Revolutions in post-communist countries, while Francisco (1995) looks at patterns of repression and protest in a sample of three states. At the same time, causal inference in small-N comparisons is more difficult, since the observed outcomes may be due to factors that we simply fail to observe. Also, due to the limited number of cases studied, it is often difficult to draw inferences about other cases or contexts. In quantitative comparisons with larger samples, this problem is less severe, as there are many realizations of the causal mechanism in question. This reduces the influence of alternative explanations or at least gives researchers the possibility of statistically controlling for them. For our analysis, we follow the latter path and utilize a large-N quantitative design.

Large-N designs have frequently been employed in the study of protest covering many countries over time (Brancati, 2014; Carey, 2006; Hollyer, Rosendorff and Vreeland, 2015). In these studies, the main (independent and dependent) variables are measured at the country level, for example by using country-year aggregated dichotomous and count indicators of protest (Ulfelder, 2005; Teorell, 2010) or the proportion of Internet users in a country (Ruijgrok, 2017). These aggregated indicators, however, carry the risk of not being able to capture the causal process well. If we find a relationship between Internet coverage and protest using indicators measured at the national level, we cannot know whether protest actually takes place in locations with Internet coverage. It could, for example, be that countries with high Internet coverage experience more protest, but that these protests mainly take place in those parts of the country where Internet coverage is low. Hence, if protest is catalyzed or inhibited by the availability of Internet service, we need to study the effect of *local* coverage on the *local* occurrence of protest, rather than correlate national indicators. This shortcoming of aggregated, macro-level studies has been recognized in the study of civil war, which led to a new generation of disaggregated research in this field (Cederman and Gleditsch, 2009). This research uses fine-grained data on violence and its correlates at a high level of spatial resolution, for example in spatial grid cells (Buhaug and Rød, 2006), settlement regions of ethnic groups (Weidmann, 2009), or even individual districts or cities (Toft and Zhukov, 2015). Some disaggregated studies also exist for political protest. However, these are usually limited to one country, for example Russian regions (Reuter and Robertson, 2015) and, most frequently, cities in the United States (Andrews, 2006; Eisinger, 1973; Myers, 2000).

While they are an important advancement over aggregated, cross-national studies, disaggregated analyses can introduce other problems. Often, they focus exclusively on local conditions and fail to take into account that the local drivers of outcomes such as violence or protest can play out differently depending on the national environment they occur in. This approach may be suitable if we study purely local processes, such as local economic conditions, but is too limited for our research on digital communication technology and protest, since the (local) effect of Internet coverage on protest is likely to depend on how the Internet is used by certain governments for indoctrination, surveillance, or co-optation. Thus, what we require for our analysis is a comparative research design that allows us to leverage the power of local, disaggregated data, but at the same time is able to model variation between different countries, political regimes, and other country-level conditions. In the remainder of this chapter, we outline a research design that can meet these requirements.

A Multilevel Research Design

Multilevel analysis has been developed for analyzing processes and data at different levels of resolution. Typical applications of these models in the social sciences include educational performance evaluations where students are nested in classes (Gelman and Hill, 2006) or survey responses from individuals across different national contexts (Busemeyer and Iversen, 2014). How do we get from the event reports contained in the MMAD to a multilevel research design that combines both the local and national level? For our analysis, we need to define the spatial and temporal units of observation, the variables required at the local and national level, and the statistical model.

UNIT OF ANALYSIS

As explained in Chapter 4, the MMAD contains event reports of protests in 68 autocracies from 2003 to 2012. Each protest event in MMAD is tagged with precise spatial (city or town) and temporal (day) coordinates. This fine-grained data leaves us with a number of options for processing the data for empirical analysis. First and foremost, we need to decide on a unit of analysis along two dimensions: space and time. Regarding the former, there are several possibilities. Some analyses use subnational administrative units such as districts or provinces as the spatial unit of analysis (Cunningham and Weidmann, 2010). For our analysis, however, this has several shortcomings. First, administrative boundaries may not be particularly relevant for the emergence of protest. The type of political protest we are focusing on in this study is directed mostly at national political administrations, and the protest issues are relevant to the entire country. Second, when comparing different countries, these units can be of vastly different size, which would require us to implement different standardizations and controls to enable a valid comparison.

In order to create more comparable spatial units, several researchers have resorted to using artificially defined grid cells. In this approach, a regular, quadratic grid is overlaid on the study area, with each of the cells constituting one spatial unit. For example, the PRIO-Grid dataset (Tollefsen, Strand and Buhaug, 2012) divides the world up into cells of 0.5 × 0.5 decimal degrees (about 55 km by 55 km at the equator), with each cell assigned to a particular country. This approach has several advantages. First, it avoids the heterogeneity we oftentimes see across administrative units by using cells of similar size. Second, using borders that have no political meaning reduces cases where borders have been drawn based on other political variables (such as ethnicity), thus avoiding potential endogeneity.

For our analysis, however, spatial grid cells have several disadvantages. First, they are created without taking into account the uneven population distribution within a country. Some areas may be densely populated, while others may have few, if any, human settlements (deserts, for example). While most studies try to statistically control for this, there is still a risk of failing to capture various underlying differences between cells, which can render results from the analysis difficult to interpret. Second, focusing on relatively large grid cells obviously misses variation within them. In densely populated areas, grid cells can easily contain many different towns, which we would not be able to distinguish if we were to observe protest only at the grid cell level.

Therefore, we turn to an even finer resolution and use cities as the spatial units of analysis. This is possible since our protest data from the MMAD includes information on the protest location (city). Cities are a natural choice for our analysis, since political mass protest by definition is a phenomenon that requires a certain number of participants. In addition, protest is highly unlikely to occur in small settlements, since it aims to gain attention from a larger audience. A city is typically defined as a populated place of a certain size and/or population density, distinguishing it from smaller places such as villages or hamlets. Including all cities of a certain size in our analysis would quickly render a large-N quantitative analysis computationally infeasible. For example, using a population density cut-off of around 200 people per square km to select larger settlements, we would end up with a sample of more than 28,000 cities across all countries in our sample. Together with a fine temporal resolution (see below), this would result in an extremely large number of observations.

For this reason, it is necessary to include only cities of a certain size into our sample. We include the five largest cities in each country in our analysis, as well as all cities larger than 250,000 (estimated population within a radius of 5 km from the city center, see below). The combination of absolute and relative size criteria has three advantages. First, the absolute threshold ensures that we include all major cities worldwide. Second, since many countries have small populations and therefore no or few cities larger than 250,000, the relative threshold allows us to include at least five cities from each country. If we excluded the largest cities in smaller states, we would not only exclude entire countries, but also many important political and economic centers where anti-regime protests are likely to occur. The capitals of Swaziland (Mbabane, 76,000 inhabitants) and Gambia (Banjul, 34,000 inhabitants), for example, are much smaller than the absolute threshold. Third, in combination, the absolute and relative size criteria allow us to keep most observations with protests while dropping the majority of the total observations. The size thresholds reduce the total number of observations by 90 percent while retaining 75 percent of the observations of protest.[11]

When it comes to the temporal dimension, we conduct our analysis with two different resolutions: *years* and *weeks*. Since our main independent variable—Internet penetration—is measured annually (see below), we use yearly time periods in the analysis of protest occurrence (Chapter 6). However, when analyzing short-term changes in protest behavior that the yearly interval cannot pick up, we use weekly intervals. Indeed, in order to study the relationship between

Internet technology, protest persistence, and spatial diffusion, we require a temporal resolution that is fine enough to capture these dynamics. Since anti-regime protests tend to ebb and flow within short time intervals, we would lose most of the variation in the data if we used longer time windows (e.g., months or years). In addition, anecdotal evidence suggests that mobilization often occurs on a weekly basis on a specific day of the week. This was the case in the Monday demonstrations in former East Germany as well as the Friday prayer protests during the Arab Spring. Aggregating to weeks has the practical advantage of limiting the inflation of observations that would accompany shorter time windows, for example days. Thus, taking both theoretical and practical concerns into consideration for the study of protest dynamics, the week level constitutes a useful compromise between time windows that reduce complexity but eliminate a lot of interesting variation in the data (months, years), and time windows that retain complexity but make inference difficult (days).

In sum, the research design uses city-years and city-weeks from 1,564 cities in 61 countries over eight years (2005–2012) as the basic units of analysis. We omit the first two years included in the MMAD (2003–2004) because the Internet penetration data cover 2004–2012 and Internet penetration needs to be lagged one year to ensure that the temporal order in the analysis is correct. Therefore, the final analysis includes the 2005–2012 time period. Moreover, of the 68 countries included in the MMAD (see Chapter 4), we omit seven countries due to the fact that they were autocratic in 2003–2004 only or for a period of less than two years in the 2005–2012 time period. These countries are Haiti, Liberia, Thailand, Bangladesh, Burundi, Georgia, and Guinea-Bissau.

The following sections describe the variables we require to carry out our analysis according to the research design above. In this chapter, we focus on the city-level variables that we use for most of the empirical analyses. However, several of the subsequent chapters also require additional variables at the city or country level, and we describe these in the respective chapters.

MEASURING PROTEST AND ITS DETERMINANTS IN CITIES

Our statistical analysis aims to establish a causal effect between Internet penetration on the occurrence of protest, its persistence over time, and diffusion over space. For this, we need variables that capture protest events and Internet penetration at the city level. However, establishing a causal effect is only possible if we can exclude alternative factors that account for the co-variation between our independent variable (Internet penetration) and the outcome we are interested in (protest). For example, failing to account for the level of economic development of a given location could lead to spurious inferences about the relationship between Internet and protest, since economic development can lead

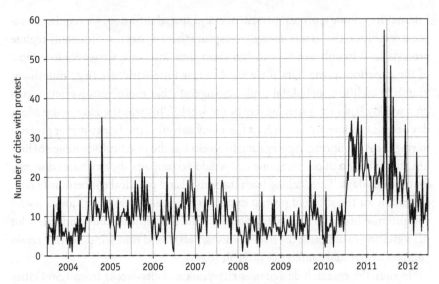

Figure 5.1 Number of cities in which protest occurred each week during our observation period

to higher levels of Internet coverage which in turn affects protest. In a regression framework such as the one we are using, we can control for these potential confounding variables in the regression. Below, we introduce the different city-level control variables, some of which were generated with the help of Geographic Information Systems (GIS) software (Gleditsch and Weidmann, 2012).

Protest.   In order to use the event reports in the MMAD (see Chapter 4) for this design, we prepare the data in two steps. First, we aggregate event reports that refer to anti-regime protests that took place in the same city on the same day to a single event.[12] We are, of course, aware that multiple anti-regime protests can occur in the same city on the same day. However, with the information at hand, it is often difficult to reliably separate two event reports into two events in the same city on the same day. This is due to the fact that anti-regime protests are often carried out by multiple actors and address multiple issues. Thus, it is almost impossible to know whether two event reports that refer to a protest in the same city on the same day, but with diverging information on actors and issues, constitute one or two events. In the second step, we aggregate events to yearly and weekly intervals for each city. These intervals start January 1, 2005, and end December 31, 2012.

For each of the temporal intervals, we calculate the number of protest events that took place. In the *city-year analysis*—in which we study the relationship between Internet penetration and protest occurrence—1,223 of the 12,244 observations experienced anti-regime protest, 691 of which experienced two or

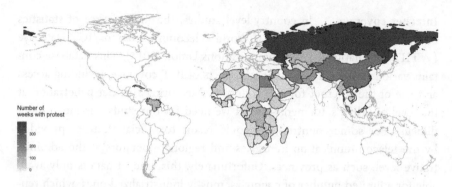

Figure 5.2 Number of weeks with at least one protest event per country, aggregated over the entire period of analysis (country borders from the CShapes dataset; Weidmann, Kuse and Gleditsch, 2010)

more protests. Therefore, we use two dependent variables in the city-year analysis. The main analysis uses a binary variable, taking a value of 1 if at least one protest occurred in a city-year. We also carry out additional analyses using a count variable of anti-regime protests per city-year. In the analyses using *city-weeks*— in which we examine the persistence of protest over time and its spatial diffusion over time—we have 128,979 (persistence) and 620,611 (diffusion) observations and only 4,829 and 4,941 city-weeks experiencing anti-regime protest, respectively. Moreover, higher counts of protest in a single week are very rare; in the dataset we use to study protest persistence, only 1,254 city-weeks have two or more protest events and only 77 have five or more. This variation makes it difficult to model protest size at the weekly level, and we therefore limit our analysis to the occurrence of protest. In other words, our main dependent variable at the city-week level is binary and takes a value of 1 if there is at least one protest event in a given city-week.

In Figure 5.1, we plot the number of cities in which protest occurs for each week from 2004 to 2012. Overall, we can see that the frequency of protest in our sample remained relatively low without major eruptions until 2010. The massive wave of protests in the Middle East and North Africa explains the major increase at the beginning of 2011. Later that same year, protests in Russia escalated in December around the time of the parliamentary elections.

At the same time, rates of protest differ widely by country, as we can see in Figure 5.2. During the 2004–2012 period, we observe that large countries such as Russia and China experience high numbers of protests, not least because of their size. In Africa, where several countries experienced only short episodes of protest, it remains a rare occurrence overall.

Internet coverage.   In country-level studies, the main source of statistics on Internet penetration is the ITU World Telecommunications/ICT Database (WTID; International Telecommunications Union, 2013). This database contains various indicators on different aspects of ICT coverage, including access and use of the Internet for 192 countries. Measuring Internet penetration at the level of urban settlements—what we need for our study—is much more difficult. For some countries, we could resort to official statistics provided by the telecommunication ministries and regional operators at the administrative level, such as provinces. Unfortunately, this kind of data is only available for a limited number of countries, mostly industrialized ones, which renders this approach useless for a study of autocracies. Another potential data source are the large surveys that are periodically conducted by international agencies to describe trends in development, health, and demographics. For example, the *Demographic and Health Surveys* (DHS) include questions about technological access among the population, such as whether a household has Internet access or people use certain Internet services (US Agency for International Development, 2016). However, while these surveys are generally representative at the country level, this is not necessarily the case at the subnational level. Hence, these kinds of surveys do not meet our data requirements, either.

In the absence of good subnational measures of Internet penetration, we rely on earlier work and use network traffic observations to estimate Internet coverage. The key idea behind this approach is that Internet traffic data can be used to identify how well connected a certain location is. The advantage of this method is that it relies on actual Internet use and is therefore less subject to inaccuracies and potential biases that affect other methods. In order to explain how this method works, we briefly describe the basic architecture of the Internet. The Internet is essentially a global network of interconnected electronic devices such as personal computers, smartphones, and servers (Kurose and Ross, 2013). The data to be transmitted—webpages or e-mails, for example—are split up into small packets, which are then routed from their origin to their destination. Similar to a package that is sent through the postal service, each data packet has two components: the information to be transmitted (the data), and the instructions that allow the system to deliver the packet to the right destination. Among other information, this metadata includes the sender's address (the device that generated the packet) and the destination (the computer it is supposed to be delivered to). Internet addresses are expressed as a set of numbers called Internet Protocol (IP) addresses, which uniquely identify both the source and the destination. Packets travel from origin to destination through a set of intermediate nodes (the routers), where each node sends the packet on to the next until it reaches its destination.

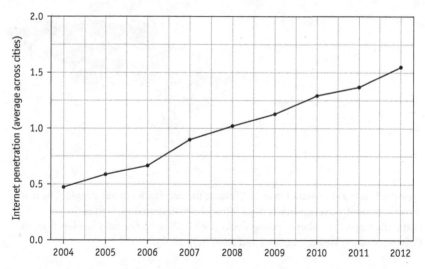

Figure 5.3 Average Internet penetration across the cities in our sample over time

Our method of measuring Internet traffic is based on traffic logs from a large Swiss Internet provider. The origin addresses of all routed packets are aggregated to the level of subnetworks (groups of around 255 addresses) to balance spatial resolution and privacy. A geolocation database is then used to determine the physical location of the observed subnetworks (Maxmind, Inc., 2014). This database translates the addresses of these networks into geographic coordinates that approximate where on the globe these networks are located. More details on this procedure are given in Weidmann et al. (2016) and Benitez-Baleato et al. (2015). In particular, Weidmann et al. (2016) shows that this method is able to track the spatial distribution of Internet coverage across countries at a reasonable level of accuracy. For our analysis, we create a city-level measure at yearly time intervals of Internet coverage by using the number of active subnetworks within a 50-km radius of a city. As in Weidmann et al. (2016), we use the logarithmized, per 1,000 capita number of subnetworks as our indicator for Internet penetration in order to avoid simply picking up differences between small and large urban areas. This approach allows us to apply a consistent estimation technique to a large sample.

Overall, as we would expect, the rate of Internet penetration has been increasing steadily over time. Figure 5.3 shows this as the average across the cities in our sample over the period of our analysis. Between 2004 and 2012, Internet penetration increased roughly threefold. At the same time, Internet penetration is distributed unevenly across the autocratic countries in our sample. Figure 5.4 plots the average city-level Internet penetration estimates at the country level for the year 2010. While some countries such as Russia

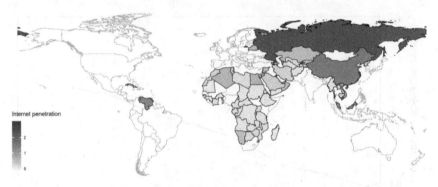

Figure 5.4 Internet penetration in 2010 across the autocracies in our sample. The map shows the country average of city-level Internet penetration measured as the (naturally-logged) number of subnetworks per 1,000 capita (country borders from the CShapes dataset; Weidmann, Kuse and Gleditsch, 2010).

and China have relatively high penetration rates, African countries rank much lower.[13]

The city-level variables for protest and Internet penetration constitute the main ingredients of our statistical analysis. However, as discussed, we also need a number of control variables. Due to the fact that data for several of these variables are unavailable in the form of conventional measurements, such as surveys, we use spatial approximations computed using Geographic Information Systems (GIS) software. In particular, we use a so-called overlay where a map of the cities in our sample is combined with a map showing data on one of the control variables. Integrating cities' geographical information with another map allows us to calculate approximations for the variables "population" and "development" at the city level.

Population.   In order to estimate the population size of a given city, we use data from the LandScan population dataset (Oak Ridge National Laboratory, 2014). LandScan is a spatial dataset that approximates the spatial distribution of the human population at a resolution of approximately 1 km. We aggregate these estimates within a 5-km radius of the city center. As described above, we use a combination of absolute and relative criteria to select the cities in our sample to balance the precision of the dataset vs. its size. In the final sample, population varies from 30,240 to 3,992,000.

Development.   We approximate the level of development at the city level using a spatial overlay computation similar to the population variable. Controlling for the level of development is important, since it could be driving Internet expansion and protest behavior, potentially introducing a spurious correlation between Internet penetration and protest. Following earlier work, we approximate development using per capita nighttime light emission at the city level. These emissions have been proposed as an alternative measurement of economic performance (Henderson, Storeygard and Weil, 2011; Chen and Nordhaus, 2011) and have recently been shown to correlate strongly with local levels of wealth as measured by surveys (Weidmann and Schutte, 2017). Our variable relies on data from the US Defense Meteorological Satellite Program (National Geophysical Data Center, 2014). Since satellite images of the earth at night can be affected by a number of issues, the images we use are yearly aggregates, where error sources such as forest fires and other non-stationary light emissions have been removed.

Capital cities.   We include other variables that capture the political status of a city. In particular, cities that are the seat of a national or regional government can potentially confound the relationship between the occurrence of protest and Internet coverage. We therefore control for whether a city is a national or provincial capital using information from the GeoNames database (see http://www.geonames.org/). Each populated place in the database is assigned a type, and we flag those coded as PPLC (national capital) or PPLA (regional capital).

Lagged protest and spatial lag of protest.   We expect cities and countries that recently experienced protest to be more likely to see protest in the future. To capture this autoregressive nature of anti-regime protest, we control for recent protest in the same location and in a different location in the same country. We operationalize these variables differently in the city-year and city-week analyses. In the city-year analyses, we use a simple lagged dependent variable (protest last year in the same location and in the same country). In the city-week analyses, we calculate the number of weeks since the last protest in the same location and in the same country.[14]

Civil war   Finally, since our sample includes a number of politically unstable countries with frequent episodes of large-scale political violence, we estimate our models with an indicator of whether there is ongoing civil war in the country, according to the *Armed Conflict Dataset* (Gleditsch et al., 2002). We need to control for ongoing civil war, since it potentially hampers the introduction and expansion of Internet technology to affected areas, and at the same time has an impact on the occurrence of anti-regime protest. In total, 23 of the 61 autocratic countries in our sample experienced civil war in the period under study in this book.

BAYESIAN MULTILEVEL MODELING

For the analysis, we use Bayesian multilevel regression models. As stated, we are interested in how local Internet coverage influences protest, but need to take into account how the effect varies across different national systems. Multilevel modeling is designed for this and is typically applied to data that are grouped in different ways. In our case, for example, we have city-year and city-week observations. Each observation belongs to a specific city, is located in a particular country, and takes place in a particular year. While we include a number of city-level predictor variables, it is highly likely that there are unobserved city- and country-level differences in protest behavior. In order to take these differences into account, we estimate both city- and country-level random effects in our models. Cities are modeled as nested in countries. In addition, there are likely to be time trends in protest (e.g., Arab Spring) as well as Internet penetration (see Figure 5.3), which is why we also group our observations by year.

The multilevel specification, together with the skewed distribution of the dependent variable, makes it difficult to estimate our regression models (especially for the city-week analysis). A typical solution in political science research is to estimate these models using a frequentist approach (Jackman, 2009). For our analysis, however, we opted for a Bayesian estimation for mainly two reasons. First and foremost, Bayesian analysis provides a convenient setting for our chosen estimation strategy, the multilevel model (Gelman and Hill, 2006). Importantly, as we discuss in the empirical chapters, the posterior samples generated by Bayesian estimation enable us to reliably verify the convergence of our models. In our case, estimating multilevel models with both non-nested and nested levels, a small number of groups (e.g., eight years), a number of control variables, and a rare events outcome, we are especially wary of convergence issues (see, e.g., Bryan and Jenkins, 2016). While Bayesian analysis is often used to incorporate prior knowledge about the relationship in question, we are simply interested in estimating the relationship between digital technology and anti-regime protest based on the data at hand, and therefore use uninformative (flat) priors.

A second, more practical, reason for using Bayesian estimation allows us greater flexibility in the specification of our models within a reliable framework compared to other (frequentist) implementations in R. Indeed, it is difficult to find reliable packages using frequentist estimation that support certain model specifications (e.g., multilevel multinomial logistic regression models and multilevel negative binomial count models).[15] Therefore, we estimate all our multilevel models using the *brms* package in R (Bürkner, 2017), a front end that facilitates the estimation of Bayesian multilevel models using the STAN language (Carpenter et al., 2017). Since some of the main dependent variables are continuous while others are binary, we estimate logit, OLS, and count specifications.

All results presented in the subsequent chapters are based on estimation with 3 chains with 500 beta draws (500 burn-in draws, thinning = 2), totaling 750 beta coefficients per variable in each analysis.

In the empirical chapters of this book, we present the results from our multilevel models in a number of ways. The most basic presentation is the *coefficient plot*—a graphical way of showing output from regression tables that displays the variables in the regression model on the y-axis and the size of each of the coefficients with 95 percent credible intervals on the x-axis. In our coefficient plots, estimates significant at the 5 percent level are black, while estimates that fail to reach significance at the 5 percent level are shown in gray. Since raw coefficients are difficult to interpret in non-linear models, we often visualize our results by using plots of *absolute probabilities*. For these plots, we use model coefficients to simulate probabilities of our outcome for different values of a given predictor (while holding the others constant). These plots show how the absolute probability of the outcome (in our case, political protest) changes for different predictor values (Internet penetration) with 95 percent confidence intervals.

The third way we visualize findings is in *first difference plots*. Similar to the absolute probabilities plots, we begin by using model estimates to simulate probabilities of our outcome for different values of our predictor. We then compute the difference in probability of our outcome given a change from one value to another in our predictor. For example, we compute the difference in probability of protest in a city with low Internet penetration and in one with high Internet penetration. The first difference plots show the magnitude of change in the probability of protest given an increase or decrease in the predictor (y-axis) for different values of the predictor or a conditioning variable (x-axis). In the text, we use the terms "first difference," "marginal effect," and "change in probability" interchangeably when interpreting these plots.

Conclusion

There are different methodological approaches in political science to test causal relationships. In this book, we opt for a large-N, disaggregated research design that captures both local- and national-level determinants of protest. This design allows us to analyze the effect of Internet technology on anti-regime protest at the local level. This is crucial, since theoretical arguments imply that the local availability of Internet coverage should lead to the occurrence or repression of protest. This is a significant improvement over existing studies that rely exclusively on aggregated, national-level indicators to test the relationship between digital technology and political protest.

At the same time, there is likely to be considerable variation across different political environments regarding the Internet's effect on protest. For this reason, we employ a multilevel research design that can capture variation in national-level conditions while estimating the local effect of digital communication. A Bayesian estimation strategy is used to estimate this model, as it is able to deal with both between-group variation and the imbalance in the sample, that is, the fact that protest only occurs in a small fraction of all observations. Moreover, the design allows us to study how the impact of Internet technology on anti-regime protest differs depending on factors that vary nationally, locally, and temporally. This lets us go a step further than studies that look at the local-level effect of digital technology on political activism in a single city or country and/or over short time periods.

In the next part of the book, we build on our theoretical framework introduced in Chapter 3 to carry out fine-grained analyses of how the availability of Internet technology plays out at different phases of protest over time and across national contexts. According to our theoretical discussion, the use of the Internet should have different effects depending on whether protest has already started or not. In Chapter 6, we analyze how Internet penetration at the city level affects protest in general, before later turning to the analysis of ongoing protests in Chapters 7 and 8.

6

Internet Coverage and
the Occurrence
of Protest

How is Internet coverage related to protest? Equipped with event data from the MMAD, subnational estimates of Internet coverage, and the multilevel research design introduced in the previous chapter, we are ready to present the first part of our empirical analysis. In our theoretical discussion in Chapter 3, we argued that the use of Internet technology by autocratic governments and opposition activists can have very different implications for anti-regime protest depending on the local and national conditions in which it is used. Importantly, we need to distinguish between the occurrence of protest and the continuation of a protest episode that has already started: The challenges activists face in getting people to turn out for the first time are very different from those during ongoing protest. In this chapter, we focus on the former and how the availability of Internet technology is related to the occurrence of protest by comparing cities with different rates of Internet penetration. In this chapter, we study all cities for which we have data, regardless of their protest history. In the following chapters, we shift our focus to the dynamics of ongoing episodes by analyzing cities after they have experienced protest to see whether Internet communication helps activists sustain protest locally (Chapter 7) or whether it fosters national-level diffusion of protest to other cities (Chapter 8). The chapter starts with a short summary of our argument, namely that governments have the power to limit the introduction and expansion of the Internet among the public, and that this helps keep dissent low and limits the opportunities for protest. We then present the empirical analysis, starting with descriptive results and later moving to the multilevel regression model described in Chapter 5. Finally, we conduct a number of robustness tests.

How the Internet Can Reduce the Occurrence of Protest

As discussed at length in Chapter 3, the view that Internet technology can be a catalyst of protest has been challenged in a number of ways. A first set of arguments question whether the technology is an effective tool for catalyzing protest. Some argue that the degree to which the technology can change peoples' beliefs and behavior is overestimated. Selective exposure to information was well known long before the advent of the Internet (Chaffee and Miyo, 1983; Sears and Freedman, 1967). In the digital age, the news landscape has become even more fragmented, with different outlets and websites catering to different audiences. If people only consume information in line with their political views and preferences, it is difficult to imagine that the Internet can really lead to the emergence of new grievances against a regime. Negroponte (1995), for example, argues that Internet access will lead to an individualized experience of society, where problems and issues shared between large societal groups become much less relevant. Anecdotal evidence from Iran supports this view. According to Aday et al. (2010), online heterophily (i.e., interacting with people outside one's narrow personal network) only increased *after* the controversial 2009 presidential election and the protests that surrounded it. This indicates that awareness of alternative political opinions may be a result of collective external shocks, and not the result of increasing Internet use itself.

Other arguments challenge whether the technology is effective for solving collective action problems. Strong interpersonal networks have been shown to be key drivers of collective action, and the assumption that such ties can be established via the Internet may simply not hold (Gladwell, 2010). Similarly, Morozov (2011) argues that Internet technology does not affect costly forms of collective action (such as political protest), but rather leads to showy, ineffective types of activism, such as digital petitions or "liking"/sharing material on social media platforms to support and promote a cause. Often referred to as "clicktivism" (or the more pejorative "slacktivism"), this type of political action may be counterproductive, and "may even harm the social and political causes people are attempting to support by conferring a false sense of accomplishment that forestalls more effective engagement" (Harvey, 2013, 282). The Kony2012 campaign by the NGO "InvisibleChildren" is often held up as a prominent example of clicktivism. InvisibleChildren published an online video with information about the war crimes of Joseph Kony and the Lord's Resistance Army (LRA). The reception of the video was unprecedented, receiving 100 million views in the first six days after it was published online. However, the outreach of the campaign had a limited impact, as most viewers' contribution was to share the video. In other words, while the video may have led to awareness about the war crimes of Kony and the LRA (at least in the short term), it did not produce policy changes. Similar comments have been made about the #BringBackOurGirls campaign after the armed organization Boko Haram kidnapped hundreds of schoolgirls in Nigeria.

Finally, the perception that digital communication fuels the emergence of protest could simply be driven by the fact that outside audiences can now observe these events more easily and directly. For example, as shown by Lotan et al. (2011), news coverage today relies heavily on social media, which creates an increase in the information streams about protest (but not necessarily an increase in protest itself). This effect is often amplified due to social media coverage "bursts"—short-term spikes in coverage of ongoing events—which leads to fast and extensive reception outside the affected countries (Starbird and Palen, 2012).

These arguments question whether opposition activists can successfully use the Internet to mobilize anti-regime protest and whether more information due to Internet access drives a perception of increased mobilization. Yet the arguments do not necessarily imply that the Internet makes protest *less* likely. However, the discussion ignores the fact that governments can also use the Internet in their favor, as discussed in Chapter 3. Since Internet technology is rolled out across a country only with the permission and under strict control of the government (Boas, 2006; MacKinnon, 2011), the Internet in autocracies is usually not the new and independent public sphere some consider it to be. Moreover, autocratic governments, while keen to reap the economic benefits of modern technology, have the means to interfere with Internet communication in different ways once it is introduced. In doing so, they affect the three determinants of protest: They can reduce peoples' *motives* for protest, limit popular *mobilization* by activists, and change political *opportunities* such that protest becomes unnecessary or infeasible. In the following, we discuss these three factors in detail.

Individual grievances as motives for protest can be affected by online communication in different ways. The availability of online entertainment can depoliticize the population and make it less likely to be critical of the autocratic regime. Online propaganda, whereby governments actively contribute online content that favors the regime, is another way to achieve the same result. A prominent example is the hiring of regime-friendly bloggers by the Chinese government. The members of the so-called 50 cent party seem to strategically divert public attention to prevent discussion of controversial topics, essentially diffusing public unrest before it escalates to large-scale collective action (King, Pan and Roberts, 2017). Resource mobilization using online channels can also be undermined by government interference and censorship. King, Pan and Roberts (2013) show that censorship in China is very fast and largely centers on content that could trigger collective action. What matters here is that censorship is visible and public: Users immediately see that their posts (or those of others) have been removed, which signals that the government is watching. This may have a lasting effect in suppressing future attempts to mobilize for collective action.

Internet technology can also help governments shift political opportunities for protest. In democracies, examples show that e-governance can increase transparency and responsiveness. Tolbert and Mossberger (2006) find that e-government increases trust in the government by improving interactions with citizens and perceptions of responsiveness. In the United Kingdom, users generally appreciate the personalization and ability to communicate directly that e-government tools offer (Kolsaker and Lee-Kelley, 2008). This enthusiasm has led to a general praise of ICTs for preventing or reducing corruption and for promoting transparency (Bertot, Jaeger and Grimes, 2010). A similar effect has been shown in certain autocratic countries. Some argue that ICTs (and in particular, the Internet) have led to an increase in the quality of government services. For example, Kalathil and Boas (2003) discuss the case of China, where Internet-based government services have helped to strengthen bureaucratic efficiency and quality, thereby leading to increased citizen satisfaction. Case studies in Singapore and Cuba illustrate a similar result (Kalathil and Boas, 2003). Politically, the Internet can be used as a vehicle to probe, and respond to, public sentiment. Since much information on social media is publicly visible, criticism and complaints posted by users can be publicly addressed by the government, which sends a widely visible signal that these complaints are taken seriously. This mechanism is part of what MacKinnon (2011) calls "networked authoritarianism." The key here is that the grievances voiced online can make it easier for local and/or liberal officials to propose governance reforms to hardliners, which can lead to better governance and increased legitimacy, but without real reform at the national level (see also Zheng, 2007, for a similar reasoning). This way, the Internet leads to the emergence of a "deliberative authoritarianism," which can stabilize the regime by bolstering legitimacy (He and Warren, 2011).

At the same time, the Internet can also serve more sinister purposes for a government by enabling it to repress social movements. Online surveillance is commonplace in many autocratic countries and is even on the rise, as several reports by Freedom House show (Freedom House, 2011, 2012, 2013, 2016d). Digital channels provide a number of advantages for surveillance. In autocracies, online services are often provided by state-run telecommunication agencies (e.g., in Belarus and Iran). These agencies link individual PCs with the larger Internet backbone, meaning that they can monitor all the traffic generated by these computers and also have information on subscribers. Even when the suppliers of Internet connections are privately owned, they are often obliged to comply with government requests. In addition, since information on the Internet is disseminated in digital form, it can be automatically searched for problematic content, which facilitates the detection of emerging dissent (Gohdes, 2016).

Summarizing the discussion in this chapter and Chapter 3, we have seen that there are a number of ways in which governments can use digital channels in their favor. Since autocratic governments usually are in charge of introducing and expanding Internet technology in a country, they enjoy a tremendous advantage over opposition activists from the start. Moreover, once in place, governments can effectively reduce motivations and political opportunities for protest and make it difficult for opposition activists to use digital communication for subversive purposes. Yet we believe that many of the opposing mechanisms identified in Chapter 3 operate in parallel: Internet technology does not exclusively empower autocrats; it can also provide opposition activists with new tools and opportunities. However, even if activists can benefit from Internet technology, the advantage the government enjoys will be much more powerful and profound. Therefore, when observing the net effect empirically, we expect it to be negative, such that *higher Internet penetration decreases the occurrence of anti-regime protest.*

Studying the Effect of Internet Penetration on Protest Occurrence Empirically

In this section, we start our empirical investigation of whether Internet penetration is related to the occurrence of political protest in autocratic countries. Following our theoretical argument, we expect cities with high levels of Internet penetration to be less prone to protest than cities with low Internet penetration due to the strategic introduction and expansion of the technology and the governments' ability to use it to reduce motives for protest, impede popular mobilization, and shape political opportunities so that protest becomes less useful and feasible. We examine a large sample of cities across 61 autocratic countries. Our disaggregated approach allows us to explore variation within as well as across countries and involves several steps. First, in a descriptive analysis, we examine the relationship between local Internet penetration and protest incidence rates without modeling it statistically. Specifically, we look at overall trends in the sample, but also show the individual results for a set of selected countries. Later, we turn to regression analysis and model the relationship between access to Internet technology and the occurrence of anti-regime protest using Bayesian multilevel models as discussed in the previous chapter. Finally, we present a number of robustness tests to show that our results do not depend on particular modeling choices.

A FIRST LOOK AT THE DATA

We start by plotting the data on local Internet penetration against protest occurrence at the city-year level. Our sample contains the five biggest cities in each country and all cities with a population larger than 250,000 (computed using the spatial approximation described in the previous chapter). The dependent variable—protest occurrence—is dichotomous, taking the value 0 if no protest occurred in a particular city and year and 1 if at least one protest occurred. The main independent variable, Internet penetration at the city level, is continuous. Since we measure protest with a binary variable, we show plots of how the probability of anti-regime protest occurrence (y-axis) varies depending on the level of Internet penetration in a city (x-axis). We first present a plot generated using a linear specification. The shape of the line in Figure 6.1 (left panel) strongly supports our theoretical expectation: At low levels of local Internet penetration, the probability of anti-regime protest occurrence is around 15 percent (top left). As Internet penetration increases, the probability that a city will experience protest decreases sharply. In cities with high Internet penetration (values of around 2), the probability is less than 5 percent—a threefold decrease compared to cities without Internet penetration. Some readers may be concerned that the linear plot constrains the relationship between Internet coverage and protest unnecessarily, and that it is non-monotonic (i.e., it first increases and then decreases or vice versa). For that reason, we also estimate the bivariate relationship with a more flexible specification that includes polynomials up to the order of three. Yet Figure 6.1 (right panel) shows that the result remains almost unchanged in this more flexible specification, and that the probability of protest occurring declines sharply as Internet penetration goes up. These initial results indicate that Internet technology plays into the hands of autocratic regimes and lowers the potential threat from opposition activists. Importantly, Figure 6.1 (right panel) shows that Internet penetration reduces protest irrespective of its absolute level.

How does the overall pattern in Figure 6.1 map onto individual countries? Do the patterns across countries diverge, or are they largely consistent? In the following we discuss the relationship between local Internet penetration and protest occurrence in cities in Russia, Iran, and Egypt. There are several reasons for focusing on these countries. First, all of them have featured prominently in the debate about whether Internet technology can aid autocratic regimes in their aim of quiescence or whether it helps opposition activists organize protests against dictators. For example, Egypt was among the countries most affected by the Arab Spring protests, and has been at the center of the discussion surrounding the political impact of communication technology during these events (Hussain and Howard, 2013; Hassanpour, 2014). Similarly, in Russia, observers claim that the massive post-election protests in 2011–2012 were catalyzed by activism on social

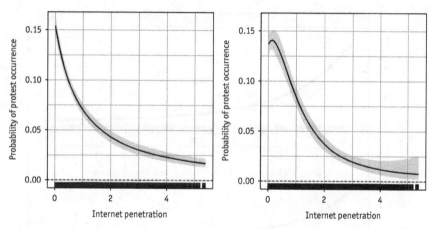

Figure 6.1 Smoothed conditional means plots, cities in all countries. Left panel: linear specification. Right panel: cubic specification.

media platforms (Freedom House, 2012). In the aftermath of these events, the Russian government has launched a large-scale crackdown on online activists, which includes long prison sentences and physical violence as punishment for sharing certain material online (Freedom House, 2016d). Moreover, in Iran, Internet technology was reportedly central for the growth of the Green Movement in 2009 (Grossman, 2009; Morozov, 2009). However, as in Russia, the government has responded by implementing new bills to curb online activists. Indeed, as underlined by Freedom House (2016d, 441), "Internet use in Iran remains a cat-and-mouse game in which tech-savvy individuals try to push red lines and circumvent the harsh restrictions imposed on them by state security." A second reason for focusing on Russia, Iran, and Egypt is that these countries experienced a high number of protests in the period under study. This allows us to estimate and plot the probability of protest against Internet penetration for each of them separately. In Russia, 261 out of 1,544 city-year observations saw protest, in Iran 82 out of 240, and in Egypt 78 out of 328.

Figure 6.2 plots the same relationship as in Figure 6.1 above, but using only data for Russia (top), Iran (middle), and Egypt (bottom). There are large overall differences in the maximum level of city-level Internet penetration, as we can see from the different ranges along the x-axis. Russia, for example, has several cities with high levels (4), while Iran scores much lower (less than 2). Moreover, Russia has higher protest rates (high values along the y-axis) compared to the other two countries. Yet the main message from the figure is that the negative relationship between Internet penetration and protest holds across all three cases: We see the highest levels of protest at low levels of Internet penetration. This is consistent with the trend for the entire sample in Figure 6.1.

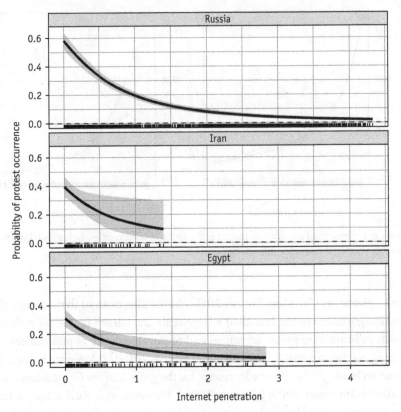

Figure 6.2 Smoothed conditional means plots, cities in Russia (top), Iran (middle), and Egypt (bottom).

A REFINED ANALYSIS USING STATISTICAL MODELS

The descriptive evidence we presented in the previous section gives some indication that higher levels of Internet coverage go along with a generally lower frequency of protest. However, so far our analysis has not taken into account other factors that might impact the relationship between city-level Internet penetration and anti-regime protest. Therefore, we might be worried that the results above are driven by other conditions that vary between countries and cities. For example, it may be that local wealth accounts for the relationship we find: A wealthy city will on average have a higher level of Internet coverage and possibly lower levels of protest. This could produce a spurious negative correlation between Internet penetration and the occurrence of protest. In our regression models, we take several measures to rule out this possibility. First, we add a number of control variables. These include variables controlling for temporal and spatial dependence of protest: an indicator for whether protest occurred in the same city last year $(t-1)$ and a spatial lag of protest in the same country last

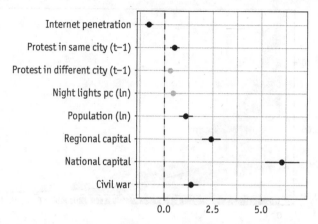

Figure 6.3 Regression results for the main model. The plot shows the coefficients for the different variables and their credible intervals. Coefficients where the credible intervals includes zero are shown in gray (city-year resolution, logistic regression). Reference: Table A.2 (all regression results can be found in the Appendix).

year (t−1). We also control for the amount of night light emission per capita to measure the level of wealth and development. Furthermore, we separate out effects due to the size and importance of the respective locations by controlling for city population and by including indicators flagging regional and national capitals. Finally, we control for ongoing civil war to take into account the effect organized political violence can have on levels of relatively peaceful dissent and Internet penetration. Second, in order to control for unobserved differences between cities, we estimate the regression models with random intercepts by cities (nested in countries), countries, and year.

The results from our main multilevel model are displayed in Figure 6.3. The variables are shown on the y-axis, and size of the coefficients with 95 percent credible intervals are shown on the x-axis. To indicate the precision of the estimates, we display estimates with 95 percent probability of being negative or positive in black (in conventional terms: significant at the 5 percent level), while the gray estimates have a higher degree of uncertainty (in conventional terms: insignificant at the 5 percent level). The regression table output can be found in the Appendix. In line with the descriptive evidence presented above, Figure 6.3 shows a negative coefficient of local Internet penetration on anti-regime protest occurrence ($\beta = -0.79$). Moreover, the credible intervals indicate that there is a 95 percent probability that the effect is between −1 and −0.59. In other words, we can be confident that local Internet penetration is negatively correlated with protest. This result demonstrates that as more inhabitants in cities gain access to the Internet, the likelihood of protest occurring decreases. The multilevel model thus further corroborates our expectation that autocratic regimes benefit from

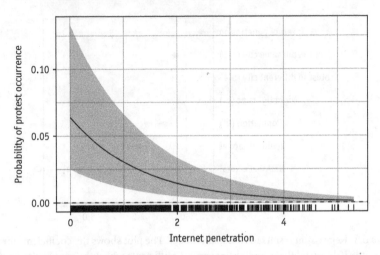

Figure 6.4 The effect of local Internet penetration on anti-regime protest occurrence (city-year resolution, logistic regression, 95 percent confidence intervals). Reference: Table A.2

the expansion of Internet penetration and successfully suppress the occurrence of protest.

To see the substantive effect of local Internet penetration, we plot simulated probabilities of protest occurrence for different levels of Internet penetration in Figure 6.4.[16] Similar to the plots above, Figure 6.4 visualizes how the probability of protest decreases as Internet penetration increases using the results from our multilevel model. First, we note that the shape of the line is very similar to the descriptive evidence in Figures 6.1 and 6.2. Second, the magnitude of the probabilities is smaller in Figure 6.4 than in the previous plots. This is to be expected. As explained above, some of the variation between Internet penetration and protest can be explained by other factors such as local wealth, which are subtracted in the multilevel model and therefore decrease the effect sizes. Figure 6.4 indicates that cities without Internet access have a probability of anti-regime protest occurrence of 6.6 percent. In cities with the median value of Internet penetration (0.39), the probability is 5 percent, and at Internet penetration levels higher than 1.47 (75th percentile) the probability is below 2.2 percent. In other words, comparing cities without Internet coverage to those at the 75th percentile, we observe a threefold decrease in the probability of anti-regime protest.

The control variables in our main model yield results in the expected direction (see Figure 6.3). Protest exhibits a strong temporal and spatial correlation, as we can see from the positive effect of the lagged protest indicator. Overall, richer and more developed cities are also more likely to see protest, which is in line with Lipset's (1959) classic modernization argument. Not surprisingly, the results also show that protests are more likely to occur in populous cities (positive coefficient of population variable). Moreover, because regional and national capitals typically are political focal points, we also find that they tend to experience more protest. Finally, the estimates show that protests are more likely when there are ongoing civil wars in the country. Since we are measuring civil war at the county-year level, this may be because anti-regime protests escalate into civil wars, because the opposition pursues a range of different tactics, or because protesters oppose the government's war policies.

On a more technical note, the multilevel model provides us with useful information about unobserved heterogeneity of the outcome (political protest) between countries, cities, and years. The large estimated between-group variation (see the standard deviation for the country, city, and year random effects in Table A.2 in the Appendix) indicates that there is a lot of unexplained variation not captured by the variables included in the model. By dividing the estimated standard deviation reported in Table A.2 by 4, we can approximate the difference between the groups (Gelman and Hill, 2006, 304). This reveals a mean estimated $+/-41$ percent variation in political protest between countries, $+/-39$ percent variation between cities (nested in countries), and $+/-19$ percent variation between years. These numbers emphasize the importance of accounting for the considerable heterogeneity across our units of observation in our multilevel modeling framework.

The results from our main multilevel model provide strong evidence in favor of our expectation that cities with high Internet penetration experience less protest. However, this conclusion may be too simple. Internet technology has changed profoundly over the last two decades, most importantly with the introduction of Web 2.0, as it enabled new and much more comprehensive communication between users. This is important for our study, because social media platforms such as Facebook, Twitter, and YouTube opened new possibilities for users to upload content and interact with each other, making Web 2.0 fundamentally different from the one-directional web services in early generations of the Internet. Within our period of analysis (2005–2012), the ways that social networks affected peoples' everyday lives changed drastically. In 2005, Facebook was only available to students, and sharing anything other than text (for example, pictures) was a new addition. In 2006, the first version of Facebook for cell phones was released and the site was made available to the general public for the first time. In 2008, a chat function was introduced. In 2010, Facebook reached 500 million members, a phenomenal difference to the 1 million student members in 2005. As the platform developed and the number of users increased, the sharing of news articles and videos became increasingly popular. Moreover, Facebook merged with other social media tools, for example in 2012, when the company bought the picture-sharing tool Instagram. Similar developments

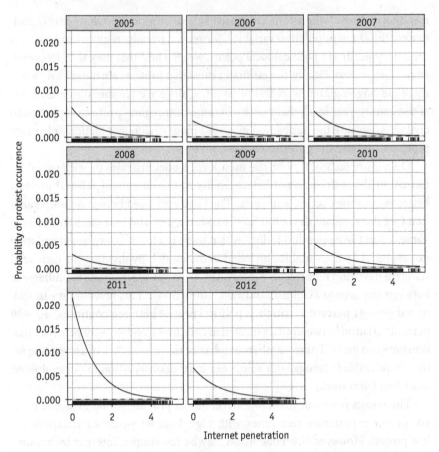

Figure 6.5 The effect of local Internet penetration on anti-regime protest occurrence (city-year resolution, logistic regression, 95 percent confidence intervals), varying slopes per year. Reference: Table A.3

can be seen in other social media tools as well, such as Twitter, Snapchat, and WhatsApp.

If social media, and not the Internet more generally, are the key technology that makes the Internet either a catalyst of political protest or a vehicle of government propaganda and censorship, the effect of Internet penetration on protest should vary over time. In particular, the negative effect of Internet penetration on protest should be *weaker* in absolute terms during the age of social media if it really helps activists mobilize for protest. Conversely, if social media improves the governments' ability to spread propaganda and spy on their citizens, the negative effect should be *stronger* in absolute terms. These considerations prompt us to explore temporal variation in addition to the overall relationship in the empirical analysis below.

How stable is this effect over time as the technology changes? To investigate this empirically, we re-estimate our multilevel model with varying slopes by year, the results of which are shown in Figure 6.5.[17] As in the descriptive plots above, the model estimates show that Internet penetration is consistently negatively correlated with anti-regime protest in every year between 2005 and 2012.[18] This consistency is reflected in the estimated variance term in the varying slope model (Table A.3), which indicates that the effect of Internet penetration only varies by 5 percent between years. In sum, the results indicate that changes in Internet use in the period under study have little consequence for the relationship between local Internet penetration and the occurrence of protest.

IS THE EFFECT ROBUST?

A common challenge in empirical research in the social sciences—and in the study of democratization and conflict in particular—is that findings are not robust to minor changes in model specification or across studies (Hegre and Sambanis, 2006; Rød, Knutsen and Hegre, 2017). In order to make sure that the specification of our main model is not driving the result, we estimate a number of additional models. We opt for a condensed display of our main quantity of interest: Figure 6.6 shows the effect of our main independent variable—local Internet penetration—across the different models. Again, estimates displayed in black are significant at the 5 percent level, while the gray estimates are not. The regression table output for each model can be found in the Appendix.

First, we estimate two models in which we change the dependent variable from occurrence to onset. We do this to check whether the negative effect we find in the main model is driven by the repeated occurrence of protest in cities with low Internet penetration. In order to do so, we exclude observations of repeated occurrence in two ways. In the first onset model, we exclude observations if a protest occurred in the same city in the previous year. In the second onset model, we exclude all subsequent years after a city has experienced a protest. The first and second rows in Figure 6.6 show that the results from the main model hold in this specification. In fact, the size of the coefficient increases from −0.79 to −1.01 and −1.2, respectively (see Tables A.9 and A.10), indicating that the effect is even larger for onsets than for overall occurrence.

Second, we estimate the same model as above with a continuous dependent variable: the number of protests in a city-year. The third and fourth rows in Figure 6.6 show the results of (i) a linear regression using a log-transformed dependent variable (Table A.4) and (ii) a count model with negative binomial distribution (Table A.5). The plotted estimates are both negative and significant, demonstrating that the protest-suppressing effect of Internet penetration is robust to these model changes.

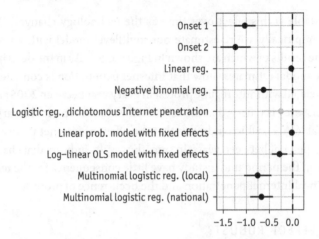

Figure 6.6 Coefficient plot for the Internet penetration variable across different alternative regression models

Third, in the above analysis we assume a linear effect of Internet penetration that is the same regardless of the actual level of access available to the general public. However, it is possible that even small levels of Internet coverage are sufficient to affect protest, for example by allowing a small group of activists to coordinate their mobilization efforts. In other words, the Internet could have a presence rather than a scale effect. In order to test this, we estimate the main model with a binary indicator for the presence of Internet connectivity, rather than the continuous one we use in the main model above (Table A.6). As we can see in the fifth row in Figure 6.6, this assumption does not bear out empirically, since we find no clear effect of the presence of Internet on anti-regime protests. In line with the descriptive evidence in Figure 6.1 (right panel), the result suggests that our main findings are driven by levels of Internet penetration rather than the introduction of the technology.

Fourth, the effect we observe in the multilevel model setup may be disproportionately driven by between-unit variation (countries, cities, years), and the random effects we include in our models are not sufficient to control for this. In order to test whether the results hold within units, we estimate linear probability models with fixed effects by city and year (Table A.7). As in the models above, we use two different outcome variables: the occurrence of protest (binary, sixth row in Figure 6.6) and the number of anti-regime protests (log-transformed, seventh row in Figure 6.6). As the plotted estimates show, the results from the main analysis remain unchanged: The higher the level of local Internet penetration, the fewer protests occur.

Finally, it is possible that digital communication technology impacts different types of protest in different ways. One way to distinguish protest is by the scope

of the demands made. While some protests are about issues of national importance (e.g., replacing a member of the central government), others are triggered
by local issues (e.g., a planned construction project in a particular neighbor-
hood). Mobilization between these different types of protest may be different, as
the former may involve much higher risks for participants. Also, our protest coding could be systematically biased toward the former, as local issues are of less
interest to news consumers and may therefore go unreported. To test whether
the negative effect is driven by one type of protest (national or local), we use
the "scope" variable in our protest data. This variable distinguishes protests surrounding issues of national relevance from those of regional or local relevance.
Correspondingly, we create a dependent variable with no protest as the base-
line category and two alternative outcomes: protest surrounding (i) *local* and
(ii) *national* issues (Table A.8). Using this variable, we estimate a multinomial
logit model. The results, displayed in rows eight and nine in Figure 6.6, show
that the protest-suppressing effect of Internet penetration pertains to both local-
and national-level protests.

   In sum, results from the alternative models are in line with our main finding
above and suggest that Internet penetration suppresses, rather than triggers, the
occurrence of protest.

Conclusion

Much of the public and scientific discourse surrounding the role of Internet technology has identified it as a catalyst of public opposition and protest. While
digital technology can certainly be a powerful weapon in the hands of activists,
in this chapter we have shown that places with higher rates of Internet coverage
generally experience lower levels of protest. In other words, the Internet seems
to suppress, rather than catalyze, open political opposition against an autocratic
government. This result remains unaffected by changes in Internet technology
over time, such as the introduction of social media. Moreover, the results hold
across various specifications of our regression models.

   At the same time, these results are only the first piece of the puzzle. So far,
we have not examined how Internet technology affects the dynamics of ongoing
unrest. Once protest has started, activists face very different challenges in keeping it going or even expanding it across the country. Hence, our next task is to
shift our analysis to cases with a history of protest. In the next chapter, we study
the persistence of protest in a city and how Internet penetration contributes to
it. In Chapter 8, we analyze whether digital communication channels foster the
spread of protest from one city to others in the country.

7

Internet Coverage and the Temporal Dynamics of Protest

In the previous chapter, we showed that a higher level of Internet coverage seems to benefit autocratic governments and reduces the overall occurrence of anti-government protest. As we have argued, governments are usually either directly in charge of providing Internet services to citizens, or they maintain a high level of control over external providers of the technology within their borders. This allows them to withhold access altogether or to implement various strategies to use the technology in their favor: Online propaganda reduces citizens' dissatisfaction and therefore their motivation to protest; online mobilization attempts by activists can be censored; regimes can use the technology as a tool to improve governance and thus boost their image; and surveillance allows governments to identify opposition activists, thereby reducing opportunities for protest. Overall, these strategies are well suited to prevent political protest from erupting in the long run, and our results in the previous chapter confirm this.

Still, these findings tell only part of the story. The analysis so far only examines whether Internet communication has an impact on the overall occurrence of protest. But what role does digital communication play for the continuation of protest once it has started? At least some dictators seem to believe that information technology plays a key role in facilitating ongoing protest. At the height of the Arab Spring in Egypt, for example, President Mubarak's government ordered national Internet services to be shut down. As Internet traffic data reveal, almost all of Egypt's telecommunications providers went offline at the same time, interrupting communication between citizens within the country as well as between Egypt and the rest of the world (Dainotti et al., 2014). This and similar incidents in other countries such as Libya and Syria suggest that autocratic rulers see Internet shutdowns as a temporary measure to prevent the further escalation of ongoing anti-government mobilization. The assumption behind this reasoning is that online communication facilitates participation in ongoing protest.

For our analysis, these considerations indicate the need to separate the effect of Internet coverage on the occurrence of protest, and its effect on protest dynamics *once protest has started*. Having examined the first question in the previous chapter, we now focus on the latter issue. More precisely, we study the effect on protest *persistence*—in other words, whether protest continues at a given location after the initial occurrence of protest there.[19] In addition, we examine how the government's repressive response to anti-regime protests affects the relationship between Internet penetration and future protest. In the sections below, we first develop theoretical expectations for the effect of Internet penetration on protest persistence and then test these expectations empirically. A related phenomenon is (spatial) protest diffusion, which is the onset of protest in new locations as a result of previous incidents elsewhere. We cover protest diffusion in the next chapter.

How the Internet Can Make Protest Last and Grow

Before we turn to an in-depth discussion of how Internet technology can be used by activists to sustain anti-regime protests, it is first necessary to contrast the conditions for remobilization after protest has happened with "first-time" mobilization. As we emphasized in the previous chapter, autocratic regimes enjoy a high level of control over Internet infrastructure and content, which allows them to implement a number of measures aimed at keeping public dissent low. However, these measures are not always successful in preventing protest mobilization. Indeed, protest sometimes occurs despite these measures, which changes the conditions for mobilization. In cities where activists have been successful in staging anti-regime protest in the past, conditions are conducive to remobilization because individual motives are present, restrictions on resource mobilization are low, and/or political opportunities are ample. In other words, in cities that have previously experienced protest, conditions for future mobilization are more favorable because long-term strategies by the government to prevent it have failed.

A large amount of literature has researched the dynamics of dissent over time. Some of this literature addresses the existence of waves of protest, where previous protest increases the likelihood of future episodes (Tarrow, 1989a). Some authors attribute these waves to characteristics of the underlying political system, which periodically provides opportunities for protest to emerge (Robertson, 2010). According to these explanations, protest exhibits temporal persistence not because prior incidents affect subsequent ones, but rather because of an underlying political contest between different groups. In other theoretical accounts, prior protest is causally related to future occurrences. This literature often focuses on groups and organizations and examines how their behavior changes over time. According to Tarrow (1989b), for example, organizational learning, where protest repertoires diffuse between organizations/groups, makes the persistence of protest more likely. Almeida (2003) makes a similar argument and shows that over time, organizations become more experienced and can therefore better respond with protest should the need arise. A related branch of literature studies shifts in protest tactics as a result of learning, where organizations can shift between non-violent and violent tactics depending on the perceived chances of success (Moore, 1998). However, since this literature largely focuses on changes within the same actor or group over time, information about prior protest and the outcomes of these actions is assumed to be present. Consequently, the availability of information via modern communication technology has little relevance for this literature.

This is different for much of the classic rational choice literature on protest dynamics, which attributes protest persistence to the rational cost-benefit calculations of individuals. According to Granovetter's (1978) threshold model, citizens have an individual participation threshold—in other words, a minimum size of a protest that they would be willing to join. The assumption behind this logic is that individuals carefully weigh the potential benefits of collective action (a change in the political status quo) against the dangers involved (the risk of being injured, imprisoned, or even killed). The larger the size of a protest, the higher the chances of success (Rasler, 1996), and the lower the odds of suffering negative consequences. A population of citizens is assumed to be heterogeneous when it comes to the level of risk they are willing to incur, which means that some will join at early stages of a protest, while the majority will "jump on the bandwagon" only later after the protest has grown to a certain size. For this process to work, however, a small population of extremists must be present. These extremists protest despite the potential costs, and can therefore incite a protest movement before others join.

Other models in this literature posit similar dynamics, where protest triggers subsequent participation by affecting the cost-benefit calculation of individual citizens. According to Kuran (1989), citizens who are critical of a regime usually do not reveal their preferences publicly for fear of repression. However, once ongoing protest reveals that discontent is more widespread than previously assumed, citizens abandon this "preference falsification" and join ongoing protests. This leads to quick escalations of protest that may seem surprising, because they lack any prior indication of widespread discontent. Similar to Granovetter's threshold model, Kuran also assumes a prior distribution of preferences in the population that provide the motive to join collective action. Hence, the key assumption of these models is that prior protest opens up opportunities for future collective action.

What role does the availability of information play in these classic models of protest mobilization and participation? As the above discussion reveals, knowing about previous or ongoing protest is absolutely essential for the individual's decision about whether to participate. The information about previous or current levels of participation and the response of the government affects individual perception of the expected costs and benefits of participation and their willingness to abandon preference falsification. As discussed in Chapter 3, the Internet provides effective and accurate channels through which this information is communicated: While governments try to limit coverage of ongoing events in the traditional media, online communication is more likely to circumvent such limitations, allowing information to flow and giving an unbiased account of the dynamics on the ground. In this way, online communication can facilitate the spontaneous coordination of anti-regime protest.

The mechanism of spontaneous coordination has been connected to the escalation of protests during the Arab Spring. Breuer, Landman and Farquhar (2015) argues that social media triggered higher turnout in Tunisia by conveying overly optimistic participation numbers in ongoing protests. This emphasizes that the turnout perceived by individuals via social media need not necessarily correspond to the actual numbers; it is sufficient if citizens expect a high-enough turnout. Moreover, Hassanpour (2014) shows that after President Mubarak's government unexpectedly shut down the Internet in January 2011, the protest movement became more fragmented and smaller protests emerged in different neighborhoods of Cairo. This implies that the Internet also had a coordinating function during these protests, which—once it was removed—led to smaller and less coordinated protest events. For our analysis, these theoretical mechanisms suggest that better information about ongoing protest as provided by the Internet should reinforce protest once it has started. In other words, *we expect that higher Internet penetration increases the likelihood of anti-regime protest persistence.*

In Chapter 3, we discussed the use of conventional tools of authoritarian control in the digital age. This is relevant for this chapter, since how the Internet affects the continuation of protest once it has started likely depends on how the government has reacted to anti-regime protests in the recent past. We can only briefly summarize the vast literature on repression here. On a general level, state repression refers to a regime using either violent or nonviolent action as a deterrent or punishment against citizens who are perceived as challenging the government (Davenport, 2007a, p. 2). Repression includes a large variety of state actions, ranging from the bureaucratic harassment of opposition members to the mass killing of certain groups. As underlined by Svolik (2012), repression is an inherent part of autocratic rule, and dictators typically engage in a range of repressive actions. In this chapter, we are interested in one particular form of re-pression: the violent countering of public protest by state security agencies such as the police or the military. These interventions typically involve beating and arresting protesters, but can also include lethal action.

What do we know about the effect of violent repression on protest? Decades of research on the repression-dissent nexus have yielded conflicting theoretical arguments and empirical evidence. Some scholars have found that repression discourages protests, while others report that repression encourages protests. According to some studies, moderate-intensity repression fuels protest while high-intensity repression deters it. Yet others find that repression leads to a shift in dissenters' strategies (for an overview, see Davenport, 2007a; Earl, 2011). The evidence is backed up by theoretical arguments grounded in value rationality, instrumental rationality, or social-psychological perspectives focusing on emo-tional responses (Lichbach, 1987; Varshney, 2003; Pearlman, 2013). At the same time, however, the conflicting findings in the literature indicate that the effect of repression on dissent is likely conditioned by contextual (e.g., political insti-tutions, media freedom) and/or conflict-specific (e.g., history of repression or armed conflict) factors.

How does the Internet affect the impact of repression on future protest? As stated, better communication flows are assumed to be key here: The Internet can be used to spread information not only about ongoing protest, but also about re-pression of previous protests. By making government action more widely known among the public, the Internet may be able to exacerbate the dynamic relation-ship between protest and repression discussed in the previous paragraph. This notion is reflected in research that focuses on how an informational war in the wake of state repression affects the future trajectory of dissent (Hess and Martin, 2006; Sutton, Butcher and Svensson, 2014). As discussed, this relationship can manifest itself in one of two ways. Repression can trigger more protest through a backlash effect. As several studies show, violent repression can lead to outrage in the population, which can convince more people to turn out to protest events. The example of the 2009 protests in Iran illustrates this. On June 20, 2009, Neda Agha-Soltan was shot dead during the unrest surrounding the presidential elec-tion. The incident was videotaped and broadcast worldwide via social media. It triggered subsequent calls for protest, which led to an escalation of protest in Tehran and elsewhere.

This example shows vividly how new types of digital content disseminated via the Internet can have a massive effect on the escalation of protest. From a ra-tional point of view, this escalation may be difficult to understand: If the costs of protest increase as a result of repression, citizens should be deterred from participating. However, this account ignores the powerful role of emotions that can be essential drivers behind collective action (Aytaç, Schiumerini and Stokes,

2018). As Schock (2005) observes, repression can invoke sympathy for activists among the population, which convinces previously uninterested people to join a movement. A similar effect is postulated by Lichbach (1987), who argues that repression can lead to the mobilization of hitherto apathetic citizens, but also to a radicalization of protesters more generally. Analyzing the specific role of social media during the Arab Spring using survey data, Breuer, Landman and Farquhar (2015) attribute a protest-increasing effect to social media, since they can inform large audiences about government atrocities carried out in response to previous protests (see Bellin, 2012, for a similar argument). In our analysis, this means that the backlash effect should be more powerful if the Internet helps to distribute information about repression more widely. In our analysis below, we expect *the Internet's positive effect on protest continuation to be stronger if prior protest was violently repressed by the government.*

As mentioned, however, other scholars have reached different conclusions with regard to the impact of repression on subsequent protest. One argument is that the effectiveness of repression depends on the level of violence employed by the state. While repression may provoke a response when it is not too severe, higher levels of violence can indeed deter opposition. As Gurr (1970) puts it, "the threat and severity of coercive violence used by a regime increases the anger of dissenters, thereby intensifying their opposition, up to some threshold of government violence beyond which anger gives way to fear." This conclusion is echoed by Hibbs (1973) and Muller and Weede (1990) in their empirical studies, and by Pierskalla (2010) in a game-theoretical model. Other research also shows that repression does not necessarily backfire as discussed above, but that it can deter future protest. As Rasler (1996) shows, repression in Iran under the Shah had a negative short-term effect and a positive long-term effect on dissent. In other words, repressive action by the government was able to reduce protest levels.

Yet another example from the Arab Spring shows how social media can contribute to this deterrent effect. In her discussion of the events in the Middle East, Bellin (2012) discusses how governments in the region were surprised by the the protests. Traditionally, turnout for political action in the Arab world had been low despite the fact that the grievances motivating the protests had existed for a long time. Relating this to the role of social media in triggering sudden escalations of protest, Bellin (2012) mentions the fact that social media quickly disseminated information about the government's response. More precisely, in Tunisia a video was circulated showing the military standing idly by, which convinced protesters that no violent response was to be expected from the government. An alternative response (violent repression) could have altered people's expectations to the extent that they refused to turn out for future protests. For our analysis, the observable implication of this mechanism is that

*the Internet's positive effect on protest continuation should be stronger if prior protest
was not repressed.*

Does the Internet Help Protest to Last?

We once again turn to our empirical data on the Internet and protest. To study
the effect of the Internet on protest persistence, we shift our unit of analysis from
years to weeks. As discussed in Chapter 5, observing protest at the level of cities
and weeks allows us to better analyze the short-term dynamics of protest. Because we are interested in the emergence of future incidents once protest has
already happened, we restrict the sample to city-weeks following the onset of
local protest—in other words, to those cities that have experienced protest in
the past. The structure of the analysis is similar to that for protest occurrence
in Chapter 6. First, we inspect the relationship between local Internet penetration and protest persistence using descriptive statistics. We start out using all the
data in the sample before taking a closer look at the data for Russia, Iran, and
Egypt. Second, we use multilevel regression analysis as described in Chapter 5
to strengthen our confidence in the descriptive evidence, to examine variation
over time, and to identify the difference between repressed and non-repressed
protest. Finally, after discussing the results of the main models, we estimate a
number of alternative models to test the robustness of our findings.

A SIMPLE BIVARIATE ANALYSIS

We first take a look at the relationship between city-level Internet penetration
and protest persistence by plotting the data for the complete sample of 61 autocracies in Figure 7.1. The y-axis shows the probability of anti-regime protest
persistence for different levels of local Internet penetration (x-axis). As before,
we display the descriptive evidence using both a linear (left panel) and a more
flexible third-order polynomial specification (right panel).

Figure 7.1 shows initial support for our expectation that Internet technology can be used by opposition activists to strengthen ongoing protest. In both
the left and the right panels, the probability of anti-regime protest persistence
increases as city-level Internet penetration increases. In the linear specification,
for example, the probability of protest continuing is around 6 percent in cities
that are not connected to the Internet, whereas it is almost 18 percent in cities
with higher Internet penetration. This threefold increase in the probability of
protest persistence also holds when using the more flexible third-order polynomial specification (right panel). However, the right panel also shows that the
increase flattens at the highest levels of Internet penetration, indicating that the

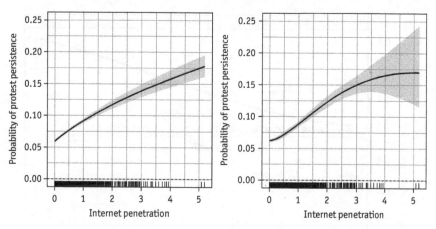

Figure 7.1 Smoothed conditional means plots, cities in all countries. Left panel: linear specification. Right panel: cubic specification

advantage that Internet technology affords to opposition activists tapers off once a high number of people are connected.

Do these general patterns also hold for the individual countries—Russia, Iran, and Egypt—that we discussed in Chapter 6? In Figure 7.2 we show the same plot as above for each of these countries. As indicated in Figure 7.2, the top panel shows the relationship for cities in Russia, the middle panel for Iran, and the bottom panel for Egypt. All of the panels show a strikingly similar pattern: As Internet penetration increases, so does the chance of protest continuation. This result underscores our theoretical expectation and the overall trend shown in Figure 7.1, namely that digital technology gives opposition activists an advantage once protest has happened. At the same time, Figure 7.2 highlights that there may be important differences between countries. Most prominent, the relatively flat line for Iran compared to Russia and Egypt indicates that Internet penetration is more effective in facilitating protest in the latter countries. We return to a more in-depth discussion on the determinants of these differences between countries in Chapter 9.

LEVERAGING THE POWER OF REGRESSION MODELS

Here, we again model the relationship between Internet penetration and the persistence of anti-regime protest in autocracies using multilevel regressions. As in Chapter 6, the statistical model is a logistic regression with protest occurrence as the dependent variable. However, as described above, we increase the temporal resolution to the week level and include only those cities in our sample that have experienced protest before. As in our analysis in the previous chapter, we

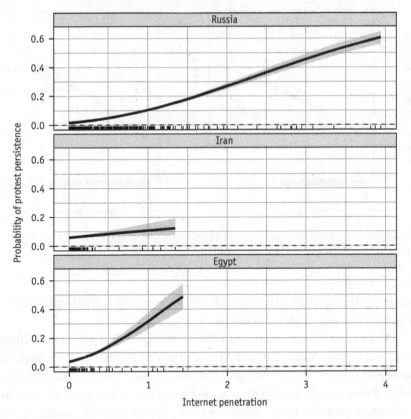

Figure 7.2 Smoothed conditional means plots: cities in Russia (top), Iran (middle), and Egypt (bottom)

specify random intercepts by city, country, and year; control for the level of development, city population, and civil war; and include dummy variables for cities
that are a regional or a national capital. In addition, our models take into account
the fact that protest often triggers more protest in the same city by including a
control variable for the number of weeks since the most recent protest. Similarly,
protest in a given city may be affected by protest elsewhere in the country, which
is why we include a control variable for the number of weeks since protest last
occurred in a different city in the country.

We first specify a model to estimate the overall effect of local Internet penetration on the continuation of protest in previously affected cities. Figure 7.3
displays the results from this model. For the reader's convenience, we once again
show our results in a coefficient plot, where the model's predictor variables are
aligned along the y-axis and the respective effects along the x-axis. The first line
in Figure 7.3 shows that the correlation between Internet penetration and the
persistence of anti-regime protest in autocracies is positive when controlling for

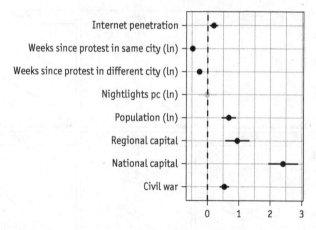

Figure 7.3 Regression results for the main model. The plot shows the coefficients for the different variables and their credible intervals. Coefficients where the credible intervals include zero are shown in gray (city-week resolution, logistic regression). Reference: Table A.11

a number of other city- and national-level characteristics. This result corroborates the evidence in Figures 7.1 and 7.2: In periods of ongoing protest activity, higher Internet connectivity is related to a higher probability of renewed outbreaks, which suggests that the Internet enables opposition activists to sustain protest. This result stands in stark contrast to the suppressing effect of Internet penetration on overall protest occurrence in Chapter 6, and highlights the importance of unpacking protest dynamics in order to better understand the political impact of Internet technology.

The model confirms other expectations about the dynamics of protest. In particular, the negative coefficients for the weeks since the last protest, both in the same city (second line in the plot) and elsewhere in the country (third line), show the strong temporal dependence in protest activity: Renewed protest is more likely if previous occurrences happened recently, an effect that declines as more time passes. Other city-level attributes such as high population and the status of the city as an administrative capital also contribute to an increased risk of protest. Finally, we find that protest is more likely during episodes of civil war.

These results indicate an overall protest-sustaining effect of local Internet penetration on protest persistence. But how stable is this effect over the years in our analysis? As discussed in the previous chapter, it is possible that the impact of Internet penetration on anti-regime protest persistence in autocracies has changed over time as digital technology developed. In particular, new online tools (e.g., social media) may have provided activists with improved means of mobilizing citizens for protest. In order to test this in a rigorous manner, we estimate a second multilevel model in which we vary the slope of Internet

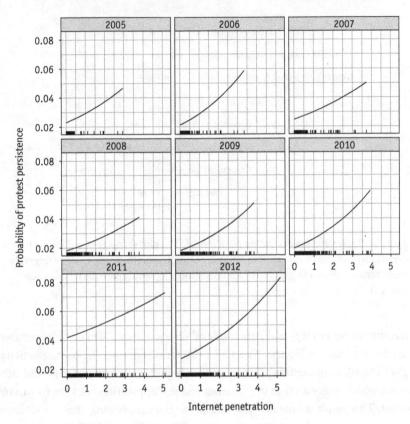

Figure 7.4 The effect of local Internet penetration on anti-regime protest persistence (city-week resolution, logistic regression), varying slopes per year. Reference: Table A.12

penetration by year. The slopes for each year (2005–2012) are displayed in Figure 7.4. The most striking pattern is that the effect of Internet penetration on anti-regime protest persistence is highly prominent in all years. The consistency of the result over time is confirmed by the estimated variance for the effect of Internet penetration on anti-regime protest persistence over time, which is only 2.5 percent (see Table A.12 in the Appendix).

While the two previous analyses take into the account the fact that protest is influenced by prior protest, they do not tell us whether the effect of digital communication on protest emergence changes depending on when the last protest occurred. For example, the Internet might reinforce protest only shortly after previous events, but not in the longer run. In order to test this, we specify a third model where we interact an indicator for the (logged) number of weeks since the most recent protest with the Internet penetration variable. This specification allows us to estimate the effect of Internet penetration on anti-regime protest conditional on when protest last occurred (recently or long ago). To enable the

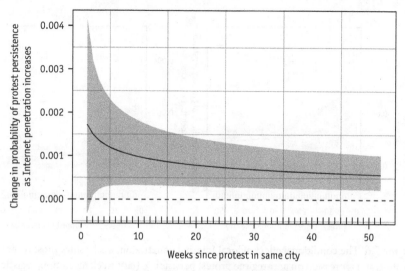

Figure 7.5 The conditional effect of local Internet penetration and weeks since most recent protest on anti-regime protest persistence (city-week resolution, logistic regression, 95% confidence intervals). Reference: Table A.13

interpretation of the interaction, we skip a discussion of the model coefficients and plot the estimated effects in Figure 7.5 (for a more technical discussion of interactions in logistic regression models, see Ai and Norton, 2003; Friedrich, 1982).

Figure 7.5 displays the change in probability of protest given an increase in Internet penetration (y-axis) for different values of weeks since the last protest (52 weeks, x-axis). The simulated probabilities were calculated by holding the continuous variables at their means, the number of weeks since protest in a different city at 12, regional capital at 1, and national capital and civil war at 0. The plot reveals three important insights. First, it confirms the finding from our previous models: As we can see from the positive change in probability of protest persistence in Figure 7.5, Internet technology seems to benefit opposition activists and allows them to sustain protest. Second, the facilitating effect is positive in the long run, as evidenced by the positive probability of protest over the one-year period plotted in Figure 7.5. Third, the gains from Internet technology diminish over time—as more time passes after a first protest (toward the right of the plots), the change in probability of protest persistence decreases. In our model, Internet penetration increases the probability of protest by about 0.16 percent in the first week after protest, but only by about a third of this (0.05 percent) a year after the last protest. At the same time, the second difference reveals that there is some uncertainty surrounding this third conclusion (95 percent confidence intervals overlap with 0).

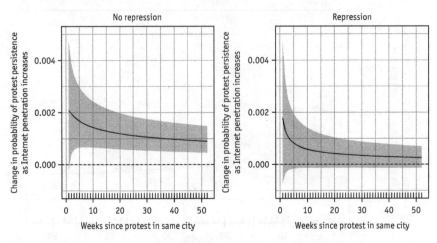

Figure 7.6 The conditional effect of local Internet penetration, weeks since most recent protest, and repression on anti-regime protest persistence (city-week resolution, logistic regression, 95 percent confidence intervals). Reference: Table A.14

Finally, can autocratic governments influence the effect of Internet penetration on protest persistence by responding with violent repression? Or does modern communication technology disseminate information about violent crackdowns in such a way that citizens are deterred from participating? We investigate this empirically by adding an indicator of the government's response to the model discussed in the previous paragraphs. This variable takes a value of 1 if security forces engaged in non-lethal or lethal repression (crowd dispersal, arrests, beating, shooting) of the protesters, and 0 otherwise. The information on security force involvement is part of the MMAD and was introduced in Chapter 4. We interact the repression indicator with our variables for Internet penetration and weeks since the last protest (logged), which allows us to produce the previous results separately for those situations where the last protest was repressed, and those where it was not. Similar to the previous model, we plot the change in probability depending on the temporal proximity of the last protest and whether it was repressed or not without discussing the regression coefficients.

The results are shown in Figure 7.6. The plots reveal considerable heterogeneity depending on the government's response to the most recent protest. The left panel indicates that an increase in Internet penetration increases the probability of protest persistence when the government does not respond with violent repression. In the right panel, the estimated effect is still positive, but the uncertainty is considerable. This makes it difficult to conclude that Internet penetration has a discernible effect on protest persistence when the last protest was met with violent repression from the government. In sum, these results indicate that activists can benefit from Internet-enabled communication only under certain circumstances: While information about the absence of repression seems to help activists successfully mobilize from that point on, this effect becomes much more uncertain when governments countered the last protest using violent means.

CHECKING THE ROBUSTNESS OF OUR FINDINGS

As in the previous chapter, we estimate alternative models to check the robustness of our results. For the results above, we are particularly concerned that the positive effect of Internet penetration on anti-regime protest persistence is an artifact of the data collection process. Since the protest data is generated using news reports, there may be issues related to reporting bias. Previous research has shown that the decision to report an event varies considerably by source, remoteness, degree of violence, and the issue of the event (see, e.g., Davenport and Ball, 2002; Earl et al., 2004). In addition, reporting can be influenced by the availability of communication technology (Weidmann, 2016). For the analysis in this chapter, this means that a positive relationship between Internet penetration/repression and protest might be caused by Internet penetration/repression influencing the *reporting* of protest rather than its actual occurrence. If this was the case, there would be an upward bias in our coefficients for Internet penetration, since events in well-connected places would be more likely to be reported. This could lead to the estimation of a spurious positive effect (Weidmann, 2016). We take reporting bias into account by including an indicator of reporting intensity at the city-week level to the three main multilevel models discussed above. Using the unique structure of the MMAD that distinguishes the different reports of an event, we create a variable that captures reporting intensity by dividing the number of news reports on protests by the number of protest events. This indicator allows us to identify how extensive media coverage of previous anti-regime protest was, and whether this intensity explains high levels of subsequent protest according to our data.

Does the inclusion of the report ratio variable affect the conclusion that Internet penetration facilitates the persistence of protest in autocracies? To check this, we replicated the plots above using the estimates from the robustness test models that include the report ratio indicator (see regression output in Tables A.15, A.16, and A.17 in the Appendix). The plots displayed in Figures 7.7, 7.8, and 7.9 reveal that the findings reported in the main models are robust to this change in model specification. As expected, however, the reporting indicator is strongly and positively related to protest persistence (see third row from the top in Figure 7.7).

Conclusion

In this chapter, we further pursued our inquiry into how Internet technology influences popular mobilization in autocratic regimes. While the previous

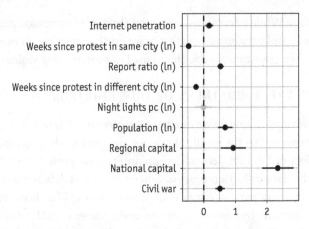

Figure 7.7 Regression results for the main robustness test. The plot shows the coefficients for the different variables and their credible intervals. Coefficients where the credible intervals include zero are shown in gray (city-week resolution, logistic regression). Reference: Table A.15

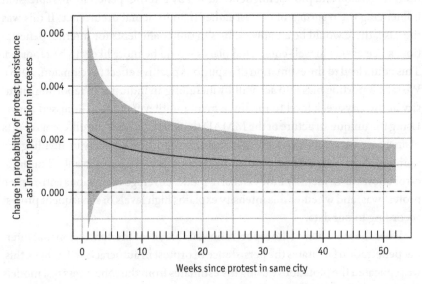

Figure 7.8 The conditional effect of local Internet penetration and weeks since most recent protest on anti-regime protest persistence, controlling for reporting (city-week resolution, logistic regression, 95 percent confidence intervals). Reference: Table A.16

chapter examined the occurrence of protest and found that Internet penetration can suppress it, this chapter focused on the continuation of ongoing protest episodes. In contrast to the previous chapter, we find that the Internet facilitates ongoing protest *after it has started*. In other words, once protesters have successfully mobilized, the Internet helps coordinate future protest and convinces more

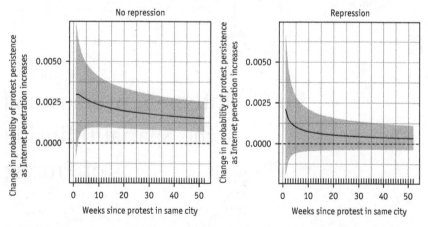

Figure 7.9 The conditional effect of local Internet penetration, weeks since most recent protest, and repression on anti-regime protest persistence, controlling for reporting (city-week resolution, logistic regression, 95 percent confidence intervals). Reference: Table A.17

people to join. This effect, however, does not seem to stem from the use of social media, as it is consistent over the entire period of our empirical analysis. At the same time, our results show that the effect is to a certain extent conditional on the amount of time that has passed since the last protest occurred, as well as the government's response to previous protests. The effect is more pronounced if protest occurred recently, and if the government did not respond with violent repression. The latter finding illustrates that the nature of information distributed through the Internet is key. If protest is met with violence by the government and citizens learn about this via the Internet, repression can be effective in deterring participation.

These divergent findings in our first two empirical chapters underscore the need to disaggregate the effect of the Internet for the different phases of protest. As we have seen, its effect differs strongly depending on whether we focus on the overall occurrence of protest or the continuation of ongoing episodes. According to our results, the Internet effectively suppresses the occurrence of protest. However, it facilitates its continuation and persistence once protest has started. As these results show, Internet technology sometimes plays into the hands of the government and sometimes into the hands of activists. In the next chapter, we continue our analysis of the dynamics of ongoing protest—specifically, the spatial diffusion of anti-regime protests between different cities in a country. Given the onset of protest in one city, does Internet technology make it more (or less) likely that protests will also occur in other cities?

8

Internet Coverage and the Spatial Diffusion of Protest

Earlier in the book, we discussed how mass political protest can lead to significant political transformation when it gains momentum. As the Arab Spring and Color Revolution illustrate, dictators may find themselves without a job when people take to the streets, potentially paving the way for democracy. However, the impact of political protest depends on its size, and a single, isolated incident is unlikely to achieve the protesters' desired outcomes. For protest to be successful, it is important that it lasts and grows. As shown in the previous chapter, Internet technology contributes to the continuation of protest events in a given city. In short, once protesters have mobilized successfully, digital technology can improve communication and thus make it easier to sustain protest over time. Can Internet technology also facilitate the spread of protest from one city to others, giving rise to a larger, coordinated protest campaign across a country? In this chapter, we set out to answer this question.

The simultaneous emergence of a particular social phenomenon across space—in other words, its spatial "clustering"—has been a frequently studied topic in political science. Scholars have shown that political events and transformations such as the adoption of particular policies (Braun and Gilardi, 2006), transitions to democracy (Gleditsch and Ward, 2006), and political violence (Buhaug and Gleditsch, 2008) often occur at the same time or in quick succession in different locations. In the international relations literature, these locations typically correspond to entire countries, with the phenomenon in question traveling between them. However, clustering can also be observed at the subnational level, for example between different districts or cities within a country, which is the focus of this chapter.

As Elkins and Simmons (2005) argue in their discussion of policy clustering, there are three kinds of mechanisms that explain the simultaneous occurrence

of political events in different places. First, clustering may be the result of similar conditions at nearby locations, which independently give rise to the phenomenon in question. Applied to the clustering of protest within a country, a
sudden shock such as a sharp increase in food prices could trigger mass mobilization in particularly poor locations. Since these locations are likely to be close to
each other, protest will exhibit spatial clustering without the different instances
having necessarily been "caused" by each other (Smith, 2014). Second, clustering can be the result of coordination by a higher-level entity. For the example
of protest, this can happen if several protest events in nearby cities are coordinated by a single opposition actor. This is a frequent argument in the contentious
politics literature, which underlines that protests grow "out of pre-existing institutions and organizational forms" (Morris, 1981, 744). However, despite their
simultaneous occurrence, these events are not causally related to each other.

In the third mechanism, according to Elkins and Simmons (2005), clustering of a social phenomenon happens because prior instances trigger new ones in
other locations. In the case of protest, this means that events occur in new cities
within a country because dissenters follow the lead of those who have successfully mobilized protest elsewhere in the recent past. This mechanism is what we
refer to as *diffusion*, and it constitutes the main focus of this chapter. Typically,
diffusion is studied in a spatial sense, where a phenomenon gradually expands
over space (Hägerstrand, 1967). This spatial element separates diffusion from
escalation (growth of a movement over time) and persistence (sustained protest
over time, see previous chapter), both of which typically do not have a spatial
component (Myers, 2000). Importantly for our analysis, the above discussion
indicates that studying a diffusion process is not straightforward. While diffusion
leads to spatial clustering of a particular phenomenon, the reverse does not hold:
Spatial clustering is not necessarily indicative of diffusion. In order to plausibly
test the diffusion mechanisms of interest to us, we first need to properly identify
how Internet technology can facilitate protest diffusion between cities in autocracies in a theoretical argument. We then need to set up an empirical design that
can measure and estimate diffusion effects. In the next section, we link Internet
technology to protest diffusion by building on existing arguments in sociology
and political science. Thereafter, we present our empirical analysis.

How the Internet Can Foster the Diffusion of Protest

For a political phenomenon to diffuse from one location to another, four elements are necessary (McAdam and Rucht, 1993): a *transmitter* of the phenomenon at the location of origin, an *adopter* at the destination, an *item* that is
diffused, and a *channel* of information. In our application of this framework, the

first three elements are easily defined. The transmitter in the original location is the dissenters in a city where protest has already occurred. They have managed to successfully mobilize people to protest, which can lead the adopter—the potential dissenters in another location—to do the same. Note that this implies that the occurrence of protest elsewhere is a necessary condition for diffusion to be possible. In our application of the above framework, the item that is diffused is protest. Now that we have identified the transmitter, the adopter, and the item, we also need to determine the channel through which the item (protest) is spread over space. For this, there is a wide range of possibilities. For the diffusion of political violence, for example, it has been argued that resources (weapons, fighters) constitute the item that makes violence spread from one place to another (Weidmann, 2015). These weapons and fighters are moved via transportation channels between locations. In contrast to the physical transportation of tangible resources, our argument focuses on how *information* can lead to diffusion. In line with much of the literature, we argue that information about ongoing protest is the channel through which dissent can be incited elsewhere. To further build on this informational mechanism theory, we need to ask (i) what information travels and (ii) how this information is transmitted from one place to another.

Information transmission can lead to the diffusion of protest in two ways. In the previous chapter, we argued that the occurrence of protest and the spreading of information about it can lead to surges of dissent in a city where protest has previously occurred. Similar mechanisms can play out between different locations. If information about prior instances of protest elsewhere reaches other cities in the country, this can set in motion bandwagoning effects as described by Kuran (1989) and Lohmann (1994) across space. In such cases, dissenters in locations that have not previously experienced protest are stimulated to ramp up mobilization efforts themselves. When people learn about prior instances of protest, they may grow more optimistic about the number of people that will join protests in their city and their chances of success, and thus be more likely to participate themselves. Information about dissent elsewhere is thus a first way in which protest can diffuse. A second way concerns information about *how* protests were conducted. Indeed, studies have shown that protest movements adjust their tactics over time, and that prior instances of collective action can inspire future ones using similar tactics (Wang and Soule, 2016). In the Color Revolution, for example, one tactical commonality was the use of one color that symbolized opposition to the regime. This illustrates that a prior instance of collective action can lead dissenters to employ a similar tactic elsewhere (Soule, 1997; Andrews, 2006).

If information about prior protest elsewhere is vital for protest diffusion, how does it get from one place to another? Scholars have noted that diffusion can be either relational or non-relational (McAdam and Rucht, 1993; Crabtree,

Kern and Pfaff, 2018). In the former, direct contact between the transmitter and the adopter facilitates diffusion (Andrews, 2006). Before the advent of mass communication technology, this was the main informational channel that contributed to diffusion, and spatial proximity was one of the main factors that determined whether information was able to spread quickly or not. For example, one study reveals that the spatial diffusion of riots in the 1830s can be explained by the accessibility between the locations (Aidt, Leon and Satchell, 2017). In the case of non-relational diffusion, impersonal channels are responsible for the transmission of information. Before the advent of mass communication, non-relational diffusion occurred, for example, through printed newspapers. The introduction of telecommunication and mass media, however, changed this dramatically. Radio, television, and telephones enabled news to spread quickly from one location to others, thus making both relational and non-relational diffusion virtually independent of geographic distance (Weidmann, 2015).

Both relational and non-relational information diffusion can benefit tremendously from the availability of Internet technology. Relational diffusion is crucial for potential dissenters to overcome the collective action problem (Tufekci and Wilson, 2012). Similar to what we argued in the previous chapter, the Internet can act as an amplifier of relational diffusion because it facilitates low-cost communication between online activists and potential dissidents. The most obvious form of communication is peer-to-peer, where e-mails or other forms of private messages are transmitted online. It is equally important to note, however, that the Internet enables relational diffusion even when online activists do not specify the audience. For example, when a popular blogger posts material about anti-regime protests and encourages others to take similar action, already-existing levels of trust and intimacy between the blogger and readers can make the information especially effective for mobilization. The type of content that can be spread online further enhances this relational effect. Internet technology enables users not only to spread personal accounts of events and appeal to others to mobilize, but also to send photos and videos. The use of imagery can be especially powerful in motivating others to take action because it brings events to life in a way that text does not. Photos and videos also serve as evidence, convincing potential dissidents that reports of ongoing protests are real. For non-relational diffusion, much like the mass media, the Internet enables users to spread information about protests elsewhere without having to specify who the receiver is (Bimber et al., 2005). The key advantage of Internet technology in particular in the age of social media is that unlike traditional means of mass communication, virtually any user can disseminate information through these channels, which can then motivate users to mobilize. In sum, Internet technology can amplify both the relational and non-relational diffusion of information about ongoing dissent. This may be particularly important in authoritarian regimes, where crucial vehicles for information dissemination, such as the mass media and political organizations, are often controlled or severely restricted by the government.

If digital technology can be a catalyst of protest diffusion, why do governments not take measures to prevent this? As argued in the previous chapter—and as our empirical results so far have confirmed—we need to distinguish between the long-term effect that Internet technology has on protest and the short-term effect. In the long term, digital communication can work in the government's favor and prevent protest from erupting in the first place. Once open dissent has broken out and protesters have overcome the collective action problem, however, it can lead to further escalation of protest, as it is very difficult for governments to quickly stop the spread of new information without taking drastic measures (such as shutting down all Internet services). The results of the previous chapter confirmed that protest is more likely to persist in places with higher Internet penetration. For the same reasons, we expect this technology to contribute to the diffusion of protest.

However, empirically testing Internet-based diffusion poses a number of challenges. Many analyses of diffusion measure the channels through which information gets from one location to another directly. For example, if we are interested in diffusion between two countries via the telephone network, we can capture this by measuring the volume of calls between these countries (Weidmann, 2015). Performing a similar analysis for Internet-based diffusion is more difficult. Essentially, we would have to know the volume of Internet traffic that travels between two locations in order to approximate whether these locations are well connected to each other. Since we are conducting our analysis on a global scale, this is virtually impossible. We therefore opt for a different approach and assume that two locations are well connected if they both feature high Internet penetration rates. This is a plausible assumption, since the Internet as a global network can relay information from almost any place to any another, especially if the two locations are within the same country. This simplifying assumption means that the diffusion of protest should be affected by Internet penetration rates in two places: the location where protest first occurred, since high Internet coverage means that information about protest can diffuse quickly, namely, the "sending" city, and the location where protest diffuses to, that is, the "receiving" city. However, since the receiving city perspective is identical to our analysis in Chapter 6, we focus on the effect of Internet coverage in the sending city and hypothesize that *the higher Internet penetration is in the sending city, the more likely diffusion of protest will be.*

As discussed in the previous chapter on the continuation of protest, the diffusion effect is presumably also conditional on how the government has responded to previous instances of protest in the sending city. On the one hand, if protest was violently repressed, this may send a signal to potential protesters elsewhere that the government is taking a hard line against public dissent, which may ultimately prevent them from staging a protest themselves. In line with this logic, we expect *the positive effect of Internet connectivity on protest diffusion to be weaker if prior protest was violently repressed.* However, in line with the literature on repression of dissent outlined in the previous chapter, a violent response from the government can also backfire. If this is the case, then *the positive effect of Internet connectivity on protest diffusion should be stronger if prior protest was violently repressed.* In the remainder of this chapter, we test these propositions empirically.

Using Quantitative Analysis to Study Protest Diffusion

As in Chapters 6 and 7, we rely on both descriptive statistics and multilevel regression models to empirically study the diffusion of protest within countries. To do so, we build on the analyses of protest occurrence and persistence presented in previous chapters. Recall that we analyzed city-years in the occurrence analysis (Chapter 6) and then zoomed in to the city-week level to model the dynamics of protest persistence (Chapter 7). Similar to protest persistence, spatial diffusion of protest is a highly dynamic process, and we therefore continue with city-weeks as our unit of analysis. However, in the persistence analysis, we only looked at the cities and weeks that had previously experienced anti-regime protest. Following a similar logic in this chapter, we analyze *all city-weeks in countries where other cities had previously experienced protest.* In other words, we look at those cities and weeks that are possible candidates for protest to spread to, due to the fact that at least one other location in the same country had been affected by protest previously. This design results in a sample of approximately 620,000 city-week observations.

Each of these city-weeks is "at risk" of being affected by protest diffusion, and our aim is to determine whether information about prior protest elsewhere can contribute to protest breaking out in these "receiving" cities and weeks. In order to do this, we need information about the city (or cities) where protest may potentially diffuse from. As introduced above, the main focus of our empirical analysis is the use of Internet technology as a channel for the out-diffusion of protest from particular cities. These "sending" cities are defined as locations where the most recent protest event happened in the same country. In many instances, the most recent protest was a single event, which means that our main independent variable—Internet penetration of the sending city—is simply the Internet penetration of that city. If, however, there were multiple protest events elsewhere at the same time, and those events were the most recent ones, we take the maximum value of Internet penetration across these cities as our independent variable. This logic captures that *one* prior protest event in a well-connected city is sufficient to make protest diffuse, which is why we prefer the maximum over, for example, the mean level of Internet penetration across these cities. The computation of our indicator takes into account only the most recent protest elsewhere. Moreover, the values of the indicator remain constant for subsequent city-weeks in which no protest takes place in other sending cities.

With these explanations in mind, we first take a look at the relationship between Internet penetration and protest diffusion using descriptive analysis. We initially present the overall picture in all 61 countries for which we have data and then take a closer look at three individual countries (Russia, Iran, and Egypt). In a second step, we estimate multilevel regression models as described in Chapter 5. Last, we test the robustness of our findings in a number of alternative model specifications.

DOES PROTEST DIFFUSE, AND DOES INTERNET TECHNOLOGY FOSTER IT?

In this section, we shed light on two interrelated questions pertaining to the diffusion of protest. First, does prior protest in a city affect whether protest occurs elsewhere in a country? And second, does Internet technology affect the chances of protest traveling from one city to others? To answer these questions, we first show descriptive plots in Figure 8.1 using data from all 61 countries for which data are available. Specifically, we display the overall probability of local protest depending on whether protest occurred elsewhere in the country in the previous week.[20] The left dot in the left panel in Figure 8.1 shows that the overall probability of protest is approximately 0.8 percent if there was no prior mobilization elsewhere in the country in the week before. This contrasts sharply with the right dot in the left panel, which shows that in countries where protest recently occurred, the probability of local protest is about 1.3 percent. This is initial evidence that protest, once started, can diffuse to other cities in the country. But does Internet penetration affect the probability of protest once successful mobilization has occurred in a country? In order to investigate this, we split the city-weeks that had experienced protest previously into places with high levels of Internet coverage and places with low levels.[21] As argued above, if the Internet plays a crucial role in protest diffusion, protests in places with high penetration should generate more protest diffusion. The results are shown in the right panel in Figure 8.1. Clearly, there does not seem to be much of a difference between sending cities with low vs. high Internet penetration. If anything, the probability is slightly lower in sending cities with high Internet penetration (left dot, 1.2 percent) than in sending cities with low Internet penetration (right dot, 1.4 percent). This is a first indication that the level of Internet availability may not facilitate diffusion.

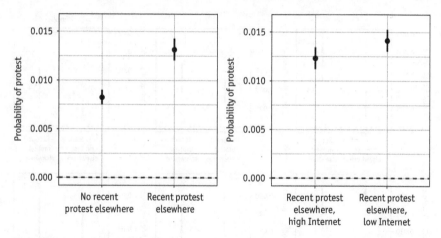

Figure 8.1 Probability of protest, cities in 61 countries

Do cities in Russia, Iran, and Egypt conform to the overall patterns discussed above? Analogous to Chapters 6 and 7, we replicate the plot shown in Figure 8.1 for each of these countries. The descriptive patterns are displayed in Figure 8.2. As we can see in the plots for Russia (left), Iran (middle), and Egypt (right), we get a very similar picture to the analysis of the full set of cases: The probability of protest is overall lowest when protest did not occur elsewhere in the country recently, and is much higher for cases where it did. Moreover, in none of the three countries do we observe a clear difference in the diffusion effect between low and high Internet penetration in the sending cities.

In sum, these first descriptive results show clear evidence of a diffusion effect. However, they do not indicate that the Internet plays a major role in facilitating it. At the same time, it is important to emphasize that this is a first look at the data using a simple bivariate comparison and a dichotomous indicator of Internet penetration in sending cities. Moreover, the evidence discussed here does not take into account differences between cities and countries. We remedy these drawbacks in the next section by estimating the relationship in our multilevel modeling framework.

INTERNET AND PROTEST DIFFUSION AT THE CITY LEVEL

The descriptive evidence above reveals that protest seems to cluster in time and space, as protest events in one location are often immediately followed by protests in others. However, this analysis does not provide much compelling evidence regarding the role of Internet penetration as a facilitator of protest diffusion between cities. While protest often seems to occur in the wake of previous events elsewhere, we need to analyze carefully whether the spread of information

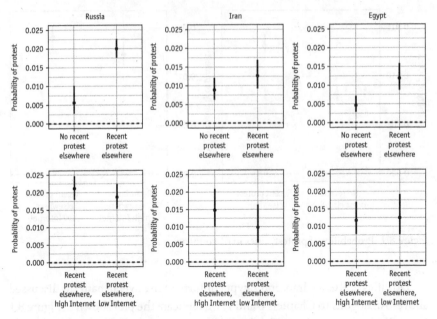

Figure 8.2 Probability of protest, cities in Russia, Iran, and Egypt

via the Internet partly accounts for this. The next step in our analysis employs a design that models the spread of protest from sending to receiving cities, the latter constituting our unit of observation. These are cities that are "at risk" of being affected by protest, given that protest recently occurred elsewhere in the country. As in Chapters 6 and 7, we use a dichotomous dependent variable indicating successful protest diffusion, which takes the value 1 if protest occurred in a particular week in the receiving city and 0 if not. Our estimated models are Bayesian multilevel logistic regressions with varying intercepts for country, receiving city (nested in countries), and year. As before, we account for temporal dependence of protest using a counter of the weeks since protest in the receiving city, but also control for economic development (night lights per capita), population, ongoing civil war, and the political importance of the receiving city (i.e., its status as a national or regional capital).

We start by amending our base model from the previous chapters by adding a variable that gauges the level of Internet penetration in the sending city/cities. This variable allows us to measure whether prior protest occurred in a well-connected location, and therefore is more likely to diffuse to other places. The results from this first model are displayed in Figure 8.3. As in previous coefficient plots, each predictor in the model is displayed on the y-axis and the dots and lines indicate the size of each coefficient and its standard error. Variables for which the 95 percent credible intervals of the posterior draws do not cross 0 (equivalent to 5 percent significance level) are shown in black, others in gray. In the first row of

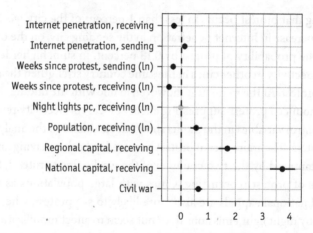

Figure 8.3 Regression results for the main model. The plot shows the coefficients for the different variables and their credible intervals. Coefficients where the credible intervals include zero are shown in gray (city-week resolution, logistic regression). Reference: Table A.18

the coefficient plot, we see that Internet penetration in the receiving city (i.e., the city whose protest occurrence we are attempting to explain) has a negative effect on anti-regime protest. This result is consistent with the main finding in Chapter 6: Local Internet penetration plays into the hands of autocrats and suppresses protest.[22]

The second row of the plot shows the coefficient we are primarily interested in in this chapter: the effect of Internet penetration in the sending city on protest elsewhere. Does better information flow as provided by the Internet lead to a higher likelihood of out-diffusion of protest? According to our model, the effect of Internet penetration in the sending city on protest is positive. This indicates that higher Internet penetration in the cities that most recently experienced protest strengthens the diffusion of protest to other cities. This positive effect deviates somewhat from the descriptive evidence above where we did not see a difference between sending cities with low vs. high Internet penetration. Given the strength of the multilevel models compared to the descriptive plots—for example, taking into account differences between cities and the ability to control for confounding factors—we are more confident in these latter results than the descriptive plots. The size of the facilitating effect of Internet penetration in a sending city is comparable to the suppressing effect of Internet penetration in a receiving city. To see this more clearly, we estimated the change in probability of protest given a change in Internet penetration in the receiving and sending city from 0 to the 50th percentile.[23] The estimated changes in probability indicate that an increase in Internet penetration in the receiving city reduces the probability of protest by about 0.13 percent, a substantial change considering that protest occurs in less than 1 percent of the city-week observations. An increase in Internet penetration in the sending city, on the other hand, increases the probability of protest by 0.18 percent. In sum, higher levels of Internet connectivity in other cities in the same country strengthen the spatial diffusion of protest. At the same time, however, in line with the findings in Chapter 6, the pronounced protest-suppressing effect of local connectivity remains.

The control variables in the model show effects similar to the analyses in previous chapters. The more recent protest occurred in both receiving and sending cities (as captured by the two counters of the weeks since protest), the higher the chance of protest reoccurring. Cities with large populations as well as regional and national capitals are also more likely to see protest, whereas wealth measured by night light emissions does not seem to affect mobilization. Finally, cities located in countries with civil wars experience more unrest overall than other countries.

As in the previous chapters, we also analyze whether there are temporal patterns in the relationship between Internet penetration and protest diffusion. First we look at the temporal variation that could be introduced by changes in Internet technology. To gauge whether our main diffusion effect becomes stronger in the age of social media, we allow the main effect in our models to vary by calendar year. To see how the slopes vary across years, we plot them in Figure 8.4. Each plot indicates a different year, with the probability of protest shown on the y-axis and the level of Internet penetration of the sending city shown on the x-axis. The plots highlight two main findings. First and foremost, the strengthening effect seems to hold across the years in the analysis, as the effect is positive throughout. However, Figure 8.4 also shows that the steepness of the slopes vary over time. Overall, the slopes are steeper in more recent years, and we can observe a steady increase in the years 2008–2012. These patterns are consistent with theoretical expectations about how changes in Internet technology over time, in particular the advent and proliferation of social media, can facilitate protest diffusion.

A second temporal aspect we examine is whether Internet technology is particularly conducive to protest diffusion immediately after a preceding event. In the previous chapter, we found that this is the case for protest persistence. Is the diffusion-inducing effect of Internet technology restricted to instances when previous protest in the country occurred recently? In order to investigate how Internet-based diffusion is affected by the temporal proximity of protest, we interact Internet penetration in sending cities with time since protest in sending cities. This allows us to gauge whether the pattern identified in the analysis above changes as time since the most recent protest increases. We visualize the findings from this model by plotting the change in probability of protest when Internet penetration in sending cities is increased from 0 to the 50th percentile (y-axis) for different values of weeks since protest in sending cities (x-axis) in Figure 8.5.

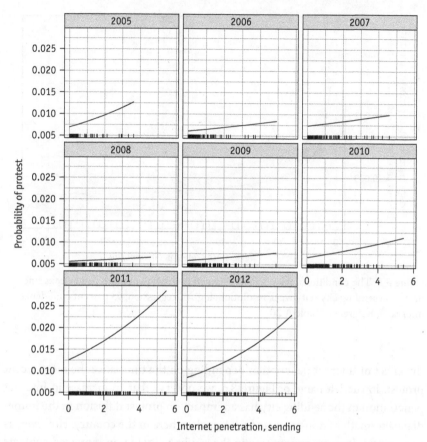

Figure 8.4 The effect of Internet penetration in sending cities on anti-regime protest diffusion (city-week resolution, logistic regression), varying slopes per year. Reference: Table A.19

The figure shows that high Internet penetration in the sending city is associated with a higher probability of out-diffusion only in the immediate aftermath of protest, and that the effect quickly diminishes and becomes negative as time since the last protest increases. When protest occurred last week, an increase in Internet penetration in the sending city increases the probability of diffusion by 0.3 percent. However, 20 weeks after protest occurred in the country, Internet penetration in the sending city reduces the likelihood of protest by 0.03 percent. This indicates that online information about the *absence* of unrest can decrease the chance of protest occurring in well-connected cities.

Third, as laid out in the theoretical discussion, we are also interested in how violent government response to anti-regime protest affects diffusion. As outlined above, repression can deter or exacerbate diffusion. Figure 8.6 displays the results of an interaction with repression of previous protest in the sending city, plotting

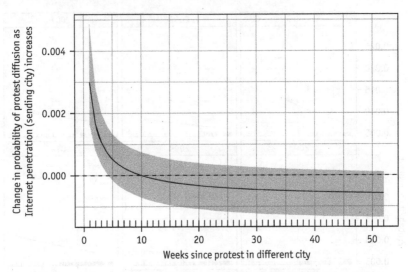

Figure 8.5 The conditional relationship between Internet penetration and weeks since protest in sending city (city-week resolution, logistic regression, 95 percent confidence intervals). Reference: Table A.20

the effect of Internet penetration depending on the time since the most recent protest. In the left panel of Figure 8.6, we observe that an increase in Internet penetration in the sending city has an impact on protest diffusion in the immediate aftermath of non-repressed protest elsewhere in the country. However, as time passes, Internet penetration in the sending city in non-repressed contexts suppresses protest diffusion. This result corroborates our earlier finding that information about quiescence in the country decreases protest in well-connected cities. In the right panel of Figure 8.6, we observe a similar strengthening effect of Internet penetration in the sending city on diffusion in cases where the government has responded violently to anti-regime protests. In other words, even when protesters are arrested, beaten, or killed in the sending cities, Internet technology contributes to the diffusion of protest to other well-connected cities in the country. This result may seem surprising in light of our findings in the persistence analysis in the previous chapter, where repression reduced the positive effect of Internet technology. Taken together, these results suggest that repression may create a spatially displaced backlash effect, where a violent government response triggers an outbreak of protest not at the location of the repressed protest, but elsewhere in the country.

Fourth, as discussed earlier in this chapter, it is often difficult to separate the effect of Internet technology on diffusion from related processes that lead to the clustering of events in time and space. For our analysis here, it could be that we see protest in multiple locations concurrently because conditions in the sending

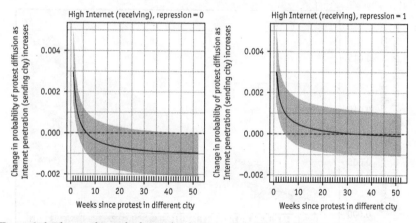

Figure 8.6 The conditional relationship between Internet penetration, weeks since protest, and repression in sending city (city-week resolution, logistic regression, 95 percent confidence intervals). Reference: Table A.21

and receiving cities are similar. For example, it could be that sudden price increases affect people similarly in different locations, giving rise to independent mobilization. It could also be that information is spread via channels other than online communication, for example by people traveling between cities. If these other processes are correlated with Internet coverage, it can produce spurious results. In order to lower concerns that the alternative processes are driving our findings in the above analyses, we consider whether geographic distance between sending and receiving cities impacts the effect of Internet technology on protest diffusion. If information transmitted via digital channels is driving diffusion, then the effect of Internet coverage should increase with distance for two reasons. First, since cities close to each other tend to be similar, conditions conducive to independent protest mobilization could be the main driver of concurrent dissent. In these cases, information can also easily be spread in other ways. Second, and importantly, information traveling via online channels is not limited by distance, which is why more of the diffusion effect should be attributed to Internet technology as distance increases. In sum, this means spatial patterns can to a large extent be attributed to factors other than Internet technology when distance is small. However, as distance grows, so should the effect of Internet coverage.

To examine this empirically, we amend the model in the first step by interacting Internet penetration in the sending city with its distance to other cities in the country. The interaction is displayed in Figure 8.7. The (logged) distance between sending and receiving city is on the x-axis and the change in probability of protest diffusion when increasing Internet penetration in the sending city from 0 to the 50th percentile is on the y-axis. In line with our expectation, the figure shows that the effect of Internet penetration on protest diffusion increases

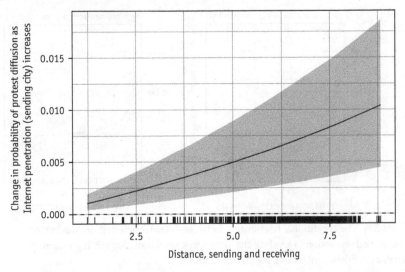

Figure 8.7 The conditional relationship between Internet penetration in sending cities and distance to receiving city (city-week resolution, logistic regression, 95% confidence intervals). Reference: Table A.22

as distance between cities increases. When two cities are approximately 50 km apart, increases in Internet penetration in the sending city heighten the probability of diffusion by 0.38 percent. At the mean distance between cities (900 km), the increase is 0.72 percent. In sum, the results of this test provide additional evidence that Internet technology can facilitate the spread of protest over space.

Finally, we explore the divergent effects of Internet coverage in the sending and receiving cities. As the results above have shown, local Internet coverage reduces the likelihood of protest, while at the same time giving rise to spatial diffusion to other places. At first glance, this result seems counterintuitive, given that the exchange of information via the Internet should be highest if *both* the sending and receiving cities have high rates of Internet penetration. To inspect this more closely, we estimate our base model with an interaction between Internet penetration in the receiving and sending cities, which allows us to test whether the two jointly affect protest diffusion. The results from this second model specification are displayed in Figure 8.8. We plot the change in probability of protest diffusion given an increase in the level of Internet penetration in the sending cities (y-axis) for different values of Internet penetration in the receiving cities (x-axis). As before, we used an increase in Internet penetration in the sending city from 0 to the 50th percentile to calculate the first difference in Figure 8.8.

What does Figure 8.8 reveal about how Internet technology is related to protest diffusion? The plot shows that the relationship is counter to our

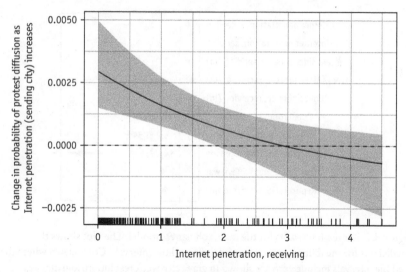

Figure 8.8 The conditional relationship between Internet penetration in sending and receiving cities (city-week resolution, logistic regression, 95 percent confidence intervals). Reference: Table A.23

expectation that levels of Internet penetration in sending and receiving cities jointly facilitate diffusion. Rather, the effect of diffusion is strongest when receiving cities have low to intermediate levels of Internet penetration (left half of the x-axis). Under these conditions Internet penetration in the sending city facilitates diffusion (positive effect along the y-axis). As Internet penetration in receiving cities increases, however, the effect of Internet penetration in the sending city decreases, and at very high levels the effect vanishes. To see this more clearly, consider a comparison between two receiving cities, one with low Internet penetration (0.16, 25th percentile) and one with high Internet penetration (2.6, 75th percentile). In the city with low Internet connection, the connectivity of other cities that recently experienced anti-regime protest leads to more local protest. The predicted change in probability is 0.29 percent. In the city with high Internet penetration, the predicted change in probability is 0.08 percent. This indicates that there are two counteracting effects of digital technology in autocracies: First, the Internet can quickly disseminate information about ongoing events elsewhere, which can lead to diffusion and the outbreak of new protest in other places. At the same time, however, this is partly offset by the protest-reducing effect of Internet coverage we found in the first chapter. In highly connected cities, Internet technology is used by the autocratic regime to co-opt and repress local populations through online propaganda, governance initiatives, and surveillance, which decreases individual motivation and opportunities for protest. Thus, we see successful diffusion only in places where this counteracting effect is unlikely to apply due to low levels of coverage. Low levels

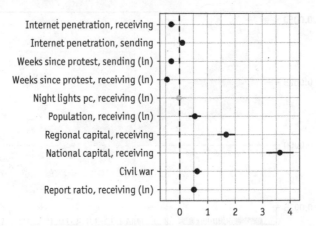

Figure 8.9 Regression results for the main robustness model. The plot shows the coefficients for the different variables and their credible intervals. Coefficients where the credible intervals include zero are shown in gray (city-week resolution, logistic regression). Reference: Table A.24

of coverage, however, are sufficient for information about protest elsewhere to flow in.

ADDITIONAL STATISTICAL CHECKS

In this section, we present robustness tests of the main results. As discussed in the previous chapter, the positive effect we find in the diffusion models could be driven by reporting bias, which would drive the effect upwards. Once again, we take advantage of the unique structure of the MMAD to deal with this potential problem. We control for previous reporting in the receiving city and re-estimate the multilevel models discussed above. As before, we created the reporting variable by dividing the number of news reports on protests by the number of protests events.

Figures 8.9, 8.10, 8.11, and 8.12 show that the findings are robust when reporting is taken into account: Internet penetration can lead to protest diffusion in autocratic regimes. The technology is especially conducive to strengthening diffusion in the immediate aftermath of protest and to locations that are far away from the sending city. Moreover, note that, as expected, the coefficient for the report ratio in Figure 8.9 is positive in the robustness test. This indicates that cities that have been extensively reported about are more likely to see protest in the future. All results can be found in Tables A.24–A.27.

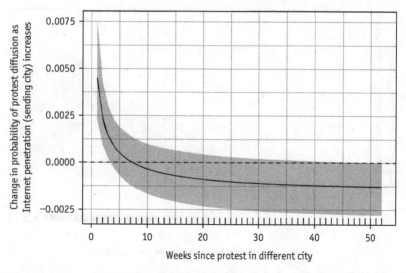

Figure 8.10 The conditional relationship between Internet penetration and weeks since protest in sending location (city-week resolution, logistic regression, 95 percent confidence intervals). Reference: Table A.25

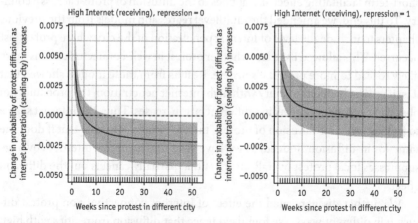

Figure 8.11 The conditional relationship between Internet penetration, weeks since protest, and repression in sending location (city-week resolution, logistic regression, 95 percent confidence intervals). Reference: Table A.26

Conclusion

In the previous chapters, we showed that Internet technology can be used by autocratic governments to suppress the outbreak of popular unrest in the long run, but that it benefits protesters and increases the likelihood of protest persistence once mobilization has been successful. In this chapter, we examined whether this

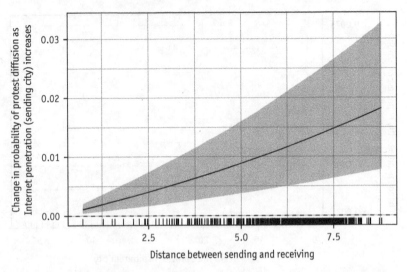

Figure 8.12 The conditional relationship between Internet penetration in sending cities and distance to receiving city (city-week resolution, logistic regression, 95 percent confidence intervals). Reference: Table A.26

short-term facilitating effect also applies to the diffusion of protest across a country. To this end, we amended the multilevel regression models from the previous chapters to include the level of Internet penetration of the city where protest last occurred. This allowed us to test whether protest in well-connected cities is more likely to lead to more protest elsewhere. Results from these models showed that it is; if protest happens in a city with high Internet penetration, the probability of observing another outbreak in a different city increases. Thus, the Internet seems to facilitate the out-diffusion of protest, but we cannot conclude that it does the same for in-diffusion. Indeed, as we have seen in Chapter 6, Internet coverage suppresses local protest overall, an effect that partially cancels out the diffusion effect.

We further disaggregated the effect of Internet connectivity on protest diffusion in different ways. We found evidence that diffusion from cities with high Internet connectivity has changed over time, becoming stronger in the age of social media. Moreover, as we saw for protest persistence in Chapter 7, Internet-induced diffusion seems to be happening in the short term. Our models show that the facilitating effect is strongest in the first weeks after a protest has occurred elsewhere. In addition, as expected, the effect is more pronounced when the distance between cities is large. Finally, we did not find evidence that a violent government response to protest hinders diffusion. Together with the results from the previous chapter, this means that police brutality can discourage protesters in the sending city from continuing their efforts, but this does not prevent outbreak in other locations. There are multiple possible explanations for this disparity. For example, there can be varying degrees of security forces deployed in different locations, or the perception of the regime's resolve may be lower outside those places where security forces have already intervened.

In sum, our results once again highlight that ICTs are a double-edged sword for autocratic governments. In the long run, governments can use the technology to prevent unrest among the population and keep dissidents at bay. However, once protest has started, the Internet enables activists to sustain collective mobilization, and even diffuse it to other places in the country. Thus, once the technology is in place, autocrats face additional challenges when countering ongoing dissent.

With these findings in mind, we are ready to move on to the final analysis in this book. A crucial gap in the analysis so far is that we have not examined variation across different types of autocracies. While we employ different empirical strategies to ensure that single countries are not driving the results we see, the results are average effects across a large sample of heterogeneous autocratic countries. Thus, our approach cannot tell whether the Internet effect plays out differently depending on existing national-level political institutions. This requires a deeper examination of the theoretical literature in comparative politics and a further modification of our analysis, which we tackle in the following chapter.

9

Reinforcement or Substitution?
Internet and Protest across
Different Autocracies

In the previous chapters, our theoretical discussion and empirical investigation showed that the introduction and expansion of Internet technology suppresses the occurrence of anti-regime protests in dictatorships. Once protests have started, however, the technology can facilitate dissent at the local and national level. At this point, our analysis of the relationship between Internet technology and protest turns to look at the diverse institutional context in which these dynamics play out. Autocratic regimes employ a number of strategies to constrain political mobilization and dissent. At the same time, we know that autocracies differ from each other as much as they differ from democracy (Geddes, 1999, 121). Some autocratic regimes go to great lengths to repress any form of political organization and influence public opinion to prevent collective action, while others tolerate a fairly competitive political arena where government criticism and regular elections are key political ingredients.

In this chapter, we explore whether and how the impact of digital technology on protest varies across different authoritarian institutional contexts. In doing so, we follow Wolfsfeld, Segev and Sheafer (2013), who argue that Internet technology may play out very differently depending on the political environment it operates in. Our focus in this chapter is on how traditional forms of authoritarian control (or lack thereof) shape the relationship between Internet technology and political protest. Specifically, we develop a theoretical argument about how this relationship varies depending on a regime's restrictions on freedom of association and political organization—a cornerstone of authoritarian control. We contend that new technology can either reinforce or substitute these traditional forms of authoritarian control. Reinforcement means that repression via modern ICT operates *in addition to* traditional means of control, while substitution refers to Internet-based repression being used *in place of* conventional methods.

After a brief review of the literature on different autocratic regimes in the next section, we elaborate on the mechanisms of reinforcement and substitution in more detail.

Not All Autocracies Are Alike

Political science has a long tradition of developing classifications and categorizations for political regimes. Much work in this area has focused on the distinction between democratic and autocratic regimes (see Chapter 2). This literature has mainly been concerned with democratization and has therefore paid little attention to variation across non-democracies. In fact, an autocracy is often defined as the absence of democracy (Alvarez et al., 1996). Early attempts to distinguish between different forms of autocracy placed autocratic regimes in the categories of "authoritarian" and "totalitarian" (Arendt, 1973; Friedrich and Brzezinski, 1965; Linz, 2000). According to this literature, totalitarian regimes are headed by a strong charismatic leader, rely heavily on a national ideology, and use physical and psychological coercion. In these regimes, the government aims to penetrate all aspects of the daily lives of its citizens. In the words of Mussolini: "everything in the state, nothing outside the state, nothing against the state." The literature on totalitarianism was largely based on descriptions of Italy under Mussolini, Nazi Germany, and the Soviet Union under Stalin.

However, totalitarianism is a less relevant descriptor for recent non-democratic countries. Pioneered by Linz (2000), the next generation of scholars therefore developed the broader concept of authoritarian regimes, defined as polities in which there is political pluralism but mobilization is discouraged, ideology is unimportant or absent, and individual leaders exercise limited power. As Linz (2000) and a large number of other scholars have underlined, regimes belonging to the broad category of autocracies differ in a number of ways. Indeed, Geddes (1999, p. 121) observes that autocracies "have different procedures for making decisions, different ways of handling the choice of leaders and succession, and different ways of responding to society and opponents." How a given autocratic regime approaches these issues determines how it is classified. For example, according to the Geddes, Wright and Frantz (2014a) typology of regimes, in a *monarchy* such as Saudi Arabia, a small group of people, usually the royal family, have established rules for selecting the leader. In contrast, in a *party regime* such as China, the party is responsible for selecting political leaders who make political decisions together with the top echelons of the party (see Cheibub, Gandhi and Vreeland, 2010, for an alternative regime type classification).

A different strand of the literature classifies autocracies according to the political rights and civil liberties they allow. As Linz (2000) noted long ago, unlike totalitarian regimes, many autocracies tolerate a degree of political pluralism. Moreover, scholars have documented an increase in the number of these "hybrid" or "competitive authoritarian" regimes in the post–Cold War era (Diamond, 2002; Levitsky and Way, 2010). These regimes occupy the gray area between closed autocracy and liberal democracy (Carothers, 2002), and are characterized by varying degrees of political competition. Although Saudi Arabia and China choose leaders and policies using different procedures, both countries restrict political freedoms to such a degree that independent organization is impossible. By contrast, Venezuela under Hugo Chávez and Zimbabwe under Robert Mugabe allowed for varying degrees of political organization, to the extent that extremely heated competitive elections were held during their administrations.

Given that contemporary autocracies differ to a great extent in the political freedoms they grant their citizens, we need to study how these differences affect the relationship between Internet penetration and protest dynamics. After all, our results in Chapter 6 provide evidence that Internet technology can help governments reduce the occurrence of dissent. How does this align with other, more traditional strategies of authoritarian control? From a theoretical perspective, we can distinguish between two possible scenarios. The first is that Internet technology is yet another way by which control of the population can be achieved and sustained in closed autocracies. In this scenario, digital repression is used in parallel with more traditional means of autocratic government control, *reinforcing* control where it is already practised. The second scenario is that, in autocratic countries that have liberalized and exercise less control over their population by repressing political freedoms, digital repression can act as a replacement for traditional strategies. In other words, control and appeasement of the population using Internet technology can fill the gap left by the lack of control over political competition. In this scenario, traditional autocratic means are *substituted* by digital ones. In the following discussion, we consider how the cornerstone of traditional autocratic rule—restrictions on freedom of association—interacts with Internet technology to produce different dynamics of dissent.

Traditional Control, Digital Control, and Anti-regime Protest in Autocracies

One of the fundamental challenges of autocratic rule is mass control (Svolik, 2012). In particular, large-scale popular dissent undermines the legitimacy of the regime and can threaten its survival. Traditionally, autocrats have relied on a number of strategies to counter this threat. When it comes to political protest, one of the most important ways for autocrats to prevent it is to restrict citizens'

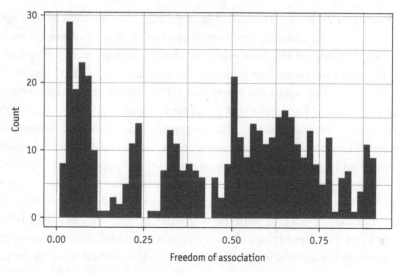

Figure 9.1 Distribution of the level of freedom of association in autocracies
(2003–2010). Data from the V-Dem Dataset, Version 7.1 (Coppedge et al., 2011)

freedom of association (McCarthy and Zald, 1977). Associations such as political parties and civil society organizations can be catalysts of open political
dissent; they provide activists with a cadre of members with common interests and a structure that enables coordination. To mobilize protests, activists
can use organizational structures and membership ties to spread information
about planned events. Furthermore, members are crucial in reaching the broader
population, for example by recruiting and mobilizing local communities. Thus,
autocratic governments would be ill-advised not to severely restrict the formation and operation of political associations. Yet, when we examine the global
pattern, it is obvious that many do not.

Figure 9.1 displays the distribution of freedom of association in autocratic
countries from 2003–2010, using data obtained from the Varieties of Democracy
Dataset (Coppedge et al., 2011). The index ranges from 0 (tightly controlled) to
1 (free). The figure shows that autocratic regimes occupy the entire range of the
index: A number of regimes maintain strict control over association, while others
allow more or less unconstrained political organization. In the former category,
we find countries like Syria, China, and Saudi Arabia, and in the latter Venezuela,
Burkina Faso, and Namibia. Figure 9.1 also shows that many regimes occupy the
middle ground, where political organization is neither banned nor unrestricted.
Instead, legal hurdles and the threat of repression for leaders and members of opposition organizations curb both the creation of organizations and membership
rates, which places these countries somewhere in the center of the chart above.
This is the case for countries such as Belarus, Jordan, and Uganda.

The empirical pattern shown in Figure 9.1 raises the question of why auto-cratic rulers would allow any freedom of association in the first place. Broadly speaking, the existing literature gives two distinct answers to this. The first is that they have no choice but to do so. Levitsky and Way (2010) discuss the main pathways that explain the emergence of competitive authoritarian systems in recent decades. They argue that a mix of autocratic and democratic institu-tions emerged because of historical contingencies and national and international pressure. Thus, autocratic governments simply had to make some concessions, and were no longer able to exercise control over the population as they used to. In many regimes, allowing political organizations was one of these conces-sions. The second answer in the literature is that autocratic governments benefit from nominally democratic institutions (parties, legislatures, elections), as they can be helpful for identifying potential challengers and subsequently co-opting or repressing these rivals. In this way, opening up the political space can reduce the risk of coups or popular uprisings (Gandhi and Przeworski, 2007; Magaloni, 2006; Svolik, 2012).

The question of why autocratic regimes grant freedom of association to their citizens is less important for our discussion than how liberalization of the politi-cal environment operates together with Internet technology and how autocratic governments attempt to use it to their own benefit e.g., to prevent unrest). Both conventional and new control strategies serve a similar goal, but we need to analyze more closely when governments use one or the other (or both). As mentioned, digital control can *reinforce* or *substitute* traditional forms of control. Reinforcement occurs when autocracies that use traditional means to prevent protest—such as restricting freedom of association—also embrace technolog-ical progress and employ digital ICT for the same purpose. This means that if there is reinforcement, we expect *the protest-suppressing effect of the Internet on protest occurrence described in Chapter 6 to be particularly high in countries with high levels of traditional repression, or in other words, where freedom of association is low.*

However, an alternative scenario is also feasible. Our discussion above re-vealed that when autocratic regimes grant more political rights and liberties to citizens, they face increasing potential threats to their rule as a result of popu-lar mobilization. The emergence of modern digital communication technology helps governments make up for the loss of control they concede as a result of allowing political organization. This regained control can take many forms, from improved information about political opposition organizations to better governance as described in Chapter 3. In particular, while political organiza-tions can be instrumental in staging large-scale political mobilization against the regime, this threat becomes much more manageable if the government can monitor these actors online and interfere with their communication. Digital propaganda undermining the opposition can also help render mobilization attempts less effective. If this expectation is correct, we should empirically observe a substitution effect in which a decline in traditional forms of autocratic control—such as fewer restrictions on political organization—is compensated for with forms of ICT control. The latter is what Gunitsky (2015) describes as the "corruption of the cyber-commons," defined as the skillful adoption of the Internet and social media for purposes of autocratic rule. This means that if there is substitution, we expect *the protest-suppressing effect of the Internet on protest occurrence to be particularly high in countries with low levels of traditional repression, or in other words, where freedom of association is high.*

As our analysis has shown, however, the effect of Internet penetration on protest varies dramatically depending on whether we look at the onset of political protest or its continuation and geographical spread. In Chapter 7 we found that Internet penetration makes protest continuation more likely, and in Chapter 8 our analysis showed that the new technology increases the spread of protest from one city to others in the same country. Thus, once protest has started, digital communication technology can facilitate its escalation. This, of course, poses a danger for autocratic rulers: In times of ongoing protest, rulers may have less control over the situation, since the availability of modern communication technology gives protesters new and effective ways to ramp up the scale of protest.

How does this protest-facilitating effect vary between more closed vs. more open regimes? If a closed regime already relies on traditional means of autocratic control such as restrictions on the freedom of association, it should be much more difficult for protesters to escalate the situation even if they have access to the Internet. In contrast, if governments rely less on traditional forms of control, once activists have successfully started a protest, they can rely on existing organizations *and* digital technology to keep protest going, and even to take it to other locations. Under these circumstances, the expansion of Internet technology backfires, and aggravates the situation for the regime. Hence, we expect *the positive effect of Internet penetration on protest continuation and diffusion to occur primarily in autocracies where political organization is not heavily restricted.* In the remainder of this chapter, we test our expectations empirically.

A Statistical Analysis of Reinforcement and Substitution

Employing our data and methods introduced above, we aim to analyze whether the effect of Internet penetration on protest occurrence, persistence, and diffusion varies depending on whether citizens are allowed to organize politically. As discussed in the theoretical section of this chapter, there are two possible scenarios: reinforcement, where digital technology is used in parallel with traditional means of repression, or substitution, where autocratic governments that have made concessions to the political opposition exploit alternative ways to exercise control via digital channels. If autocrats substitute traditional repression with digital means, we expect the protest-reducing effect of Internet coverage to be particularly strong in regimes that grant their citizens extensive freedoms of association. At the same time, however, this means that once activists have successfully mobilized, these regimes have fewer conventional means of suppressing protest. Hence, we expect the protest-facilitating effect of Internet penetration on persistence and diffusion to be particularly strong in regimes with fewer limitations on political organization.

We follow our earlier approach and start out by looking at descriptive evidence and plotting the data. We then proceed with our multilevel models in three steps, looking at each of the three outcomes: the occurrence, persistence, and diffusion of protest. In each step, we re-estimate the main multilevel models presented in the respective previous chapters, adding an interaction between Internet penetration and a measure of freedom of association from the Varieties of Democracy (V-Dem) dataset introduced above (see Figure 9.1). This interaction term allows us to test whether there is a conditional relationship between Internet technology and institutional setting. Similar to the previous chapters, our data consist of 1,564 cities in 61 autocratic countries. Our units of analysis are city-years (occurrence) and city-weeks (persistence, diffusion). As before, the results displayed below are based on Bayesian multilevel logistic regression models with varying slopes by country, city, and year. All models include the same set of control variables as in Chapters 6–8, and the regression tables for each model can be found in the Appendix.

BASIC PATTERNS IN OUR DATA

In a first look at whether national-level institutions influence the impact of digital technology on anti-regime protest, we plot our data in Figures 9.2, 9.3, and 9.4. As in previous chapters, the plots show how the probability of anti-regime protest occurrence/persistence/diffusion (y-axis) varies depending on Internet penetration (x-axis). The left panel in each figure uses data from the sample of cities with low levels of freedom of association (below the sample mean), and the right panel data from cities with high freedom of association (above the sample mean). While dichotomizing at the mean is a crude way of operationalizing political openness, it is useful as a first step to identifying patterns in the data. The multilevel models allow us to be more flexible, and we therefore abandon the

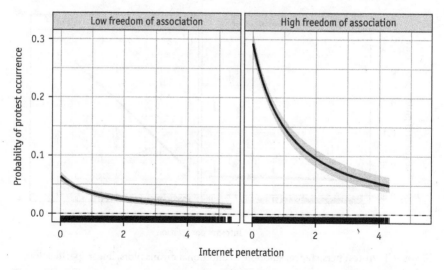

Figure 9.2 Protest occurrence: smoothed conditional means plots, linear specification, cities in 61 countries

two categories later on and estimate the conditional models using a continuous measure of freedom of association.

In Figure 9.2, we see initial evidence that national-level institutions matter for how Internet technology affects protest occurrence. Notice that the probability of anti-regime protest is much lower in closed regimes (e.g., Saudi Arabia) than in open regimes (e.g., Venezuela). This is unsurprising: It is much more difficult to organize mass protests in closed regimes that do not allow for independent organizations than in regimes that do. More important for us, however, is how Internet technology affects political protest in closed vs. open regimes. In closed regimes, the line slopes downwards, which means that the general incidence rate of protest decreases as Internet coverage goes up. This is analogous to our finding in Chapter 6. Similarly, in regimes that restrict political organization to a lesser extent (Figure 9.2, right panel), we also find that the availability of Internet technology at the city level goes along with reduced political protest. While the empirical relationship between Internet penetration and political protest is analogous in closed and open regimes, Figure 9.2 accentuates the size difference of the effect. Specifically, in closed regimes, the probability of protest is 5.9 percent if a city has no Internet connection, and 3.3 percent if a city's Internet penetration is above the median. In open regimes, on the other hand, the same increase in Internet penetration decreases the probability of protest in a city from 29.1 percent to 10.3 percent. In other words, the decrease in probability is 65 percent in open regimes, while it is 45 percent in closed regimes. This provides some initial evidence that Internet technology can be a substitute for traditional means of control in autocratic regimes by lowering the chance of activists mobilizing for

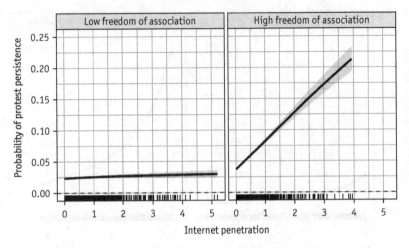

Figure 9.3 Protest persistence: smoothed conditional means plots, linear specification, cities in 61 countries

protests, even if the government theoretically allows them to do so. At the same time, we observe a considerable reinforcing effect in closed regimes.

Do we see similar differences between open and closed autocratic regimes when it comes to protest persistence? In order to investigate this, we plot the smoothed conditional means using the observations in the protest persistence dataset. Indeed, Figure 9.3 highlights a similar divergence with respect to national-level institutions. In the closed regimes (left panel), there does not appear to be any relationship between Internet connectivity and the probability of protest, and the line is essentially flat. In open regimes, however, the pattern matches our finding from Chapter 7: Internet technology strengthens the remobilization of anti-regime protest. In countries that permit some freedom of association, the probability that protest will continue in a city without Internet penetration is 4 percent, whereas it is 5 percent for cities with Internet penetration larger than the median. In combination with the result above, this empirical pattern is intriguing: In closed regimes, there is overall little protest, which can be reduced even further when the government uses the Internet for repression and co-optation. In these regimes, Internet technology does not seem to affect the persistence of protest once it has started. In open regimes, on the other hand, protest is much more frequent, but the autocratic government can reduce unrest through the use of digital technology. Once protest occurs in these regimes, however, the technology can be successfully used against the regime, benefiting activists who mobilize opposition protests.

Finally, what does the descriptive evidence indicate for our final outcome, protest diffusion? Figure 9.4 plots the probabilities of interest, distinguishing

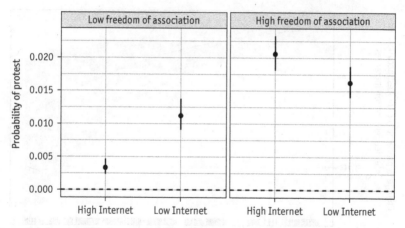

Figure 9.4 Protest diffusion: probability of protest, cities in 61 countries

between open (left panel) and closed (right panel) autocracies. We plot the probability of protest separately depending on whether the city where the most recent protest occurred (the "sending" city) had a high or a low level of Internet penetration. The figure reveals a number of interesting patterns. First, a comparison of the closed and open regimes highlights that, overall, protest diffusion is more likely in open autocracies. This is unsurprising, as the hurdles to collective action are reduced when regimes open up and grant their citizens freedom to organize politically. Second, somewhat surprisingly, the left panel in Figure 9.4 shows that in closed autocracies, the probability of protest diffusion is lower when sending cities have high (0.3 percent) compared to low Internet penetration (1.1 percent). In open regimes, on the other hand, higher Internet penetration in sending cities corresponds to higher probability of protest (2 percent in high Internet contexts vs. 1.6 percent in low Internet contexts).

However, before giving too much weight to the descriptive evidence, note that we have not taken important differences between countries and cities into account here. If, for example, closed regimes are more common in small countries, as many scholars have argued (e.g., Teorell, 2010), then these patterns may change when we account for these factors. Yet, taken together, these results indicate that the facilitating effect of Internet penetration in sending cities on protest diffusion revealed in Chapter 8 is confined to autocracies that allow a degree of independent organization.

ANALYZING PROTEST OCCURRENCE ACROSS DIFFERENT AUTOCRACIES

As discussed, we expect national-level institutions that regulate the right to organize to condition how the use of Internet technology affects anti-regime

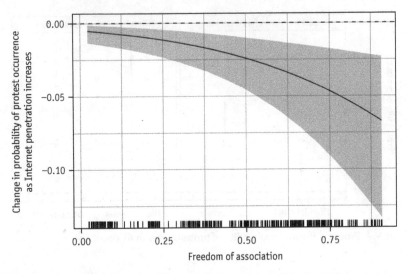

Figure 9.5 The conditional effect of Internet penetration and freedom of association on protest occurrence (city-year resolution, logistic regression, 95 percent confidence intervals). Reference: Table A.28

protest occurrence. Recall that, overall, digital technology suppresses the general incidence of protest. In Chapter 6, we argued that autocratic governments can use the technology to repress and co-opt potential dissenters by improving government responsiveness, but also to conduct surveillance and spread propaganda. However, the degree to which online repression and co-optation is effective is likely to vary depending on the threat posed by activists. In particular, in countries where activists have organizational vehicles at their disposal, the potential for protest is higher, and therefore the suppressing effect of Internet technology should be greater. In countries where freedom of association is highly restricted, on the other hand, protest mobilization is already impeded by traditional forms of control. In short, we expect that Internet technology can substitute for traditional strategies of authoritarian control and reduce protest to a larger degree where activists can organize. In the previous section, we saw some initial evidence for this argument in Figure 9.2.

Does the conditional relationship hold up in a more rigorous test? To investigate this, we plot the first differences from our multilevel model in Figure 9.5. The figure displays the change in probability when Internet penetration increases from 0 to the 50th percentile at different levels of freedom of association.

Figure 9.5 displays two interesting findings. First, we observe that the protest-suppressing effect of Internet technology is present at all levels of freedom of association. In other words, the technology can be successfully employed by governments to reduce the occurrence of anti-regime protest in countries that restrict freedom of association heavily (Saudi Arabia, China) and countries that have opened up and allowed activists to organize opposition parties (Zimbabwe, Kyrgyzstan). Second, a closer look reveals that the change in probability of protest occurrence becomes more negative in countries with a more open institutional setting. Specifically, when freedom of association is highly restricted (a value of 0), the use of Internet penetration reduces protest by 0.5 percent, whereas this probability is more than four times as high (2.2 percent) in countries with a more liberalized institutional setup (an indicator value of 0.47). A calculation of the second difference indicates that these values are significantly different. This is ample evidence that Internet technology serves as a substitute for traditional restrictions on the right to organize. While the technology is also effectively used by governments in closed autocracies to suppress unrest, the impact is smaller because traditional means of control already play a large role in reducing the threat of protest mobilization. In other words we find both a *reinforcing* and a *substituting* effect.

HOW THE INTERNET AFFECTS PROTEST PERSISTENCE IN DIFFERENT AUTOCRATIC REGIMES

In the previous section, we saw that Internet technology reduces protest occurrence by substituting traditional means of control in autocracies. How does the conditional relationship between digital technology and national-level institutions play out once protest has started? The descriptive evidence discussed above indicated that freedom of association influences the facilitating effect of Internet technology on protest persistence. Specifically, Figure 9.3 indicated that a facilitating effect exists in open autocratic regimes, but not in closed ones. In order to subject this finding to a more rigorous test, we estimated our main persistence model with an interaction term between Internet penetration and freedom of association. The first differences from the model are plotted in Figure 9.6. As for the protest occurrence analysis, the figure displays the change in probability when Internet penetration increases from 0 to the 50th percentile for different values of freedom of association. In Figure 9.6, we observe no evidence of a conditional relationship. Specifically, the slope of the interaction (indicated by the line) is almost flat. This means that Internet penetration strengthens protest persistence in both closed and open autocratic regimes. At very high levels of freedom of association, we see that the confidence intervals overlap 0. However, this is likely due to a small number of observations.

In sum, while an initial look at the data indicated a conditional relationship between national-level institutions and Internet penetration, our multilevel models do not provide compelling evidence that Internet penetration either substitutes or reinforces traditional strategies of control for protest persistence. The

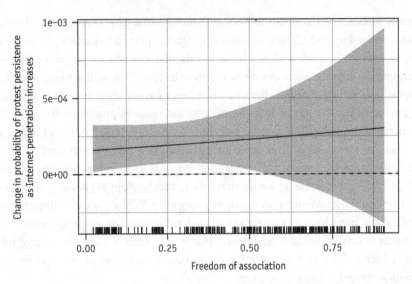

Figure 9.6 The conditional effect of Internet penetration and freedom of association on protest persistence (city-week resolution, logistic regression, 95 percent confidence intervals). Reference: Table A.29

facilitating effect of digital technology seems to be constant across national-level environments.

AUTOCRATIC INSTITUTIONS CONDITION THE INTERNET'S EFFECT ON PROTEST DIFFUSION

Do national level institutions affect the degree to which protest spreads between cities? According to our theoretical discussion above, we expect the protest-strengthening effect of Internet communication to be particularly pronounced in more liberal regimes, since governments have a harder time containing protest movements once they have started. The descriptive evidence initially indicated that there are heterogeneous effects of Internet penetration in sending cities on diffusion: In closed regimes, Internet penetration seems to reduce diffusion, while it increases it in open autocratic environments. To test this in a more rigorous way, we estimate the main diffusion model from Chapter 8 with an interaction term between Internet penetration in sending cities and freedom of association. The first differences from the model are plotted in Figure 9.7. As for the protest occurrence and persistence analyses above, the figure displays the change in probability when Internet penetration in sending cities increases from 0 to the 50th percentile for different values of freedom of association. The figures show that the interaction is positive, which is consistent with the expectation that Internet technology is more likely to lead to protest diffusion in open autocratic

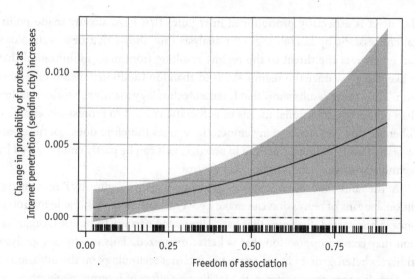

Figure 9.7 The conditional effect of Internet penetration in sending cities and freedom of association on protest diffusion (city-week resolution, logistic regression, 95 percent confidence intervals). Reference: Table A.30

regimes. In Figure 9.7, we see that an increase in Internet penetration in sending cities has a small, positive impact on protest diffusion in closed regimes, and that the effect grows substantially in open regimes. Estimation of the second difference shows that the effect is indeed significantly different in open vs. closed regimes.

To summarize the results of this section, we find evidence that the effect of Internet technology on protest diffusion varies depending on the institutional context. Our analysis shows that Internet technology and institutions reinforce each other so that as regimes liberalize, the strengthening effect of digital communication on the diffusion of political protest increases.

Conclusion

In this chapter, we have taken into account that autocratic countries differ substantially from each other. Dictatorships can be governed by kings, military juntas, warlords, or political parties, and they exhibit a great deal of variation with respect to the political rights and civil liberties they grant to their citizens. We focused on the degree to which the regime controls independent political organization, and discussed how the introduction and expansion of Internet technology interacts with this cornerstone of autocratic rule.

Our empirical analysis shows that Internet technology suppresses the occurrence of new political protest regardless of institutional context. However, the effect is especially pronounced in regimes that have already made political concessions by liberalizing. Our analysis thus shows that new technology can counteract the threat to the regime resulting from mass mobilization that is likely to grow once the regime starts to abandon traditional means of repression. Thus, these results show that Internet technology mainly substitutes, rather than reinforces, traditional means of autocratic control to repress dissent. The "liberalization" we see in many autocratic regimes therefore does not necessarily lead to more political freedom in practice, as it can be partly counteracted by technology-driven means of political control.

At the same time, our results show that opening up a regime by removing traditional means of repression can make a government more vulnerable to protest once it has started. Regimes that have eliminated barriers to political organization may face an opposition that is better organized. This is why our analysis indicates heterogeneity in the impact of Internet technology on the diffusion of protest: In more open regimes, the facilitating effect of Internet penetration on protest is stronger than in more closed ones. Essentially, the Internet's positive effect on protest diffusion becomes more pronounced in these regimes. However, we do not find a similar pattern for protest continuation—here, the strengthening effect is stable across different contexts. In sum, Internet technology is a double-edged sword for autocratic regimes. While it helps them replace traditional, and often costly, means of political control, it is difficult for regimes to contain the protest-strengthening effects once the traditional tools of repression have been abandoned.

10

Conclusion

How does Internet technology affect anti-regime protest in autocracies? In this book, we have presented a new theoretical framework to understand the complex relationship between digital communication and protest. We have also presented new fine-grained data on political protest and Internet coverage that we collected and assembled at the local level for more than 70 autocratic countries. We used the data to perform a series of empirical analyses that illuminate how autocratic governments and activists can use Internet technology to prevent or mobilize political protest. In this final chapter, we summarize the key innovations and results of our research and discuss their scientific implications. We also outline directions for future work. Finally, we discuss implications for policy derived from the research presented in this book.

Key Contributions and Findings

We began Chapter 1 by emphasizing the need to study the relationship between Internet technology and political protest—and political contention more generally—in a more nuanced fashion. In this book, we have done so through theoretical development, data collection, and rigorous statistical analyses. In the following, we discuss the key contributions in each of these three main contributions of our research.

Theoretical argument and new empirical findings. We developed a theoretical framework that explicitly incorporates the multifaceted political effects of Internet technology. Our starting point is that multiple political actors benefit from Internet technology, and they do so under different circumstances.

Sometimes, Internet technology can serve as a tool for protest mobilization for opposition activists, and at other times the technology can enhance the capacity of autocratic governments to counteract mobilization. The challenge—both theoretical and empirical—is to identify the conditions under which ICT facilitates protest mobilization by empowering opposition activists, or when it does the opposite and suppresses protest by playing into the hands of autocratic governments. We employed a distinction between motives, mobilization, and opportunities to categorize the mechanisms through which ICT can affect unrest in autocracies. The distinction highlights that digital communication can affect people's individual considerations whether to protest or not, their ability to mobilize others to join, but also the political context that permits whether protest is a feasible strategy of political opposition.

There are two main observations we make that help us identify the conditions that generate the complex relationship between Internet technology and political protest in autocracies. The first of these is that control of Internet technology is asymmetrical; since autocratic governments choose when and where to introduce and expand the technology, they enjoy a relative advantage over opposition activists when it comes to using the technology in their favor. Once established, governments also have an overwhelming resource advantage at hand for shaping the online environment. As a consequence, digital communication technology can be introduced, expanded, and used to serve the goals of autocratic governments, and should therefore benefit them in the long run.

This observation has different implications for the three phases of protest we consider in the book, namely its occurrence, persistence over time, and diffusion over space. For each of these phases, we developed theoretical arguments by linking them to asymmetric control of Internet technology and traditional forms of authoritarian control. Our first theoretical expectation is that local Internet coverage reduces the occurrence of protest. Since autocratic governments decide where to introduce the technology and enjoy a considerable resource advantage, Internet coverage should decrease individual motives for protest through regime propaganda and access to round-the-clock entertainment. Further, attempts at mobilization can be thwarted with censorship, and governments can use the digital infrastructure to improve governance and ramp up surveillance.

Following this first theoretical expectation, we examined the general relationship between Internet penetration and political protest empirically in Chapter 6. The results of the analysis showed support for our theoretical expectation: Higher levels of city-level Internet penetration are associated with significantly lower protest incidence rates. The finding remains robust across a number of different models and model specifications. Overall, this finding cautions us against viewing modern communication technology as a tool that exclusively empowers activists in autocracies. According to our results, the massive increase in coverage and use of digital communication over time is *not* accompanied by a similar increase in mobilization against autocratic rule; rather, it seems to reduce it.

But what happens once opposition activists have successfully mobilized political protests in the recent past? In this situation, local grievances are present, mobilization attempts have been successful, and political opportunities are conducive to protest. Our second theoretical expectation is therefore that Internet coverage catalyzes the persistence of protest over time and its diffusion across space, because opposition activists can use the technology to effectively spread information about ongoing unrest to receptive citizens. Both of these processes are essential for protesters to reach their goals: If activists manage to sustain protest at a particular location, or even extend it to other locations in the country, they are much more likely to be successful in achieving political concessions as a result. That our theoretical discussion revealed that Internet technology can have opposite affects on political protest depending on previous mobilization underlines the importance of appreciating the complex relationship under study.

Following up on this second theoretical expectation, we empirically analyzed how Internet technology influences the continuation of protest in a city once it has started in Chapter 7, and how it affects the spatial diffusion of protest to other cities in the same country in Chapter 8. In contrast to our first finding, our analyses of protest persistence and diffusion reveal a positive effect of Internet technology. Put simply, a higher level of Internet penetration makes it more likely that protest lasts once it has started, and that protest in a given city leads to the outbreak of more protest elsewhere. In other words, our results for protest persistence and diffusion support the notion that modern communication technology can, in the context of ongoing political protest, empower opposition activists and catalyze mobilization efforts.

Our second crucial observation is about the role of conventional tools of popular control in the digital age. Autocratic leaders have relied on a variety of means to fend off popular mobilization against the regime, and they continue to use them today. Hence, we need to keep in mind that legal restrictions of, and even violent repression against, political opposition can fundamentally affect how digital communication technology affects the dynamics of protest in autocratic political systems. The degree to which autocratic governments in different countries restrict the freedoms of their citizens and use violence against protesters varies considerably. Given the importance of such traditional forms of autocratic control, their implementation should fundamentally influence the relationship between Internet technology and political protest, and hence must be part of the puzzle we study in this book.

For that reason, we discussed how variation in traditional forms of control and repression can shape the relationship between Internet technology and protest incidence, persistence, and diffusion. Authoritarian governments use different strategies for fending off challenges to their rule. Most important, these strategies are employed to ensure a certain level of control over the population to prevent mass mobilization. Generally, this can be achieved by preventive measures such as restrictions on the freedom of the press and political associations, but also through the violent repression of emerging protest. These traditional strategies of autocratic rule do not simply disappear in the digital age. Rather, governments can and do rely on them to counter possible threats arising from the introduction and adoption of modern communication technology. Hence, an important task of this book was to theoretically and empirically investigate the impact of the Internet on protest mobilization in relation to these traditional means of autocratic control.

We examined the interrelationship between digital mobilization and conventional repression at two levels. Local-level violent responses to protest (such as beatings or killings by the police) can deter future protest by increasing the risks of participation. This effect can be amplified by online communication, since more people learn about these instances and the government's resolve. In order to investigate this theoretical expectation empirically, we amended our analyses of protest persistence and diffusion in Chapters 7 and 8. As discussed, these chapters study the continuation of protest after prior instances had occurred, either in the same location or elsewhere in the country. To test how government violence affects these dynamics, we amended our analysis to compare how Internet technology affects protest persistence and diffusion when the government used violent repression and when it did not. Evidence from these analyses provides partial evidence for a dampening effect of violent repression on the Internet's protest-catalyzing effect. In Chapter 7, where our initial results showed that Internet penetration increases the likelihood that protest will persist in a given city, we find this effect to be reduced if prior protest was violently repressed. This means that modern technology not only helps disseminate information about protest activity—which can lead to more turnout and further protest in the future—but also disseminates information about governmental actions against protesters, which can deter potential participants. However, we fail to find a similar effect in the case of protest diffusion. This suggests that the effectiveness of deterrence through prior repression is geographically limited: Protesters may assume that security forces will violently intervene again at the same place, but not in other locations.

The interplay of digital mobilization and conventional tools of repression not only applies to local cases of protest repression, but also to national-level institutions. In Chapter 9, we discussed the national level institutional context in which autocratic governments and opposition activists use Internet technology. Our discussion revolved around how the relationship between Internet technology and protest is shaped by a cornerstone of authoritarian control, namely restrictions on freedom of association and political organization. Some autocratic regimes—such as Saudi Arabia—attempt to repress almost any form of political organization to prevent collective action, while others—such as Venezuela—tolerate a fairly competitive political arena. Our theoretical expectation is that the autocratic context fundamentally shapes how digital technology affects protest in each phase. The theoretical discussion highlighted how new technology can either reinforce or substitute these traditional forms of authoritarian control. If there is reinforcement, digital repression operates alongside traditional means of control. On the other hand, if there is substitution, Internet-based repression is being used instead of conventional methods.

In the corresponding empirical analysis in Chapter 9, we examined how the effect of Internet penetration on protest explored in the first part of the book varies with the autocratic institutional context. The results of this analysis showed that the Internet reduces protest rates especially in less restrictive countries with relatively liberal citizens' rights. In other words, autocratic regimes that have relaxed their use of traditional means of political control can partly compensate for this by using Internet technology. Hence, digital repression seems to serve as a substitute for traditional forms of repression. At the same time, however, we find that these regimes are more vulnerable once protest has started, with a stronger effect of Internet penetration on protest persistence and diffusion compared to more restrictive regimes. These findings highlight that institutional liberalization in autocratic regimes can be partly counteracted by technology-driven means of political control. However, the analysis also shows that the combination of political liberalization and new technology can be an explosive mix once anti-regime mobilization has started.

New Protest Data   To enable the exploration of the theoretical framework empirically, we have collected new, disaggregated data on political protest. The result of this data collection effort is the Mass Mobilization in Autocracies Database (MMAD). The database covers protest activity in almost 70 autocratic regimes over the 2003–2012 time period (Version 1.0). The database is currently being extended; see https://mmadatabase.org for details and continuous updates and data releases. The MMAD has a number of features that make it a useful resource for researchers beyond the analyses presented in this book. First, the data collection on political protest in the MMAD is in itself an empirical contribution to the literature on autocratic regimes, and the temporally and geographically fine-grained resolution of the data opens up a number of new avenues of research for scholars of autocracy. It also includes additional information that we have not fully explored in this book, such as the scope of protest, the actors involved, and the protest issue. Second, the database contains protest event data extracted from media reports and is designed to make the coding process as transparent as possible. The coding of an individual protest event is often based on multiple reports, including from different sources. Rather than providing merely an event-level version of the data in which the reports are preaggregated, our database contains information from each individual report, which makes it possible to explore variation among multiple reports (see Cook and Weidmann, 2019, for a detailed discussion). In addition, it allows researchers to study variation in reporting *intensity*, 2018, (as for example in Hellmeier, Weidmann and Rød, 2018).

Further data used in our analyses can also be useful beyond the scope of this book. Our Internet penetration estimates were derived in collaboration with computer scientists and are based on network traffic observations. While well established in computer science, these measurements have received little attention in the social sciences, despite their considerable potential and relevance. The estimates used in this book may help other researchers study related questions concerning the impact of Internet penetration on political and social outcomes, or encourage them to tap into Internet measurement data for other purposes. Another new type of data we use is night light emissions from satellites, which helps us control for local economic performance in our analyses.

New empirical analyses on the dynamics of protest.   We presented empirical, statistical analyses that cover the relationship between Internet technology and the three protest phases at the local level. As discussed, the empirical analysis also investigated how governments' use of Internet technology relates to more traditional forms of autocratic repression and control. In order to model the relationship between ICT and political protest at the local level and explicitly embed it in various autocratic contexts, we employed Bayesian multilevel statistical models, which provided us with a flexible framework for estimation, particularly with respect to the incorporation of different levels (city, country) in the same model. All data and statistical codes are available to other researchers as part of the replication archive, which can be downloaded from https://github.com/espengroed/WR_internet_protest_book.

Our empirical, comparative approach offers rigorous evidence on the relationship between Internet penetration and political protest at the local level that extends beyond each individual location. This is a significant step forward in a literature that, to a large extent due to data restrictions, has been overwhelmingly case-based. While research on individual cases is excellent for in-depth knowledge, the methodological approach we have taken in this book has allowed us to synthesize a large body of research, develop a holistic theoretical framework to understand how Internet technology shapes protest in autocracies, and test these theoretical expectations empirically.

Our analysis that was carried out at the subnational level is a significant improvement over existing statistical work that has been largely based on national level indicators. As we discussed in detail in the Chapter 5, indicators measured at the national level may not capture the causal process of interest well. A correlation between Internet coverage and protest at the national level does not tell us whether protest actually took place in locations with Internet coverage. Such an analysis could, for example, pick up that countries with high Internet coverage experience more protest, but that these protests are located in parts of the country where Internet coverage is low. Hence, to know whether protest is affected by Internet technology, we need to study the effect of ICT on protest at the *local* level, rather than correlate national indicators.

At the same time, disaggregated data present a different set of challenges. Most problematically, disaggregated research designs fail to take into account that the local drivers of outcomes can play out differently depending on the context in which they occur. For the research conducted in this book, this is a considerable challenge, since there are strong theoretical reasons to expect that local effect of Internet coverage on protest depends on the specific authoritarian context. Therefore, we took a multilevel modeling approach that allowed us to leverage the power of local, disaggregated data, and at the same time capture variation between different countries.

Directions for Future Work

While our investigation makes a number of important contributions and pushes the debate on the political implications of new technology forward, there is ample room for future research on the topic. Partly, this is due to constraints in our empirical approach and the data and methods used, while others are the result of the scope and focus of our analysis. Below, we discuss these issues in more detail, and provide suggestions for how they can be addressed in future research.

One main result is that increasing Internet penetration reduces protest occurrence in general. Establishing this relationship is an important step forward, but the question remains which mechanisms exactly account for this. In Chapter 3, we discussed the high level of control that governments exert over the introduction of the Internet, the public's access to it, and the content that is communicated over digital channels. This gives rise to different potential mechanisms that explain the negative effect we observe in our analysis. First, higher levels of Internet access may weaken citizens' motives for protest. This could be due to real improvements in governance through digital channels, to the distraction that citizens find on the Internet, or to governments using these channels for propaganda purposes. Second, the effect may be driven by restricted opportunities for protest, where autocratic regimes strategically use digital surveillance to identify and silence potential challengers. Finally, the relationship could be driven in part by smart implementation by autocratic regimes (e.g., by expanding network services in particular in locations with populations that are likely to be co-opted).

Reduced motives, reduced opportunities for protest, and smart implementation are all explanations that are consistent with the outcomes we observe, but based on our analysis, it is difficult to determine whether one is a more powerful explanation than another. It is likely that the impact differs across the different contexts, and possibly even over time. Testing this more rigorously in future work requires better empirical measurements for each explanation, which could then be used in a comparative analysis similar to ours. This, however, is not a straightforward task, not only because concepts such as protest motivation or the extent of government propaganda are difficult to measure, but also because we would need comparable data across different countries and time periods. Similar considerations apply to our second main finding, the facilitating effect of the Internet on ongoing protest.

One way to test different mechanisms is to study particular cases, rather than employing a large-N, comparative focus as we do in our analysis. As existing work shows, it is possible to study government propaganda and censorship in great detail in selected countries (King, Pan and Roberts, 2013, 2017). We hope that our research will inspire more work along these lines, for example regarding the role of e-governance in autocracies or the effectiveness of digital propaganda for reducing citizens' dissatisfaction with the government. Similarly, when it comes to our second main finding—that the Internet can foster the persistence and diffusion of protest—case-based and more detailed analyses will be able to tell us more about the mechanisms that make protest last longer or diffuse to other places. These types of studies can serve as initial probes to confirm—or reject— candidate explanations for the general relationship we observe in our analysis. While we see ample opportunities for case-based research, we also believe that some mechanisms can be measured across countries over time, enabling a comparative large-N analysis. Data on e-governance services and functionality, for example, can be collected by country experts or in surveys. However, collecting such data requires theoretical work on the relevant facets of e-governance and consideration of the Internet users' privacy. The collection of data for comparative analysis on other mechanisms, such as online surveillance, seems more difficult.

One of the reasons why it is difficult to test particular mechanisms with our study is the relatively coarse measure of Internet penetration we use. While it has the advantage of being applicable to the different countries for a comparative analysis, measuring only Internet access ignores the content of the communications taking place via digital channels. Getting a better idea of what services Internet users access, whether these are national or international services, and what the content of those communications are is extremely difficult in both large-N comparative settings and case studies. Not only would that violate the privacy of Internet users, but it would also require collaboration with a great number of Internet service providers, especially if the aim is to cover a large sample of countries. Again, one possibility would be to implement surveys, but it is questionable whether Internet users would be willing to respond honestly to inquires about their online habits, especially those who are in a socially or politically vulnerable position.

While the limited ability of our approach to test precise mechanisms is one of the main questions we leave for future research, there are other aspects in the study of Internet and protest that can be further refined. For one, the classic literature on social movements and protest has a strong actor-centric perspective, in which the social movement organizations, their members, actions, and tactical choices constitute the main focus of the theoretical discussion and empirical analysis. While our theoretical framework incorporates opposition movements as key actors, our analysis remains at the level of outcomes (protest events). However, since our data generally enable the identification of protest actors and issues, future work can use it to pursue these questions further. This is particularly true for the tactical choices of protest actors, and how protesters can potentially benefit from modern communication technology. For example, research has shown that non-violent tactics can be highly effective for social movements (Chenoweth and Stephan, 2011). Are successful tactics adopted more often because movements learn more quickly from others through digital channels? Are tactics chosen in part based on what is likely to be considered successful and effective by an international audience following the events closely via social media? These questions regarding protest tactics should be pursued in future research.

This book also brackets out questions about the success or failure of protest. In other words, are protesters able to extract some form of concession from the government (Bratton and van de Walle, 1992)? Can protests trigger military defections or even regime change (Bellin, 2012)? There are good reasons to assume that by drawing the attention of a much larger audience to events on the ground, the Internet may be able to strengthen the effectiveness of political protest once it happens. Even though our study does not take this into account, researchers should pursue these questions further. We have made a first step in this direction by coding the scope of a protest in the MMAD, that is, whether the protest addresses issues of purely local, regional, or national importance.

A continuous challenge for scholars studying the relationship between technology and politics is that technology is constantly changing. The Internet is no exception; in fact, the Internet at the time of publication of this research is already vastly different from the Internet studied in this book. Hence, readers may wonder what our results can tell us about the Internet's political effects in the future. While we cannot be certain, we expect the patterns to be relatively consistent over time, even though the technology is changing. As our analysis has shown, the relationship between Internet technology and political protest is stable over time despite massive changes in the technology. In fact, the introduction and explosive popularity of social media after the introduction of Web 2.0 in the 2000s fundamentally changed the way the Internet was used, yet it hardly affects our results. Moreover, many of our theoretical assumptions apply regardless of the precise way that Internet technology works. Most important, autocratic governments have always been keen to control communication and take advantage of new technology—from the telegraph to the mass media revolution—and we expect similar behavior in the future. While it is certainly possible that changes in technology can change the relationship between the Internet and political protest in the short term, governments will rapidly develop responses to new threats.

Implications for Research and Policy

Looking back at the key contributions of our analysis, how does it advance scientific and political debates about the role of modern communication technology in autocratic politics? For the scholarly community, there are several key implications that readers should take away from this book.

Overall—although we are not the first to note this—our theoretical framework and empirical results show that the political and societal effects of modern communication technology are fundamentally multifaceted. Digital communication is neither inherently good, as "liberation technology" proponents in the scientific discourse tended to believe early on, nor does it exclusively serve pernicious purposes, as more recent research has argued. Rather, Internet technology affects political contention in different ways, depending on the circumstances in which it is used. The goal of our book was to identify under which conditions the Internet seems to help autocratic governments, and when it helps activists. Generally speaking, as we elaborate on below, we cannot understand the impact of new technology on politics without taking established insights from the social sciences into account, such as challenges to collective action as well as the role of political institutions and government repression. Acknowledging the multi-faceted political effects of new technology will allow social scientists to develop richer and more nuanced theoretical frameworks that can move the scholarly debate forward and be useful for policy. This will become increasingly important in the future, as digital technologies and innovations in artificial intelligence are sure to become an even more integral part of everyday life for people around the globe.

One of the main differences we found in the effect of Internet technology is related to the protest phase. Here, we showed that increased Internet penetration deters protest in general, but reinforces it once protest has started. This finding illustrates that the challenges activists face during protest mobilization are fundamentally different depending on whether or not visible turnout has already occurred, as other scholars have observed (Kuran, 1989). Perhaps not surprisingly, starting a protest is significantly more difficult than sustaining it, and according to our results, Internet communication can exacerbate this effect. Overall, our theoretical framework and empirical results emphasize the need to refine future investigations of protest and other forms of political contention in a way that explicitly takes these different phases and the different challenges to mobilization associated with them into account. At the very least, scholars should be clear on the limitations of studying specific outcomes, for example the occurrence of protest. Our analysis shows that drawing broad-stroke conclusions that are not limited to the actual protest phase in question can be misleading.

Our theoretical discussion and empirical analysis also revealed that we cannot study mobilization or repression via digital channels without taking into account the traditional, more established means autocratic governments frequently use to control the population. We showed that in some instances, gains to opposition activists arising from Internet technology are substantially smaller, or even nonexistent, when dictators counter mobilization with repressive means (violence). At the same time, digital techniques can expand a dictator's repressive toolkit, so that potentially costly and visible traditional means such as open bans on political associations can be replaced in part by digital techniques to keep dissent low. Overall, it is no surprise that dictators use Internet-based communication to their advantage. Just as businesses and democratic governments have embraced Internet technology and benefited from a centralization of services, extremely low marginal costs per user, and automatic data collection about user behavior, dictators are likely equally enthusiastic about this technology.

On the other hand, we also showed that the adaption of Internet technology by autocratic governments and a decreased reliance on traditional repressive means entails certain risk. If popular mobilization occurs, digital channels make it easier for activists to sustain protest and diffuse it to other locations. This means that dictators face a dilemma: The technology can clearly be used in their favor to prevent protest. However, if protest occurs despite these preventative measures, then the technology can play into the hands of activists. Nevertheless, domestic and international economic pressure will lead to an increased expansion of digital technology in the future. In addition, our analysis shows that this is a risk that might be worth taking, since protest is reduced overall. In sum, our results are in line with what Gunitsky (2015) has argued: Internet communication in autocracies is frequently used to co-opt people, which is why we see reduced rates of protest with increasing Internet penetration. In times of political crisis, however, modern digital communication can turn out to be dangerous to autocratic regimes and serve to strengthen ongoing mass mobilization. Future research would do well to theorize about and empirically investigate how the technology interacts with specific economic and political crises.

Overall, our discussion of the autocratic context in which Internet technology is introduced and expanded further highlights how fruitful it is to contextualize research findings. Our view is that considerations of context can and should extend far beyond the simple autocracy-democracy distinction, and there is a long tradition in comparative politics for employing finer contextual lenses for understanding political phenomena. In our analysis, we focused on traditional, institutional forms of autocratic control and repression at the national level. Future research can go even further. Contextual effects can also exist at the local level, and researchers interested in the political impacts of ICT, also in democracies, can explore how the local context shapes political outcomes. A further worthwhile consideration is to conceive of how local contexts are embedded in the national contexts.

It is difficult to derive implications for policy from our research. Policy-makers sometimes hold strong beliefs about the transformative power of the Internet, as reflected in Hillary Clinton's "Remarks on Internet Freedom" we mentioned in the introduction (Clinton, 2010). If we take such an optimistic perspective of the political and societal implications of modern communication technology, it is not difficult to conclude that policy-makers should aim to expand Internet technology wherever possible. However, as pointed out in the previous sections of this chapter, the conclusion of this book is much more cautious and highlights the pernicious effects of Internet technology in the hands of autocratic governments. What do our results mean for policy? At first glance, they appear to speak against the expansion of Internet technology, since it reduces rather than facilitates political protest against autocratic rule. There are at least two reasons why we should be careful in drawing this conclusion.

First, it is based on the premise that political protest is a welcome and necessary political action in autocracies and that it usually entails beneficial consequences for citizens. While this is certainly a possibility, it clearly does not hold in general. In some cases, most recently Tunisia in 2011, the successful overthrow of an autocratic government through popular mobilization led to (partial) democratization. However, in a number of other cases, the old autocratic government was simply replaced with a new one, for example Iran in 1976 and Kyrgyzstan in 2005 and 2010. Even Egypt, a country that held free and fair elections in the aftermath of the Arab Spring uprisings, quickly reverted to military dictatorship. In addition, as a large body of research on democratization has shown, it is a consistent historical pattern that revolt often entails an escalation of human rights abuses, protracted violence, and even international crises. Recent examples include the repressive crackdown that prompted the intervention in Libya in 2011 and the civil war that is still raging in Syria today. Hence, it is difficult to defend the notion that protest mobilization in autocracies is generally desirable and effective.

Second, the reduced occurrence of protest as a result of increased Internet penetration may not necessarily be problematic. To understand why, recall that there are different mechanisms that may account for this relationship. One of these is that improved digital communications can enable (even autocratic) governments to better perceive citizens' needs and become more accountable and to improve governance using digital channels. If this mechanism holds, expanding digital communications is clearly desirable, as it has positive implications for accountability and governance under autocratic rule. This recommendation only applies, however, if autocratic governments predominantly use digital communication technology in ways that benefit their citizens. As much anecdotal evidence suggests, this assumption may be overly optimistic. In this book, we have discussed numerous examples of how dictators rely on Internet technology to identify political rivals, eliminate dissenting opinions, and spread pro-regime propaganda. If this is what accounts for the negative relationship between Internet penetration and political protest in our analysis, better Internet coverage implies a decisively worse situation for citizens and activists living under dictatorships, and expansion is not something that policy should prioritize.

Nevertheless, our analysis can help policy-makers better understand autocratic politics in the digital age. One important insight of this book is that dictators' use of modern information technology and more traditional, often violent means of repression operate hand in hand. In particular, we showed that the suppression of protest through digital means occurs mainly in those regimes that have loosened control of the population through traditional means, for example by lifting restrictions on civil liberties. The protest-reducing effect of Internet technology is not, we assume, due exclusively to improvements in the regimes' responsiveness and digital governance. It is much more likely that Internet technology helps these regimes make up for the loss of control they conceded when they moved away from strict autocratic rule. Thus, observed shifts away from autocracy that are solely tied to changes in institutional characteristics should be treated with caution. Indeed, our results suggest that autocracies are relying less on institutional arrangements and traditional repression than they have in the past. This, however, does not necessarily mean that these systems are liberalizing; rather, power may be increasingly shifting to digital channels where governments use modern information technology for surveillance and propaganda. To paraphrase Mussolini, the Internet may be the modern version of the capillary through which the blood of dictatorship diffuses through society (see Gandhi and Przeworski, 2007, p. 1283). Hence, its importance in autocratic politics, and therefore its relevance for researchers and policy-makers, is likely to grow in the years to come.

Appendix

In the four empirical chapters, we discussed a large number of statistical models that provide empirical evidence on how Internet penetration affects political protest in autocracies. This appendix mainly displays the regression tables from the statistical models discussed in each chapter. To give readers a better overview of the choices we made for the statistical analysis in this book, we first briefly review the research design discussed in detail in Chapter 5, including the Mass Mobilization in Autocracies Database (MMAD) that we have created and that the empirical part of this book is based on.

In this book, our central research question is how Internet use by activists and autocratic governments affects patterns of protest in autocracies. We study how Internet technology influences different phases of protest, including occurrence, persistence over time, and diffusion across space. Moreover, we are interested in how the impact of Internet penetration is affected by regime institutions and violent repression of protests by autocratic governments. Our approach is comparative and draws on a large sample of observations, examining how variation in our main independent (Internet penetration) variable is related to variation in an outcome (political protest) by using data from more than 60 countries. The full list of countries and the time periods covered in the MMAD is shown in Table A.1. Due to limitations in data availability for other variables in the analysis, the time periods covered in the analysis in this book are slightly shorter.

To investigate our research question empirically, we take a disaggregated approach in which our main variables are measured at the city level. The fine-grained data on political protest from the MMAD, combined with novel geo-located data on Internet availability, enable us to study the effect of Internet penetration on protest within countries, but also between different countries. This disaggregation is one of the key innovations of our analysis. While there are studies of the effect of Internet penetration on protest measured at the country level, indicators of Internet penetration and protest at the country level carry the risk of not being able to capture the causal process well. If we find a relationship between Internet coverage and protest using indicators measured at the country level, we cannot know whether protest actually takes place in locations with Internet coverage. In fact, it could simply be that countries with high Internet coverage experience more protest, but that these protests mainly take place in those parts of the country where Internet coverage is low. This means that we need to study the effect of *local* coverage on the *local* occurrence of protest, rather than correlate variables at the country level.

Yet, disaggregated analyses introduce different issues. Commonly, they focus exclusively on local conditions and fail to take into account that the local drivers of outcomes such as violence or protest can play out differently depending on the context in which they occur. This is too restrictive for our research, since the (local) effect of Internet coverage on protest is likely to depend on how the Internet is used by certain governments for indoctrination, surveillance, or co-optation. Therefore, we opt for a comparative research design in which we leverage the power of local, disaggregated data, but at the same time captures variation between different countries. We take a multilevel approach to estimate our statistical models, in which cities are nested countries (Gelman and Hill, 2006). All statistical models are estimated using the *brms* package in R (Bürkner, 2017), a front end that facilitates the estimation of Bayesian multilevel models using the STAN language (Carpenter et al., 2017).

Our research design uses city-years and city-weeks from 1,564 cities in 61 countries over eight years (2005–2012) as units of analysis. Our dichotomous outcome variables, protest incidence, protest persistence, and protest diffusion, are created using the MMAD. Our *city-year analysis* of protest incidence consists of 12,244 observations. In the analyses using *city-weeks*—which we need to examine the more dynamic outcomes persistence of protest over time and its spatial diffusion over time—we have 128,979 (persistence) and 620,611 (diffusion) observations.

To measure Internet penetration subnationally, we rely on earlier work and use network traffic observations to estimate Internet coverage. The key idea behind this approach is that Internet traffic data can be used to identify how well connected a certain location is. More details on this procedure are given in Chapter 5 of this book as well as in Weidmann et al. (2016) and Benitez-Baleato et al. (2015). As in Weidmann et al. (2016), we use a per capita measure of subnetworks as our indicator for Internet penetration in order to avoid simply picking up differences between small and large urban areas. Finally, for many of the control variables in our analysis, such as population and economic development, we use spatial approximations computed using Geographic Information Systems (GIS) software.

In the next section, we show the list of countries and variables in the MMAD. Next, we elaborate on how to read the regression tables that are presented in this appendix. In the four following sections, we present regression tables for each of the empirical chapters in the book.

List of Countries and Variables in the MMAD (Version 1.0)

Table A.1   Countries and time periods covered in the MMAD.

Country	Start	End
Afghanistan	2009-08-20	2012-12-31
Algeria	2003-01-01	2012-12-31
Angola	2003-01-01	2012-12-31
Armenia	2003-01-01	2012-12-31
Azerbaijan	2003-01-01	2012-12-31
Bangladesh	2007-01-11	2008-12-29
Belarus	2003-01-01	2012-12-31
Botswana	2003-01-01	2012-12-31
Burkina Faso	2003-01-01	2012-12-31
Burundi	2003-01-01	2003-04-30
Cambodia	2003-01-01	2012-12-31
Cameroon	2003-01-01	2012-12-31
Central African Republic	2003-03-15	2012-12-31
Chad	2003-01-01	2012-12-31
China	2003-01-01	2012-12-31
Congo	2003-01-01	2012-12-31
Cuba	2003-01-01	2012-12-31
Democratic Republic of the Congo	2003-01-01	2012-12-31
Egypt	2003-01-01	2012-06-30
Eritrea	2003-01-01	2012-12-31
Ethiopia	2003-01-01	2012-12-31
Gabon	2003-01-01	2012-12-31
Gambia	2003-01-01	2012-12-31
Georgia	2003-01-01	2003-11-23
Guinea	2003-01-01	2010-01-16
Guinea-Bissau	2003-01-01	2003-09-14
Haiti	2003-01-01	2004-02-29
Iran	2003-01-01	2012-12-31
Ivory Coast	2003-01-01	2012-12-31

(Continued)

Table A.1 **Continued**

Country	Start	End
Jordan	2003-01-01	2012-12-31
Kazakhstan	2003-01-01	2012-12-31
Kuwait	2003-01-01	2012-12-31
Kyrgyzstan	2003-01-01	2012-12-31
Laos	2003-01-01	2012-12-31
Liberia	2003-01-01	2003-08-11
Libya	2003-01-01	2012-12-31
Madagascar	2009-03-17	2012-12-31
Malaysia	2003-01-01	2012-12-31
Mauritania	2003-01-01	2012-12-31
Morocco	2003-01-01	2012-12-31
Mozambique	2003-01-01	2012-12-31
Myanmar	2003-01-01	2012-12-31
Namibia	2003-01-01	2012-12-31
Nepal	2003-01-01	2006-04-24
North Korea	2003-01-01	2012-12-31
Oman	2003-01-01	2012-12-31
Pakistan	2003-01-01	2008-08-18
Russia	2003-01-01	2012-12-31
Rwanda	2003-01-01	2012-12-31
Saudi Arabia	2003-01-01	2012-12-31
Singapore	2003-01-01	2012-12-31
South Sudan	2011-07-09	2012-12-31
Sudan	2003-01-01	2012-12-31
Swaziland	2003-01-01	2012-12-31
Syria	2003-01-01	2012-12-31
Tajikistan	2003-01-01	2012-12-31
Tanzania	2003-01-01	2012-12-31
Thailand	2006-09-19	2007-12-23
Togo	2003-01-01	2012-12-31
Tunisia	2003-01-01	2012-12-31
Turkmenistan	2003-01-01	2012-12-31
Uganda	2003-01-01	2012-12-31
United Arab Emirates	2003-01-01	2012-12-31
Uzbekistan	2003-01-01	2012-12-31
Venezuela	2005-12-04	2012-12-31
Vietnam	2003-01-01	2012-12-31
Yemen	2003-01-01	2012-12-31
Zambia	2003-01-01	2012-12-31
Zimbabwe	2003-01-01	2012-12-31

Our MMAD coding project allows for the disaggregated analysis of political protest in autocracies. It provides disaggregated information about protest incidents, and contains a number of different variables for each incident (not all of which are used in this book). For more details about the coding of these variables please refer to the MMAD codebook (see https://mmadatabase.org/).

- Event date (type: date): Date of incident.
- Location (type: string): City of incident, according to the GeoNames database of place names (http://www.geonames.org).
- Actors (type: string): Actors involved in the protest incident. In a general sense, this string variable captures the label given by the article to the actors involved. If more than one actor is given in the article, we separate them with a semicolon.
- Number of participants (type: string): Estimate of the number of participants. Can be either an *integer number* or a *phrase*.
- Issue (type: string): Reported issue / motivation for incident. Described by one or two terms using the original wording in the event report. More than one issue can be reported for each incident, separated with a semicolon.
- Side (type: dichotomous): Takes the value 1 if incident was anti-government. Anti-government is understood in a broad sense. It is not necessary that protesters demand the resignation of the central government, but that they are protesting actions made or sanctioned by it. This includes national, regional, and local authorities' actions, since the hiring and firing of state employees at all levels of government rests on the people in charge. If 0, the protest is explicitly pro-government, staged to show support for the government or the government's actions. If NA, protest was directed at a domestic public or private non-governmental institution.
- Scope (type: categorical): Indicates which level the protest is directed at. 0 = national, 1 = regional / state, 2 = local. If NA, protest was directed at a *domestic* public or private institution. The assumption here is that local and regional protest is also anti- or pro-government.
- Level of violence by protest participants (type: ordinal): Ordinal level of violence from protest participants. NA = no report on the level of violence from protest participants, 0 = explicit report of no violence, 1 = reports of property damage or clashes with civilians or security forces, 2 = reports of people injured, 3 = reports of people killed. Protesters blocking roads or railroads do not qualify as exerting violence, unless there are explicit reports that participants were damaging cars, equipment, or exerting physical violence against bystanders. We do not consider self-immolation as violence here, because the action is not directed at other people.

- Level of official security force involvement (type: ordinal): Ordinal level of official security force involvement. NA = no report on the level of official security force involvement, 0 = explicit report of no presence, 1 = reports of presence, 2 = reports of physical intervention. Includes crowd dispersal, arrests, and beatings but excludes lethal intervention, 3 = reports of lethal intervention.

How to Read the Regression Tables

The captions of all tables below indicate the relationship that the statistical model estimates, the resolution of the data in the model, and the estimator. In Table A.2, for example, the caption indicates that the statistical model aims to estimate the effect of local Internet penetration on protest occurrence. The resolution of the data is the city-year and logistic regression was the estimator. For the relevant tables, there is also an indication of whether the slope of Internet penetration varies by year in a multilevel model (see e.g., Table A.3).

Since we estimate Bayesian multilevel models, all tables in the appendix show the values of the coefficients ("Mean Beta"), as well as the low (2.5 percent) and high (97.5 percent) values of the credible interval, also referred to as the highest posterior density interval (HPD). These numbers indicate the estimated effect of the respective variable on the outcome studied in the model. These values are computed across the posterior draws for each coefficient, with the low and high credible intervals indicating the 95 percent probability interval of the posterior distribution. For example, in Table A.2, the estimated effect of the national capital indicator on protest occurrence is 6.06. Moreover, the 2.5 percent and 97.5 percent bounds indicate that the effect of national capital is between 5.2 and 6.96 with a 95 percent probability. The only exception to this interpretation is Table A.7, which shows regression output from (frequentist) linear probability models with point estimates and standard errors in parentheses.

Finally, lagged variables are marked with $(t-1)$ and variables that we log-transformed with (ln). Interactions between variables are indicated with an * between two variables. The final rows in each table indicate the estimated standard deviation (SD) as a measure of the heterogeneity of the outcome between countries, cities, and years. For example, in Table A.2, the standard deviation of political protest SD country $(cowcode)$ is 1.64. By dividing this number by 4, we can approximate the difference between the groups (Gelman and Hill, 2006, 304). Doing so reveals a mean estimated $+/-41$ percent variation in protest between countries. These numbers emphasize the importance of accounting for the considerable heterogeneity across the units of observation in our multilevel modeling framework.

Chapter 6

REGRESSION TABLES

The following tables show the estimated coefficients for all indicators in the models discussed in Chapter 6, which estimate how Internet penetration affects the occurrence of protest in autocracies. Each table below is referenced in the caption of corresponding figure(s) in Chapter 6. For example, Table A.2 is referenced in Figure 6.3. Since we discuss the results from each individual table in the relevant chapter, we do not these results in more detail here.

Table A.2 **The effect of local Internet penetration on anti-regime protest occurrence (city-year resolution, logistic regression).**

	Mean Beta	**2.5%**	**97.5%**
Intercept	−5.1948	−6.2824	−4.2475
Internet penetration	−0.7933	−1.0012	−0.5899
Protest in same city (t−1)	0.5211	0.2781	0.7693
Protest in different city (t−1)	0.3083	−0.1213	0.7268
Night lights pc (ln)	0.4527	0.0097	0.9050
Population (ln)	1.1106	0.7722	1.4645
Regional capital	2.4244	1.9682	2.8975
National capital	6.0593	5.2039	6.9613
Civil war	1.3882	1.0389	1.7689
SD country (cowcode)	1.6401	1.2250	2.1138
SD city (geonameid)	1.5514	1.3468	1.7634
SD year	0.7422	0.3877	1.5246

Table A.3 The effect of local Internet penetration on number of anti-regime protests (city-year resolution, logistic regression, local Internet penetration slope varies by year).

	Mean Beta	2.5%	97.5%
Intercept	−5.1956	−6.1532	−4.1879
Internet penetration	−0.7836	−1.0491	−0.5270
Protest in same city (t−1)	0.5378	0.2750	0.8119
Protest in different city (t−1)	0.2985	−0.1204	0.7528
Night lights pc (ln)	0.4380	−0.0106	0.8732
Population (ln)	1.1107	0.7469	1.4546
Regional capital	2.4146	1.9874	2.8848
National capital	6.0682	5.2040	6.8786
Civil war	1.3768	1.0124	1.7540
SD country (cowcode)	1.6555	1.1972	2.2292
SD city (geonameid)	1.5458	1.3515	1.7500
SD year	0.8089	0.4057	1.5484
SD Internet penetration: year	0.1860	0.0145	0.4500

Table A.4 The effect of local Internet penetration on number of anti-regime protests (city-year resolution, OLS).

	Mean Beta	2.5%	97.5%
Intercept	0.0070	−0.0737	0.0866
Internet penetration	−0.0253	−0.0342	−0.0167
Number of protests t−1	0.3565	0.3301	0.3841
Protest in different city (t−1)	−0.0353	−0.0667	−0.0042
Night lights pc (ln)	−0.0190	−0.0501	0.0090
Population (ln)	0.0334	0.0087	0.0583
Regional capital	0.1480	0.1224	0.1741
National capital	0.8719	0.7988	0.9478
Civil war	0.1627	0.1390	0.1879
SD country (cowcode)	0.2135	0.1706	0.2651
SD city (geonameid)	0.1593	0.1466	0.1714
SD year	0.0769	0.0430	0.1398

Table A.5 **The effect of local Internet penetration on number of anti-regime protests (city-year resolution, negative binomial regression).**

	Mean Beta	2.5%	97.5%
Intercept	−5.0015	−5.7746	−4.1478
Internet penetration	−0.6261	−0.7881	−0.4556
Protest in same city (t−1)	0.3921	0.2088	0.5568
Protest in different city (t−1)	0.2749	0.0040	0.5647
Night lights pc (ln)	0.2536	−0.1247	0.6444
Population (ln)	0.9291	0.6084	1.1976
Regional capital	2.3644	1.9452	2.7821
National capital	5.3184	4.6410	6.0839
Civil war	1.3777	1.1119	1.6251
SD country (cowcode)	1.4685	1.1317	1.9016
SD city (geonameid)	1.5727	1.4121	1.7460
SD year	0.6722	0.3697	1.3255

Table A.6 **The effect of local Internet penetration on number of anti-regime protests (city-year resolution, logistic regression, Internet penetration dummy).**

	Mean Beta	2.5%	97.5%
Intercept	−5.7258	−6.7577	−4.8438
Internet dummy	−0.2523	−0.6911	0.1462
Protest in same city (t-1)	0.5071	0.2380	0.7813
Protest in different city (t−1)	0.2568	−0.1846	0.6494
Night lights pc (ln)	0.4399	0.0138	0.8879
Population (ln)	1.0088	0.6477	1.3755
Regional capital	3.0108	2.5476	3.4989
National capital	6.5839	5.7306	7.5831
Civil war	1.3830	0.9794	1.7298
SD country (cowcode)	1.7184	1.2670	2.2746
SD city (geonameid)	1.6430	1.4051	1.8913
SD year	0.6180	0.3372	1.2050

Table A.7 **The effect of local Internet penetration on anti-regime protest (city-year resolution, linear probability models with fixed effects by city and year).**

	Dependent variable:	
	Protest occurrence	Number of protests
	(1)	(2)
Internet penetration	−0.015**	−0.282***
	(0.006)	(0.084)
Protest in same city (t−1)	−0.069***	0.282**
	(0.010)	(0.128)
Protest in different city (t−1)	0.013	0.108
	(0.011)	(0.151)
Night lights pc (ln)	0.014	−1.220***
	(0.021)	(0.280)
Population (ln)	−5.164**	−14.813
	(2.621)	(34.789)
Regional capital	4.244*	11.209
	(2.178)	(28.908)
National capital	8.276**	35.186
	(3.661)	(48.590)
Civil war	0.093***	1.406***
	(0.009)	(0.121)
Constant	−3.022*	−8.597
	(1.543)	(20.474)
Observations	12,211	12,211
Note:	$^{*}p<0.1$; $^{**}p<0.05$; $^{***}p<0.01$	

Table A.8 **The effect of local Internet penetration on local and national anti-regime protests (city-year resolution, multinomial logistic regression).**

	Mean Beta	2.5%	97.5%
	Local protest		
Intercept	−6.5136	−7.7948	−5.3204
Internet penetration	−0.7555	−1.0691	−0.4609
Local protest in same city (t−1)	0.4744	−0.2417	1.1776
National protest in same city (t−1)	0.9965	0.4119	1.5824
Protest in different city (t−1)	0.3190	−0.6147	1.2982
Night lights pc (ln)	0.1661	−0.4222	0.8029
Population (ln)	0.6923	0.2069	1.1764
Regional capital	0.5928	−0.0155	1.2755
National capital	2.1046	0.7928	3.4505
Civil war	0.6339	0.0776	1.2097
SD country (cowcode)	0.8393	0.1441	1.6942
SD city (geonameid)	1.8033	1.4230	2.2200
SD year	0.2149	0.0127	0.6318
	National protest		
Intercept	−6.0015	−7.1560	−5.0092
Internet penetration	−0.6725	−0.9297	−0.4383
Local protest in same city (t−1)	1.2327	0.6751	1.8030
National protest in same city (t−1)	0.5914	0.2832	0.8814
Protest in different city (t−1)	0.3096	−0.1731	0.8157
Night lights pc (ln)	0.4746	−0.0109	0.9907
Population (ln)	1.2288	0.8664	1.6391
Regional capital	3.0893	2.5773	3.6508
National capital	6.6400	5.7637	7.6128
Civil war	1.6037	1.2119	2.0318
SD country (cowcode)	1.8906	1.4875	2.4082
SD city (geonameid)	1.3738	1.1372	1.6173
SD year	0.8630	0.4631	1.6268

Table A.9 **The effect of local Internet penetration on anti-regime protest onset (city-year resolution, logistic regression).**

	Mean Beta	2.5%	97.5%
Intercept	−4.6834	−5.6198	−3.7326
Internet penetration	−1.0291	−1.2643	−0.8046
Protest in different city (t−1)	0.4511	−0.0577	0.9974
Night lights pc (ln)	0.6386	0.1875	1.0632
Population (ln)	1.0022	0.6553	1.3364
Regional capital	1.9006	1.4793	2.3140
National capital	4.8764	4.0311	5.7495
Civil war	1.2499	0.8124	1.6966
SD country (cowcode)	1.4101	1.0498	1.8714
SD city (geonameid)	1.2232	0.9882	1.4612
SD year	0.6963	0.3812	1.3348

Table A.10 **The effect of local Internet penetration on anti-regime protest onset (city-year resolution, logistic regression).**

	Mean Beta	2.5%	97.5%
Intercept	−4.3068	−5.4670	−3.3599
Internet penetration	−1.2329	−1.5995	−0.9477
Protest in different city (t−1)	0.0224	−0.6167	0.6492
Night lights pc (ln)	0.6295	0.2050	1.0749
Population (ln)	1.0610	0.7072	1.4921
Regional capital	1.9629	1.4363	2.5614
National capital	5.6689	4.3789	7.4062
Civil war	1.4388	0.9664	1.9225
SD country (cowcode)	1.7196	1.2420	2.3386
SD city (geonameid)	0.9029	0.2668	1.7083
SD year	0.7086	0.3780	1.3303

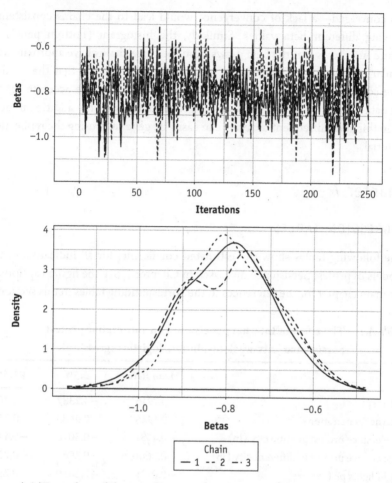

Figure A.1 Trace plot and density of Internet penetration betas from the main model.

MODEL CONVERGENCE

In this section, we inspect the convergence of one of our models. We do so by discussing the convergence of our main independent variable (Internet penetration) from the analysis in Table A.2. First, the Gelman-Rubin convergence diagnostic that takes into account between- and within-chain differences is 1, indicating that the model has converged (Gelman and Rubin, 1992). Second, Figure A.1 plots the beta draws for Internet penetration from the estimated model. The top panel shows a trace plot; the bottom panel displays a density plot of the betas for the three chains. The trace plot (top panel) in Figure A.1 shows that the beta draws have stabilized in the region between −1 and −0.6. Moreover, the trace plot indicates that the beta draws for the three chains mix well. Both the stabilization and the mixing of the chains indicate that the model has converged—a lack of convergence would lead to the chains consistently drawing different beta values. Similarly, the histogram (bottom panel) in Figure A.1 shows that the beta draws from the three chains have approximately similar means and uncertainty. In sum, these plots indicate that the models have converged and that the coefficients discussed above are accurate (given the data). For interested readers, convergence statistics for the additional models in this and subsequent chapters can easily be generated using the replication material.

Chapter 7

REGRESSION TABLES

The following tables show the estimated coefficients for all indicators in the models of protest persistence discussed in Chapter 7. See the figure captions in the main chapter for the references to the corresponding tables in this section.

Table A.11 **The effect of Internet penetration on anti-regime protest persistence (city-week resolution, logistic regression).**

	Mean Beta	2.5%	97.5%
Intercept	−3.7216	−4.2387	−3.2072
Internet penetration	0.1935	0.0683	0.3204
Weeks since protest in same city (ln)	−0.4781	−0.5076	−0.4481
Weeks since protest in different city (ln)	−0.2606	−0.2964	−0.2243
Night lights pc (ln)	−0.0174	−0.2850	0.2563
Population (ln)	0.6753	0.4571	0.8942
Regional capital	0.9495	0.5556	1.3381
National capital	2.4100	1.9512	2.8656
Civil war	0.5393	0.3894	0.6884
SD country (cowcode)	0.6634	0.4890	0.8717
SD city (geonameid)	0.6735	0.5861	0.7652
SD year	0.3442	0.1806	0.7616

Table A.12 The effect of Internet penetration on anti-regime protest persistence, varying slopes by year (city-week resolution, logistic regression).

	Mean Beta	2.5%	97.5%
Intercept	−3.7261	−4.2869	−3.1809
Internet penetration	0.2366	0.0806	0.3967
Weeks since protest in same city (ln)	−0.4786	−0.5069	−0.4471
Weeks since protest in different city (ln)	−0.2577	−0.2921	−0.2236
Night lights pc (ln)	−0.0508	−0.3124	0.2038
Population (ln)	0.6619	0.4370	0.8789
Regional capital	0.9367	0.5618	1.3071
National capital	2.3848	1.9338	2.8550
Civil war	0.5280	0.3634	0.6890
SD country (cowcode)	0.6712	0.4833	0.8990
SD city (geonameid)	0.6666	0.5781	0.7570
SD year	0.3517	0.1953	0.6463
SD Internet penetration (ln):year	0.1012	0.0269	0.2289

Table A.13 The effect of Internet penetration on anti-regime protest persistence, interaction with logged weeks since protest (city-week resolution, logistic regression).

	Mean Beta	2.5%	97.5%
Intercept	−3.6838	−4.2114	−3.2076
Internet penetration	0.1235	−0.0219	0.2760
Weeks since protest in same city (ln)	−0.4955	−0.5272	−0.4666
Weeks since protest in different city (ln)	−0.2580	−0.2899	−0.2218
Night lights pc (ln)	−0.0405	−0.3043	0.2370
Population (ln)	0.6698	0.4469	0.9115
Regional capital	0.9228	0.5320	1.3202
National capital	2.3888	1.9538	2.8591
Civil war	0.5397	0.3801	0.6861
Internet * W. s. protest same city (ln)	0.0358	−0.0035	0.0710
SD country (cowcode)	0.6670	0.4779	0.9111
SD city (geonameid)	0.6726	0.5928	0.7623
SD year	0.3250	0.1842	0.6572

Table A.14 **The effect of Internet penetration on anti-regime protest persistence, interaction with logged weeks since protest and repression (city-week resolution, logistic regression).**

	Mean Beta	2.5%	97.5%
Intercept	−3.7463	−4.2499	−3.2781
Internet penetration	0.1514	−0.0159	0.3170
Weeks since protest in same city (ln)	−0.4877	−0.5275	−0.4477
Last protest repressed	0.1243	−0.0341	0.2687
Weeks since protest in different city (ln)	−0.2560	−0.2926	−0.2233
Night lights pc (ln)	−0.0341	−0.3017	0.2149
Population (ln)	0.6585	0.4417	0.8740
Regional capital	0.9482	0.5672	1.3248
National capital	2.3993	1.9591	2.8522
Civil war	0.5347	0.3837	0.6984
Internet * W. s. protest same city	0.0618	0.0145	0.1096
Internet * Repressed	−0.0343	−0.1684	0.1060
W. s. protest same city * Repressed	−0.0273	−0.0861	0.0363
Internet * W. s. protest same city * Repressed	−0.0612	−0.1303	0.0031
SD country (cowcode)	0.6561	0.4801	0.8604
SD city (geonameid)	0.6754	0.5867	0.7723
SD year	0.3278	0.1717	0.6947

Table A.15 **The effect of Internet penetration on anti-regime protest persistence, controlling for reporting (city-week resolution, logistic regression).**

	Mean Beta	2.5%	97.5%
Intercept	−3.7374	−4.2800	−3.2296
Internet penetration	0.1742	0.0499	0.2938
Weeks since protest in same city (ln)	−0.4720	−0.5008	−0.4451
Report ratio (ln)	0.5319	0.4364	0.6296
Weeks since protest in different city (ln)	−0.2421	−0.2767	−0.2059
Night lights pc (ln)	−0.0127	−0.2954	0.2514
Population (ln)	0.6757	0.4580	0.8949
Regional capital	0.9306	0.5366	1.3523
National capital	2.3390	1.8617	2.8361
Civil war	0.5126	0.3635	0.6581
SD country (cowcode)	0.6707	0.4942	0.8813
SD city (geonameid)	0.6596	0.5791	0.7579
SD year	0.3177	0.1750	0.6170

Table A.16 **The effect of Internet penetration on anti-regime protest persistence, interaction with logged weeks since protest and controlling for reporting (city-week resolution, logistic regression).**

	Mean Beta	2.5%	97.5%
Intercept	−3.7090	−4.2586	−3.2030
Internet penetration	0.0967	−0.0564	0.2587
Weeks since protest in same city (ln)	−0.4866	−0.5188	−0.4506
Report ratio (ln)	0.5315	0.4307	0.6262
Weeks since protest in different city (ln)	−0.2411	−0.2742	−0.2046
Night lights pc (ln)	−0.0224	−0.3219	0.2480
Population (ln)	0.6718	0.4492	0.8826
Regional capital	0.9417	0.5820	1.3460
National capital	2.3506	1.9059	2.7728
Civil war	0.5027	0.3528	0.6490
Internet * W. s. protest same city	0.0364	0.0008	0.0754
SD country (cowcode)	0.6715	0.4938	0.9020
SD city (geonameid)	0.6649	0.5817	0.7573
SD year	0.3346	0.1794	0.6673

Table A.17 **The effect of Internet penetration on anti-regime protest persistence, interaction with logged weeks since protest and repression, controlling for reporting (city-week resolution, logistic regression).**

	Mean Beta	2.5%	97.5%
Intercept	−3.7486	−4.2433	−3.2608
Internet penetration	0.1263	−0.0358	0.2963
Weeks since protest in same city (ln)	−0.4828	−0.5234	−0.4425
Last protest repressed	−0.0016	−0.1498	0.1327
Report ratio (ln)	0.5587	0.4547	0.6631
Weeks since protest in different city (ln)	−0.2408	−0.2751	−0.2080
Night lights pc (ln)	−0.0130	−0.2668	0.2546
Population (ln)	0.6644	0.4392	0.8838
Regional capital	0.9566	0.6102	1.3574
National capital	2.3703	1.9497	2.8404
Civil war	0.5024	0.3502	0.6605
Internet * W. s. protest same city	0.0608	0.0186	0.1080
Internet * Repressed	−0.0368	−0.1787	0.1025
W. s. protest same city * Repressed	−0.0147	−0.0704	0.0394
Internet * W. s. protest same city * Repressed	−0.0600	−0.1284	0.0072
SD country (cowcode)	0.6555	0.4851	0.8677
SD city (geonameid)	0.6667	0.5806	0.7557
SD year	0.3147	0.1781	0.5921

Chapter 8

REGRESSION TABLES

The following tables show the estimated coefficients for all indicators in the models of protest diffusion presented in Chapter 8. See the figure captions in the main chapter for the references to the corresponding tables in this section.

Table A.18 **The effect of sending Internet penetration on anti-regime protest diffusion (city-week resolution, logistic regression).**

	Mean Beta	2.5%	97.5%
Intercept	−4.9391	−5.4726	−4.4408
Internet penetration, receiving	−0.2852	−0.4065	−0.1812
Internet penetration, sending	0.1196	0.0718	0.1652
Weeks since protest, sending (ln)	−0.3070	−0.3447	−0.2708
Weeks since protest, receiving (ln)	−0.4578	−0.4873	−0.4289
Night lights pc, receiving (ln)	−0.0227	−0.3002	0.2248
Population, receiving (ln)	0.5536	0.3344	0.7618
Regional capital, receiving	1.7012	1.3688	2.0291
National capital, receiving	3.7274	3.3026	4.2211
Civil war, receiving	0.6418	0.5102	0.7778
SD country (cowcode)	0.8570	0.6567	1.1154
SD city (geonameid)	0.9096	0.8007	1.0267
SD year	0.3722	0.2124	0.6700

Table A.19 **The effect of sending Internet penetration on anti-regime protest diffusion, varying slope by year (city-week resolution, logistic regression).**

	Mean Beta	2.5%	97.5%
Intercept	−4.9201	−5.4390	−4.4056
Internet penetration, receiving	−0.3100	−0.4381	−0.1922
Internet penetration, sending	0.1025	0.0112	0.1866
Weeks since protest, sending (ln)	−0.3125	−0.3495	−0.2754
Weeks since protest, receiving (ln)	−0.4538	−0.4810	−0.4275
Night lights pc, receiving (ln)	−0.0158	−0.2938	0.2527
Population, receiving (ln)	0.5538	0.3376	0.7774
Regional capital, receiving	1.6775	1.3573	1.9696
National capital, receiving	3.7268	3.2758	4.2146
Civil war, receiving	0.6617	0.5220	0.8212
SD country (cowcode)	0.8520	0.6477	1.1286
SD city (geonameid)	0.9190	0.8101	1.0286
SD year	0.3477	0.1814	0.6815
SD Internet penetration, sending	0.0840	0.0214	0.2073

Table A.20 **The effect of sending Internet penetration on anti-regime protest diffusion, interaction with logged weeks since protest in sending city (city-week resolution, logistic regression).**

	Mean Beta	2.5%	97.5%
Intercept	−4.9807	−5.5390	−4.4611
Internet penetration, receiving	−0.2779	−0.3981	−0.1572
Internet penetration, sending	0.1587	0.1050	0.2104
Weeks since protest, sending (ln)	−0.2833	−0.3211	−0.2450
Weeks since protest, receiving (ln)	−0.4550	−0.4829	−0.4271
Night lights pc, receiving (ln)	−0.0277	−0.2845	0.2069
Population, receiving (ln)	0.5446	0.3300	0.7696
Regional capital, receiving	1.7000	1.4184	2.0036
National capital, receiving	3.7371	3.2851	4.2103
Civil war, receiving	0.6515	0.5055	0.7815
Internet, send. * W. s. protest, send.	−0.0697	−0.1094	−0.0335
SD country (cowcode)	0.8575	0.6427	1.1150
SD city (geonameid)	0.9175	0.8103	1.0264
SD year	0.3843	0.2017	0.7606

Table A.21 **The effect of sending Internet penetration on anti-regime protest diffusion, interaction with logged weeks since protest and repression in sending city (city-week resolution, logistic regression).**

	Mean Beta	2.5%	97.5%
Intercept	−5.0238	−5.5553	−4.4785
Internet penetration, receiving	−0.2875	−0.4164	−0.1787
Internet penetration, sending	0.1641	0.0978	0.2263
Weeks since protest, sending (ln)	−0.2496	−0.2976	−0.1983
Last protest repressed, sending	0.1009	−0.0157	0.2223
Weeks since protest, receiving (ln)	−0.4536	−0.4833	−0.4257
Night lights pc, receiving (ln)	−0.0282	−0.2752	0.2149
Population, receiving (ln)	0.5428	0.3265	0.7771
Regional capital, receiving	1.6986	1.4126	2.0388
National capital, receiving	3.7468	3.2886	4.2077
Civil war, receiving	0.6467	0.4804	0.7818
Internet, send. * W. s. protest, send.	−0.0887	−0.1390	−0.0420
Internet, send. * Repr., send.	−0.0116	−0.0783	0.0533
W. s. protest, send. * Repr., send.	−0.0684	−0.1364	−0.0087
Internet, send. * W. s. protest, send. * Repr., send.	0.0443	−0.0161	0.1103
SD country (cowcode)	0.8557	0.6574	1.1107
SD city (geonameid)	0.9169	0.8095	1.0249
SD year	0.3775	0.2037	0.7207

Table A.22 **The effect of sending Internet penetration on anti-regime protest diffusion, interaction with logged distance between sending and receiving cities (city-week resolution, logistic regression).**

	Mean Beta	2.5%	97.5%
Intercept	−4.8190	−5.4169	−4.2296
Internet penetration, receiving	−0.2306	−0.3429	−0.1250
Internet penetration, sending	−0.1969	−0.3624	−0.0282
Distance, sending and receiving (ln)	0.0003	−0.0501	0.0488
Weeks since protest, sending (ln)	−0.3105	−0.3490	−0.2709
Weeks since protest, receiving (ln)	−0.4558	−0.4837	−0.4279
Night lights pc, receiving (ln)	−0.0448	−0.3039	0.1961
Population, receiving (ln)	0.5590	0.3565	0.7727
Regional capital, receiving	1.5827	1.2725	1.8772
National capital, receiving	3.5990	3.1887	4.0368
Civil war, receiving	0.6460	0.4906	0.7961
Internet, send. * Distance	0.0551	0.0303	0.0800
SD country (cowcode)	0.8771	0.6733	1.1453
SD city (geonameid)	0.8879	0.7890	0.9868
SD year	0.3739	0.2049	0.7022

Table A.23 **The effect of sending Internet penetration on anti-regime protest diffusion, interaction with receiving Internet penetration (city-week resolution, logistic regression).**

	Mean Beta	2.5%	97.5%
Intercept	−4.9950	−5.5585	−4.4548
Internet penetration, receiving	−0.1626	−0.3174	−0.0158
Internet penetration, sending	0.1755	0.1035	0.2455
Weeks since protest, sending (ln)	−0.3045	−0.3407	−0.2671
Weeks since protest, receiving (ln)	−0.4552	−0.4834	−0.4262
Night lights pc, receiving (ln)	−0.0533	−0.3299	0.2137
Population, receiving (ln)	0.5400	0.3137	0.7598
Regional capital, receiving	1.6797	1.3467	2.0088
National capital, receiving	3.7122	3.2508	4.1539
Civil war, receiving	0.6461	0.4881	0.7939
Internet, receiving * Internet, sending	−0.0583	−0.1069	−0.0112
SD country (cowcode)	0.8797	0.6681	1.1535
SD city (geonameid)	0.9166	0.8243	1.0230
SD year	0.3668	0.2014	0.7149

Table A.24 **The effect of sending Internet penetration on anti-regime protest diffusion, controlling for reporting (city-week resolution, logistic regression).**

	Mean Beta	2.5%	97.5%
Intercept	−4.9178	−5.4807	−4.3931
Internet penetration, receiving	−0.2926	−0.4026	−0.1764
Internet penetration, sending	0.1042	0.0544	0.1542
Weeks since protest, sending (ln)	−0.2925	−0.3298	−0.2546
Weeks since protest, receiving (ln)	−0.4499	−0.4788	−0.4219
Night lights pc, receiving (ln)	−0.0249	−0.3013	0.2265
Population, receiving (ln)	0.5475	0.3344	0.7625
Regional capital, receiving	1.6770	1.3700	1.9856
National capital, receiving	3.6292	3.1475	4.1457
Civil war, receiving	0.6226	0.4802	0.7673
Report ratio, receiving (ln)	0.5047	0.3954	0.6144
SD country (cowcode)	0.8375	0.6297	1.1313
SD city (geonameid)	0.8867	0.7867	1.0070
SD year	0.3819	0.2044	0.7522

Table A.25 **The effect of sending Internet penetration on anti-regime protest diffusion, interaction with logged weeks since protest in sending city, controlling for reporting (city-week resolution, logistic regression).**

	Mean Beta	2.5%	97.5%
Intercept	−4.9643	−5.4706	−4.4208
Internet penetration, receiving	−0.2916	−0.3989	−0.1820
Internet penetration, sending	0.1463	0.0919	0.2033
Weeks since protest, sending (ln)	−0.2657	−0.3062	−0.2271
Weeks since protest, receiving (ln)	−0.4455	−0.4733	−0.4166
Night lights pc, receiving (ln)	−0.0116	−0.2678	0.2229
Population, receiving (ln)	0.5508	0.3479	0.7412
Regional capital, receiving	1.6755	1.3590	1.9814
National capital, receiving	3.6472	3.2132	4.1213
Civil war, receiving	0.6203	0.4794	0.7539
Report ratio, receiving (ln)	−0.0738	−0.1131	−0.0315
Internet, send. * W. s. protest, send.	0.5095	0.4075	0.6134
SD country (cowcode)	0.8437	0.6479	1.1111
SD city (geonameid)	0.9021	0.7999	1.0157
SD year	0.3938	0.2133	0.7695

Table A.26 **The effect of sending Internet penetration on anti-regime protest diffusion, interaction with logged weeks since protest and repression in sending city, controlling for reporting (city-week resolution, logistic regression).**

	Mean Beta	2.5%	97.5%
Intercept	−5.0235	−5.5846	−4.4595
Internet penetration, receiving	−0.3017	−0.4192	−0.1888
Internet penetration, sending	0.1530	0.0886	0.2146
Weeks since protest, sending (ln)	−0.2292	−0.2807	−0.1779
Last protest repressed, sending	0.1117	−0.0234	0.2259
Weeks since protest, receiving (ln)	−0.4435	−0.4724	−0.4158
Night lights pc, receiving (ln)	−0.0193	−0.2910	0.2150
Population, receiving (ln)	0.5470	0.3288	0.7521
Regional capital, receiving	1.6762	1.3820	1.9933
National capital, receiving	3.6654	3.2222	4.1463
Civil war, receiving	0.6199	0.4807	0.7622
Report ratio, receiving (ln)	0.5171	0.4144	0.6225
Internet, send. * W. s. protest, send.	−0.0992	−0.1477	−0.0513
Internet, send. * Repr., send.	−0.0115	−0.0742	0.0646
W. s. protest, send. * Repr., send.	−0.0787	−0.1495	−0.0110
Internet, send. * W. s. protest, send. * Repr., send.	0.0592	−0.0085	0.1250
SD country (cowcode)	0.8501	0.6431	1.1126
SD city (geonameid)	0.9040	0.8097	1.0167
SD year	0.3919	0.2181	0.7813

Table A.27 **The effect of sending Internet penetration on anti-regime protest diffusion, interaction with logged distance between sending and receiving cities, controlling for reporting (city-week resolution, logistic regression).**

	Mean Beta	2.5%	97.5%
Intercept	−4.8056	−5.3712	−4.2163
Internet penetration, receiving	−0.2374	−0.3508	−0.1263
Internet penetration, sending	−0.2321	−0.3883	−0.0742
Distance, sending and receiving (ln)	−0.0056	−0.0537	0.0384
Weeks since protest, sending (ln)	−0.2960	−0.3317	−0.2581
Weeks since protest, receiving (ln)	−0.4464	−0.4715	−0.4175
Night lights pc, receiving (ln)	−0.0270	−0.2812	0.2182
Population, receiving (ln)	0.5608	0.3486	0.7731
Regional capital, receiving	1.5725	1.2738	1.8806
National capital, receiving	3.5327	3.1008	3.9962
Civil war, receiving	0.6230	0.4646	0.7886
Report ratio, receiving (ln)	0.5127	0.4029	0.6188
Internet, send. * Distance	0.0586	0.0343	0.0831
SD country (cowcode)	0.8593	0.6675	1.0913
SD city (geonameid)	0.8760	0.7809	0.9885
SD year	0.3647	0.2036	0.7010

Chapter 9

REGRESSION TABLES

The following tables show the estimated coefficients for all indicators in the models presented in Chapter 9 on how Internet penetration and national level political institutions affect protest in autocracies. See the figure captions in the main chapter for the references to the corresponding tables in this section.

Table A.28   **The conditional effect of Internet penetration and freedom of association on anti-regime protest occurrence (city-year resolution, logistic regression).**

	Mean Beta	2.5%	97.5%
Intercept	−5.9486	−7.0406	−4.8289
Internet penetration	−0.5181	−0.8620	−0.2183
Freedom of association	2.2638	0.6861	3.7019
Protest in same city (t−1)	0.5486	0.2922	0.7902
Protest in different city (t−1)	0.3007	−0.1242	0.7443
Night lights pc (ln)	0.5194	0.0771	0.9388
Population (ln)	1.1473	0.8397	1.5044
Regional capital	2.2587	1.8173	2.7312
National capital	5.8928	5.0705	6.8796
Civil war	1.4034	1.0490	1.7540
Internet penetration * Freedom of association	−1.0941	−2.0639	−0.0792
SD country (cowcode)	1.4751	1.0829	2.0029
SD city (geonameid)	1.5127	1.3082	1.7338
SD year	0.7404	0.4028	1.4678

Table A.29   **The conditional effect of local Internet penetration and freedom of association on anti-regime protest persistence (city-week resolution, logistic regression).**

	Mean Beta	2.5%	97.5%
Intercept	−4.1646	−4.7968	−3.5348
Internet penetration	0.2237	0.0107	0.4149
Freedom of association	0.9531	0.3274	1.5605
Weeks since protest in same city (ln)	−0.4787	−0.5069	−0.4514
Weeks since protest in different city (ln)	−0.2585	−0.2909	−0.2235
Night lights pc (ln)	0.0291	−0.2192	0.2936
Population (ln)	0.6791	0.4691	0.9105
Regional capital	0.9594	0.5947	1.3354
National capital	2.4349	1.9888	2.8990
Civil war	0.5580	0.4111	0.7148
Internet penetration * Freedom of association	−0.0401	−0.5719	0.5097
SD country (cowcode)	0.6134	0.4419	0.8341
SD city (geonameid)	0.6744	0.5881	0.7708
SD year	0.3278	0.1781	0.6504

Table A.30 **The conditional effect of local Internet penetration and freedom of association on anti-regime protest diffusion (city-week resolution, logistic regression).**

	Mean Beta	*2.5%*	*97.5%*
Intercept	−5.2850	−5.8892	−4.7188
Internet penetration, receiving	−0.2767	−0.3897	−0.1622
Internet penetration, sending	0.0518	−0.0445	0.1523
Freedom of association	0.7536	0.1133	1.3494
Weeks since protest, sending (ln)	−0.3057	−0.3465	−0.2665
Weeks since protest, receiving (ln)	−0.4563	−0.4830	−0.4278
Night lights pc, receiving (ln)	−0.0191	−0.2680	0.2251
Population, receiving (ln)	0.5409	0.3403	0.7317
Regional capital, receiving	1.7008	1.3966	2.0227
National capital, receiving	3.7582	3.2998	4.2663
Civil war, receiving	0.6637	0.5207	0.8197
Internet, sending, * Freedom of association	0.2388	−0.0323	0.4716
SD country (cowcode)	0.7905	0.5713	1.0374
SD city (geonameid)	0.9145	0.8218	1.0196
SD year	0.3748	0.1991	0.6994

SYMMETRIC INTERACTION PLOTS

In this section, we consider the symmetry of the interaction between Internet technology and national-level institutions presented in Chapter 9 by plotting the marginal effect of freedom of association on Internet penetration (Berry, Golder and Milton, 2012). Plotting the symmetric effect allows us to fully examine the evidence for our theoretical argument. To explain the reasoning behind this, consider that any observed relationship between freedom of association and the marginal effect of Internet penetration is accompanied by a wide variety of ways in which the marginal effect of freedom of association varies with Internet penetration (since regression model interactions are inherently symmetric). If the observed pattern of the latter is inconsistent with the underlying conditional theory, this would weaken our evidence. If it is consistent, however, it strengthens the evidence for our theory. Therefore, in Figure A.2, we display the change in probability of *protest occurrence* when freedom of association increases from the 25th to the 75th percentile at different levels of Internet penetration.

The results strengthen the evidence for our finding above. First, we see that the probability of anti-regime protest is higher in cities that are located in liberalized autocracies compared to cities in closed regimes. However, this is only the

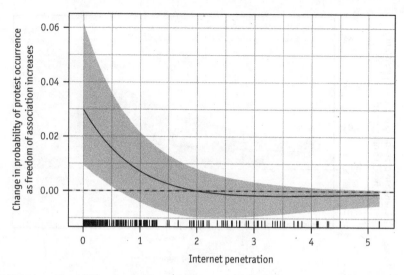

Figure A.2 The conditional effect of Internet penetration and freedom of association on protest occurrence (city-year resolution, logistic regression, 95 percent confidence intervals). Reference: Table A.28.

case in cities with low connectivity. As local Internet penetration increases, the facilitating effect of freedom of association disappears. More specifically, the estimated first differences indicate that when freedom of association increases from the 25th to the 75th percentile in cities *without Internet*, the probability of protest increases by 2.8%. The same comparison for cities *with Internet penetration at the median* yields an (insignificant) increase in protest probability of 0.2%. However, the second difference indicates that the change in probability at different levels of Internet penetration are significantly different. In other words, while countries using traditional strategies of control experience less anti-regime protest than liberalized autocracies, Internet technology can be used to reduce this difference caused by national-level institutions. Indeed, these results indicate that digital technology can substitute for a lack of restrictions on the freedom to organize politically.

In Figures A.3 and A.4, we show similar results for protest *persistence* and *diffusion*. These results also corroborate the findings presented above. In Figure A.3, we see that increasing freedom of association from highly restricted to the median value has a facilitating effect on protest persistence for all levels of Internet penetration. Finally, in Figure A.4, we observe that protest diffusion is more likely in liberalized autocracies, regardless of the Internet penetration level in the sending city.

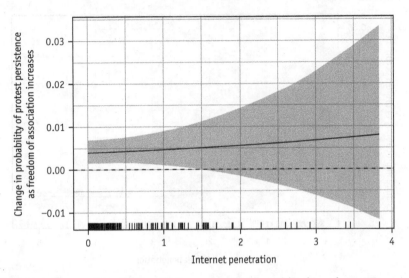

Figure A.3 The conditional effect of Internet penetration and freedom of association on protest persistence (city-week resolution, logistic regression, 95 percent confidence intervals). Reference: Table A.29.

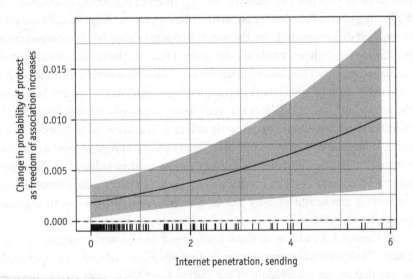

Figure A.4 The conditional effect of Internet penetration in sending cities and freedom of association on protest diffusion (city-week resolution, logistic regression, 95 percent confidence intervals). Reference: Table A.30.

Chapter 1

1. Samizdat (Russian for "self-published") was an important part of dissent against communist regimes during the Cold War. To evade censorship, activists produced independent publications by hand that were circulated among citizens.

Chapter 2

1. While the electoral dimension is fundamental to the distinction between democracy and autocracy, a number of other characteristics are also important, such as political rights and horizontal accountability (Merkel, 2004). We recognize the importance of such characteristics, but also note several problems with adding more dimensions to distinguish democracy from autocracy, in particular with regard to inclusion criteria, replicability, and measurement (Przeworski et al., 2000).
2. Note that "resource mobilization" theory also covers aspects other than the mainly informational ones considered here, such as material and human resources that can contribute to a movement's success.

Chapter 3

1. Here, we refrain from using the term "service" as in computer networking, where it refers to some specific system functionality offered by a network node. Although there is some overlap, we loosely refer to "service" as a particular way in which a user can use a remote functionality or access remote information over the Internet.

Chapter 4

1. Articles containing at least one of the following terms: "protest," "demonstration," "rally," "campaign," "riot," "picket."

2. In order to aggregate the event reports to events, we used information about the date, location, and side of the protesters (e.g., pro-government, anti-government). For example, three event reports with the exact same date, location, and side designation constitute one event.
3. This section uses material from Weidmann and Rød (2015).
4. Other variables omitted for the sake of illustration.
5. For the sake of illustration, the reported average number of participants omits the verbally specified numbers (hundreds and several thousand).
6. The MMAD also contains data on pro-regime protest, which we excluded from our analysis.

Chapter 5

1. These numbers were calculated from a complete dataset at the city-week level with approximately 7 million observations.
2. The MMAD also contains data on pro-regime protest, which are excluded from this analysis.
3. Pakistan and Nepal are excluded from this map since these countries were not classified as autocracies in 2010.
4. Note that this is likely to lead to an underestimation of the effect of Internet penetration on anti-regime protest in the city-week analyses. This is because the lagged variables can induce post-treatment bias: If Internet penetration (measured annually) influences protest occurrence, including lagged variables of protest (measured weekly) means controlling for an outcome of Internet penetration. We prefer to err on side of caution and risk underestimating rather than overestimating the effect.
5. Jackman (2009, see, e.g., Introduction and Chapter 1) also points out that there are differences in the interpretation of results from frequentist and Bayesian analyses. Inference in frequentist analysis is based on the probability that the result will be the same when analyzing a different sample, while inference in Bayesian analysis is based on the distribution of the posterior. In other words, uncertainty is expressed as a data problem in frequentist analysis, while it is expressed as a probabilistic statement about the estimated parameter in Bayesian analysis. Consider a point estimate of 0.8 with 95 percent confidence intervals at 0.7 and 0.9. The interpretation of this result from a frequentist perspective is that the point estimate will be between 0.7 and 0.9 in 95 out of 100 samples. In a Bayesian analysis, the interpretation is that the probability that the point estimate is between 0.7 and 0.9 is 95 percent. While the interpretation of Bayesian results is more intuitive, these differences are not of primary importance for us.

Chapter 6

1. The simulated probabilities were calculated holding the temporal (protest $t-1$) and spatial lags (protest in a different city $t-1$) at 0 and the continuous variables in the model at their means. Regional capital was set to 1, while national capital and civil war were set to 0.
2. The regression output is displayed in Table A.3 in the Appendix.
3. Note also that the point estimate for the fixed Internet penetration term is unchanged compared to the main model (-0.79 and -0.78 in the main model and the varying slopes model; see Tables A.2 and A.3).

Chapter 7

1. We use the terms "continuation" and "persistence" interchangeably.

Chapter 8

1. We also require that the cities in this sample did not experience protest in the past three months to make sure that the results are not contaminated by local protest surges.
2. We split the observations at the median value of Internet penetration in the sending city.
3. The model even strengthens the evidence for this claim by showing that our previous finding is robust to an alternative specification controlling for ongoing protest in the country.
4. The simulated probabilities were calculated by holding population and night lights at their means and time since protest in the receiving city at 12 weeks and sending cities at two weeks. The regional capital indicator was set to 1 while the national capital indicators were set to 0. Finally, civil war was set to 0.

Bibliography

Aday, Sean, Henry Farrell, Marc Lynch, John Sides, John Kelly, and Ethan Zuckerman. 2010. "Blogs and Bullets: New Media in Contentious Politics." *United States Institute of Peace (USIP) Peaceworks* 65.

Ai, Chunrong, and Edward C. Norton. 2003. "Interaction Terms in Logit and Probit Models." *Economics Letters* 80(1):123–129.

Aidt, Toke, Gabriel Leon, and Max Satchell. 2017. "The Social Dynamics of Riots: Evidence from the Captain Swing Riots, 1830–31." Working paper, London School of Economics. Available at http://sticerd.lse.ac.uk/seminarpapers/pspe02052017.pdf.

Almeida, Paul D. 2003. "Opportunity Organizations and Threat-Induced Contention: Protest Waves in Authoritarian Settings." *American Journal of Sociology* 109(2):345–400.

Alvarez, Mike, José Antonio Cheibub, Fernando Limongi, and Adam Przeworski. 1996. "Classifying Political Regimes." *Studies in Comparative International Development (SCID)* 31(2):3–36.

Anderson, John. 1999. *Kyrgyzstan: Central Asia's Island of Democracy?* Amsterdam: Harwood Academic Publishers.

Anderson, Lisa. 2011. "Demystifying the Arab Spring: Parsing the Differences between Tunisia, Egypt, and Libya." *Foreign Affairs* 90(3):2–7.

Andrews, Kenneth T. 2006. "The Dynamics of Protest Diffusion: Movement Organizations, Social Networks, and News Media in the 1960s Sit-Ins." *American Sociological Review* 71(5): 752–777.

Arendt, Hannah. 1973. *The Origins of Totalitarianism*. Orlando, FL: Houghton Mifflin Harcourt.

Aytaç, S. Erdem, Luis Schiumerini, and Susan Stokes. 2018. "Why Do People Join Backlash Protests? Lessons from Turkey." *Journal of Conflict Resolution* 62(6):1205–1228.

Bailard, Catie Snow. 2012. "Testing the Internet's Effect on Democratic Satisfaction: A Multi-Methodological, Cross-National Approach." *Journal of Information Technology and Politics* 9(2):185–204.

Banks, Arthur S. 2011. "Cross-National Time-Series Data Archive. Databanks International." Available at http://www.databanksinternational.com.

Barbera, Pablo, and Thomas Zeitzoff. 2018. "The New Public Address System: Why Do World Leaders Adopt Social Media?" *International Studies Quarterly* 62(1):121–130.

Bardhan, Pranab. 2002. "Decentralization of Governance and Development." *The Journal of Economic Perspectives* 16(4):185–205.

BBC. 2007. "Uzbekistan: Analysts Say Internet Obstructions Make News Blackout Worse." *BBC* December 2.

BBC. 2017. "BBC Monitoring." Electronic resource. Available at https://monitoring.bbc.co.uk/.

Beach, Derek, and Rasmus Brun Pedersen. 2013. *Process-tracing Methods: Foundations and Guidelines.* Ann Arbor, MI: University of Michigan Press.

Beissinger, Mark R. 2007. "Structure and Example in Modular Political Phenomena: The Diffusion of Bulldozer/Rose/Orange/Tulip Revolutions." *Perspectives on Politics* 5(2):259–276.

Bellin, Eva. 2012. "Reconsidering the Robustness of Authoritarianism in the Middle East: Lessons from the Arab Spring." *Comparative Politics* 44(2):127–149.

Benitez-Baleato, Suso, Nils B. Weidmann, Petros Gigis, Xenofontas Dimitropoulos, Eduard Glatz Glatz, and Brian Trammell. 2015. "Transparent Estimation of Internet Penetration using Network Observations." In *Proceedings of the Passive and Active Measurement Conference,* pp. 220–231.

Bennett, W. Lance, Christian Breunig, and Terri Givens. 2008. "Communication and Political Mobilization: Digital Media and the Organization of Anti-Iraq War Demonstrations in the US." *Political Communication* 25(3):269–289.

Berry, William D., Matt Golder, and Daniel Milton. 2012. "Improving Tests of Theories Positing Interaction." *Journal of Politics* 74(3):653–671.

Bertot, John C., Paul T. Jaeger, and Justin M. Grimes. 2010. "Using ICTs to Create a Culture of Transparency: E-government and Social Media as Openness and Anti-corruption Tools for Societies." *Government Information Quarterly* 27(3):264–271.

Bimber, Bruce, Flanagin, Andrew J., and Cynthia Stohl. 2005. "Reconceptualizing Collective Action in the Contemporary Media Environment." *Communication Theory* 15(4):365–388.

Boas, Taylor C. 2006. "Weaving the Authoritarian Web: The Control of Internet Use in Nondemocratic Regimes." In *How Revolutionary Was the Digital Revolution? National Responses, Market Transitions, and Global Technology,* ed. John Zysman, and Abraham Newman. Stanford, CA: Stanford University Press. pp. 361–378.

Boulianne, Shelley. 2009. "Does Internet Use Affect Engagement? A Meta-analysis of Research." *Political Communication* 26(2):193–211.

Boulianne, Shelley. 2015. "Social Media Use and Participation: A Meta-analysis of Current Research." *Information, Communication & Society* 18(5):524–538.

Brancati, Dawn. 2014. "Pocketbook Protests: Explaining the Emergence of Pro-Democracy Protests Worldwide." *Comparative Political Studies* 47(11):1503–1530.

Bratton, Michael, and Nicolas van de Walle. 1992. "Popular Protest and Political Reform in Africa." *Comparative Politics* 24(4):419–442.

Braun, Dietmar, and Fabrizio Gilardi. 2006. "Taking 'Galton's Problem' Seriously: Towards a Theory of Policy Diffusion." *Journal of Theoretical Politics* 18(3):298–322.

Breuer, Anita, Todd Landman, and Dorothea Farquhar. 2015. "Social Media and Protest Mobilization: Evidence from the Tunisian Revolution." *Democratization* 22(4):764–792.

Bryan, Mark L., and Stephen P. Jenkins. 2016. "Multilevel Modelling of Country Effects: A Cautionary Tale." *European Sociological Review* 32(1):3–22.

Bueno de Mesquita, Bruce, Alastair Smith, Randolph M. Siverson, and James D. Morrow. 2003. *The Logic of Political Survival.* Cambridge, MA: MIT Press.

Buhaug, Halvard, and Jan Ketil Rød. 2006. "Local Determinants of African Civil Wars, 1970-2001." *Political Geography* 25(3):315–335.

Buhaug, Halvard, and Kristian Skrede Gleditsch. 2008. "Contagion or Confusion? Why Conflicts Cluster in Space." *International Studies Quarterly* 52:215–233.

Buhaug, Halvard, and Jan Ketil Rød. 2006. "Local Determinants of African Civil Wars, 1970–2001." *Political Geography* 25(3):315–335.

Bunce, Valerie, and Sharon L. Wolchik. 2006. "Favorable Conditions and Electoral Revolutions." *Journal of Democracy* 17(4):5–18.

Bürkner, Paul-Christian. 2017. "brms: An R Package for Bayesian Multilevel Models Using Stan." *Journal of Statistical Software* 80(1):1–28.

Busemeyer, Marius R., and Torben Iversen. 2014. "The Politics of Opting Out: Explaining Educational Financing and Popular Support for Public Spending." *Socio-Economic Review* 12(2):299–328.

Carey, Sabine C. 2006. "The Dynamic Relationship between Protest and Repression." *Political Research Quarterly* 59(1):1–11.

Carothers, Thomas. 2002. "The End of the Transition Paradigm." *Journal of Democracy* 13(1): 5–21.

Carpenter, Bob, Andrew Gelman, Matt Hoffman, Daniel Lee, Ben Goodrich, Michael Betancourt, Michael A. Brubaker, Jiqiang Guo, Peter Li, and Allen Riddell. 2017. "Stan: A Probabilistic Programming Language." *Journal of Statistical Software* 76(1):1–32.

Cederman, Lars-Erik, and Kristian Skrede Gleditsch. 2009. "Introduction to Special Issue on 'Disaggregating Civil War'." *Journal of Conflict Resolution* 53(4):487–495.

Chadwick, Andrew. 2017. *The Hybrid Media System: Politics and Power.* New York: Oxford University Press.

Chadwick, Andrew, and Philip N. Howard. 2009. *Routledge Handbook of Internet Politics.* Oxford: Routledge.

Chaffee, Steven H., and Yuko Miyo. 1983. "Selective Exposure and the Reinforcement Hypothesis: An Intergenerational Panel Study of the 1980 Presidential Campaign." *Communication Research* 10(1):3–36.

Cheibub, José Antonio, Jennifer Gandhi, and James Raymond Vreeland. 2010. "Democracy and Dictatorship Revisited." *Public Choice* 143(1–2):67–101.

Chen, Jidong, Jennifer Pan, and Yiqing Xu. 2016. "Sources of Authoritarian Responsiveness: A Field Experiment in China." *American Journal of Political Science* 60(2):383–400.

Chen, Xi, and William D. Nordhaus. 2011. "Using Luminosity Data as a Proxy For Economic Statistics." *Proceedings of the National Academy of Sciences* 108(21):8589–8594.

Chenoweth, Erica, and Maria J Stephan. 2011. *Why Civil Resistance Works: The Strategic Logic of Nonviolent Conflict.* New York: Columbia University Press.

Clark, David, and Patrick Regan. 2016. "Mass Mobilization Protest Data." Available at http://dx.doi.org/10.7910/DVN/HTTWYL.

Clinton, Hillary. 2010. "Remarks on Internet Freedom." Speech at The Newseum, Washington DC, January 21. Available at http://www.state.gov/secretary/rm/2010/01/135519.htm.

CNN. 2009. "Report: Iran Blocks Facebook ahead of Presidential Election." *CNN* May 23.

Collier, David. 2011. "Understanding Process Tracing." *PS: Political Science & Politics* 44(4): 823–830.

Cook, Scott, and Nils B. Weidmann. 2019. "Lost in Aggregation: Improving Event Coding with Report-level Data." *American Journal of Political Science* 63(1):250–264.

Coppedge, Michael, John Gerring, David Altman, Michael Bernhard, Steven Fish, Allen Hicken, Matthew Kroenig, Staffan I. Lindberg, Kelly McMann, Pamela Paxton, Holli A. Semetko, Svend-Erik Skaaning, Jeffrey Staton, and Jan Teorell. 2011. "Conceptualizing and Measuring Democracy: A New Approach." *Perspectives on Politics* 9(2):247–267.

Crabtree, Charles, Holger L. Kern, and Steven Pfaff. 2018. "Mass Media and the Diffusion of Collective Action in Authoritarian Regimes: The June 1953 East German Uprising." *International Studies Quarterly* 62(2):301–314.

Crabtree, Charles, and Nils B. Weidmann. 2018. "Internet Service Provision under Authoritarian Rule: A Field Experiment in Belarus." SocArXiv. Available at https://doi.org/10.17605/OSF. IO/KUWH2.

Crandall, Robert W., and Charles L. Jackson. 2001. *The $500 Billion Opportunity: The Potential Economic Benefit of Widespread Diffusion of Broadband Internet Access.* Washington, DC: Criterion Economics, LLC.

Croicu, Mihai, and Nils B. Weidmann. 2015. "Improving the Selection of News Reports for Event Coding Using Ensemble Classification." *Research & Politics* 2(4):2053168015615596.

Cunningham, Kathleen, and Nils B. Weidmann. 2010. "Shared Space: Ethnic Groups, State Accommodation and Localized Conflict." *International Studies Quarterly* 54(4):1035–1054.

Dainotti, Alberto, Claudio Squarcella, Emile Aben, Kimberly C. Claffy, Marco Chiesa, Michele Russo, and Antonio Pescapé. 2014. "Analysis of Country-wide Internet Outages Caused by Censorship." *IEEE/ACM Transactions on Networking* 22(6):1964–1977.

Davenport, Christian. 2007a. "State Repression and Political Order." *Annual Review of Political Science* 10(1):1–23.

Davenport, Christian. 2007b. *State Repression and the Domestic Democratic Peace.* New York: Cambridge University Press.

Davenport, Christian, and Patrick Ball. 2002. "Views to a Kill: Exploring the Implications of Source Selection in the Case of Guatemalan State Terror, 1977–1995." *Journal of Conflict Resolution* 46(3):427–450.

Deibert, Ronald, John Palfrey, Rafal Rohozinski, and Jonathan Zittrain. 2008. *Access Denied: The Practice and Policy of Global Internet Filtering.* Cambridge, MA: MIT Press.

Deibert, Ronald, and Rafal Rohozinski. 2010. "Liberation vs. Control: The Future of Cyberspace." *Journal of Democracy* 21(4):43–57.

Diamond, Larry Jay. 2002. "Thinking about Hybrid Regimes." *Journal of Democracy* 13(2):21–35.

Diamond, Larry Jay. 2010. "Liberation Technology." *Journal of Democracy* 21(3):69–83.

Earl, Jennifer. 2011. "Political Repression: Iron Fists, Velvet Gloves, and Diffuse Control." *Annual Review of Sociology* 37(1):261–284.

Earl, Jennifer, Andrew Martin, John D. McCarthy, and Sarah A. Soule. 2004. "The Use of Newspaper Data in the Study of Collective Action." *Annual Review of Sociology* 30(1):65–80.

Eisinger, Peter K. 1973. "The Conditions of Protest Behavior in American Cities." *American Political Science Review* 67(1):11–28.

El-Baradei, Mohamed. 2011a. "The Next Step for Egypt's Opposition." *New York Times* February 10.

El-Baradei, Mohamed. 2011b. "Wael Ghonim: Spokesman for a Revolution." *Time Magazine* April 21.

Elkins, Zachary, and Beth Simmons. 2005. "On Waves, Clusters, and Diffusion: A Conceptual Framework." *The Annals of the American Academy of Political and Social Science* 598(1):33–51.

Evans, Peter B. 2012. *Embedded Autonomy: States and Industrial Transformation.* Princeton, NJ: Princeton University Press.

Fisher, Marc. 2011. "In Tunisia, Act of One Fruit Vendor Sparks Wave of Revolution through Arab World." *Washington Post: Monkey Cage* March 26.

Francisco, Ronald A. 1995. "The Relationship between Coercion and Protest: An Empirical Evaluation in Three Coercive States." *Journal of Conflict Resolution* 39(2):263–282.

Francisco, Ronald A. 2006. "European Protest and Coercion Data." Online resource. Available at http://web.ku.edu/ ronfran/data/index.html.

Freedom House. 2002. "Freedom in the World 2002. Kyrgyzstan." Online resource, available at: https://freedomhouse.org/report/freedom-world/2002/kyrgyzstan.

Freedom House. 2010. "Freedom in the World 2010. Iran." Online resource, available at: https://freedomhouse.org/report/freedom-world/2010/iran.

Freedom House. 2011. "Freedom on the Net 2011. A Global Assessment of Internet and Digital Media." Online resource, available at https://freedomhouse.org/report/freedom-net/freedom-net-2011.

Freedom House. 2012. "Freedom on the Net 2012. A Global Assessment of Internet and Digital Media." Online resource, available at https://freedomhouse.org/report/freedom-net/freedom-net-2012.

Freedom House. 2013. "Freedom on the Net 2013. A Global Assessment of Internet and Digital Media." Online resource, available at https://freedomhouse.org/report/freedom-net/freedom-net-2013.

Freedom House. 2015. "Freedom in the World 2015. Discarding Democracy: Return to the Iron Fist." Online resource, available at https://freedomhouse.org/report/freedom-world/freedom-world-2015.

Freedom House. 2016a. "Freedom in the World 2016. Egypt." Online resource, available at: https://freedomhouse.org/report/freedom-world/2016/egypt.

Freedom House. 2016b. "Freedom in the World 2016. Kyrgyzstan." Online resource, available at: https://freedomhouse.org/report/freedom-world/2016/kyrgyzstan.

Freedom House. 2016c. "Freedom of the Press 2016. The Battle for the Dominant Message." Online resource, available at https://freedomhouse.org/report/freedom-press/freedom-press-2016.

Freedom House. 2016d. "Freedom on the Net 2016. Silencing the Messenger: Communication Apps under Pressure." Online resource, available at https://freedomhouse.org/report/freedom-net/freedom-net-2016.

Freedom House. 2017. "Freedom of the Press 2017. Sudan." Online resource, available at https://freedomhouse.org/report/freedom-press/2017/sudan.

Friedrich, Carl J., and Zbigniew K. Brzezinski. 1965. *Totalitarian Dictatorship*. Cambridge, MA: Harvard University Press.

Friedrich, Robert J. 1982. "In Defense of Multiplicative Terms in Multiple Regression Equations." *American Political Science Review* 26(4):797–833.

Gandhi, Jennifer, and Adam Przeworski. 2007. "Authoritarian Institutions and the Survival of Autocrats." *Comparative Political Studies* 40(11):1279–1301.

Geddes, Barbara. 1999. "What Do We Know about Democratization after Twenty Years?" *Annual Review of Political Science* 2(1):115–144.

Geddes, Barbara, Joseph Wright, and Erica Frantz. 2014a. "Autocratic Breakdown and Regime Transitions: A New Data Set." *Perspectives on Politics* 12(2):313–331.

Geddes, Barbara, Joseph Wright, and Erica Frantz. 2014b. "Autocratic Regimes Code Book, Version 1.2." Available at http://sites.psu.edu/dictators/.

Geddes, Barbara, Joseph Wright, and Erica Frantz. 2018. *How Dictatorships Work*. Cambridge: Cambridge University Press.

Gelman, Andrew, and Donald B. Rubin. 1992. "Inference from Iterative Simulation Using Multiple Sequences." *Statistical Science* 7(4):457–472.

Gelman, Andrew, and Jennifer Hill. 2006. *Data Analysis Using Regression and Multilevel/Hierarchical Models*. New York: Cambridge University Press.

Gelman, Andrew, and Donald B. Rubin. 1992. "Inference from Iterative Simulation Using Multiple Sequences." *Statistical Science* 7(4):457–472.

Gladwell, Malcolm. 2010. "Small Change." *New Yorker* October 4.

Gleditsch, Kristian S., and Nils B. Weidmann. 2012. "Richardson in the Information Age: Geographic Information Systems and Spatial Data in International Studies." *Annual Review of Political Science* 15(1):461–481.

Gleditsch, Kristian Skrede, and Michael D. Ward. 2006. "Diffusion and the International Context of Democratization." *International Organization* 60(4):911–933.

Gleditsch, Nils Petter, Peter Wallensteen, Mikael Eriksson, Margareta Sollenberg, and Håvard Strand. 2002. "Armed Conflict 1946–2001: A New Dataset." *Journal of Peace Research* 39(5):615–637.

Göbel, Christian. 2012. "Das Innovationsdilemma und die Konsolidierung autokratischer Regime [The Innovation Dilemma and the Consolidation of Autocratic Regimes]." *Politische Vierteljahresschrift Sonderheft* 47:132–156.

Gohdes, Anita. 2015. "Pulling the Plug: Network Disruptions and Violence in Civil Conflict." *Journal of Peace Research* 52(3):352–367.

Gohdes, Anita. 2016. *State Repression in the Digital Age*. Book manuscript.

Goldsmith, Jack, and Tim Wu. 2006. *Who Controls the Internet? Illusions of a Borderless World*. New York: Oxford University Press.

Granovetter, Mark. 1978. "Threshold Models of Collective Behavior." *American Journal of Sociology* 83(6):1420–1443.

Grossman, Lev. 2009. "Iran Protests: Twitter, the Medium of the Movement." *Time Magazine* June 17.

Gunitsky, Seva. 2015. "Corrupting the Cyber-commons: Social Media as a Tool of Autocratic Stability." *Perspectives on Politics* 13(1):42–54.

Gurr, Ted R. 1970. *Why Men Rebel*. Princeton, NJ: Princeton University Press.

Hadenius, Axel, and Jan Teorell. 2007. "Pathways from Authoritarianism." *Journal of Democracy* 18(1):143–156.

Hägerstrand, Thorsten. 1967. *Innovation Diffusion as a Spatial Process.* Chicago, IL: University of Chicago Press.

Hammond, Jesse, and Nils B. Weidmann. 2014. "Using Machine-coded Event Data for the Micro-level Study of Political Violence." *Research & Politics* 1(2):2053168014539924.

Harvey, Kerric. 2013. *Encyclopedia of Social Media and Politics.* London: Sage Publications.

Hassanpour, Navid. 2014. "Media Disruption and Revolutionary Unrest: Evidence From Mubarak's Quasi-Experiment." *Political Communication* 31(1):1–24.

He, Baogang, and Mark E. Warren. 2011. "Authoritarian Deliberation: The Deliberative Turn in Chinese Political Development." *Perspectives on Politics* 9(2):269–289.

Hegre, Håvard, and Nicholas Sambanis. 2006. "Sensitivity Analysis of Empirical Results on Civil War Onset." *Journal of Conflict Resolution* 50(4):508–535.

Hegre, Håvard, Tanja Ellingsen, Scott Gates, and Nils Petter Gleditsch. 2001. "Toward a Democratic Civil Peace? Democracy, Political Change, and Civil War, 1816–1992." *American Political Science Review* 95(1):33–48.

Hegre, Håvard, and Nicholas Sambanis. 2006. "Sensitivity Analysis of Empirical Results on Civil War Onset." *Journal of Conflict Resolution* 50(4):508–535.

Hellmeier, Sebastian, Nils B. Weidmann, and Espen Geelmuyden Rød. 2018. "In the Spotlight: Analyzing Sequential Attention Effects in Protest Reporting." *Political Communication* 35(4):587–611.

Hencken Ritter, Emily, and Courtenay R. Conrad. 2016. "Preventing and Responding to Dissent: The Observational Challenges of Explaining Strategic Repression." *American Political Science Review* 110(1):85–99.

Henderson, Vernon, Adam Storeygard, and David N. Weil. 2011. "A Bright Idea for Measuring Economic Growth." *American Economic Review* 101(3):194–199.

Hendrix, Cullen S., and Idean Salehyan. 2015. "No News Is Good News: Mark and Recapture for Event Data when Reporting Probabilities Are Less than One." *International Interactions* 41(2):392–406.

Hess, David, and Brian Martin. 2006. "Repression, Backfire, and the Theory of Transformative Events." *Mobilization: An International Quarterly* 11(2):249–267.

Hibbs, Douglas A. 1973. *Mass Political Violence: A Cross-national Causal Analysis.* New York: Wiley.

Hollyer, James R., B. Peter Rosendorff, and James Raymond Vreeland. 2015. "Transparency, Protest, and Autocratic Instability." *American Political Science Review* 109(4):764–784.

Holmes, Amy. 2012. "There Are Weeks When Decades Happen: Structure and Strategy in the Egyptian Revolution." *Mobilization: An International Quarterly* 17(4):391–410.

Hussain, Muzammil M., and Philip N. Howard. 2013. "What Best Explains Successful Protest Cascades? ICTs and the Fuzzy Causes of the Arab Spring." *International Studies Review* 15(1):48–66.

International Telecommunications Union. 2013. "World Telecommunication/ICT Indicators Database." Available at http://www.itu.int/en/ITU-D/Statistics/Pages/publications/wtid.aspx.

Jackman, Simon. 2009. *Bayesian Analysis for the Social Sciences.* New York: Wiley.

Jenkins, J. Craig, Charles Lewis Taylor, Marianne Abbott, Thomas V. Maher, and Lindsey Peterson. 2012. *The World Handbook of Political Indicators IV.* Columbus, OH: Mershon Center for International Studies, The Ohio State University.

Jenkins, J. Craig, and Thomas V. Maher. 2016. "What Should We Do about Source Selection in Event Data? Challenges, Progress, and Possible Solutions." *International Journal of Sociology* 46(1):42–57.

Jenkins, J. Craig, Charles Lewis Taylor, Marianne Abbott, Thomas V. Maher, and Lindsey Peterson. 2012. *The World Handbook of Political Indicators IV.* Columbus, OH: Mershon Center for International Studies, The Ohio State University.

Kakabadse, Andrew, Nada K. Kakabadse, and Alexander Kouzmin. 2003. "Reinventing the Democratic Governance Project through Information Technology? A Growing Agenda for Debate." *Public Administration Review* 63(1):44–60.

Kalathil, Shanthi, and Taylor C. Boas. 2003. *Open Networks, Closed Regimes: The Impact of the Internet on Authoritarian Rule*. Carnegie Endowment for International Peace.

Kern, Holger Lutz, and Jens Hainmueller. 2009. "Opium for the Masses: How Foreign Media Can Stabilize Authoritarian Regimes." *Political Analysis* 17(4):377–399.

Khamis, Sahar, Paul B. Gold, and Katherine Vaughn. 2012. "Beyond Egypt's 'Facebook Revolution' and Syria's 'YouTube Uprising': Comparing Political Contexts, Actors and Communication Strategies." *Arab Media & Society* 15:1–30.

Khondker, Habibul Haque. 2011. "Role of the New Media in the Arab Spring." *Globalizations* 8(5):675–679.

King, Gary, and Will Lowe. 2003. "An Automated Information Extraction Tool for International Conflict Data with Performance as Good as Human Coders: A Rare Events Evaluation Design." *International Organization* 57(3):617–642.

King, Gary, Jennifer Pan, and Margaret E. Roberts. 2013. "How Censorship in China Allows Government Criticism but Silences Collective Expression." *American Political Science Review* 107(2):1–18.

King, Gary, Jennifer Pan, and Margaret E. Roberts. 2017. "How the Chinese Government Fabricates Social Media Posts for Strategic Distraction, Not Engaged Argument." *American Political Science Review* 111(3):484–501.

King, Gary, and Will Lowe. 2003. "An Automated Information Extraction Tool for International Conflict Data with Performance as Good as Human Coders: A Rare Events Evaluation Design." *International Organization* 57(3):617–642.

Kolsaker, Ailsa, and Liz Lee-Kelley. 2008. "Citizens' Attitudes towards E-government and E-governance: A UK Study." *International Journal of Public Sector Management* 21(7):723–738.

Kriesi, Hanspeter. 2011. Social Movements. In *Comparative Politics*, ed. Daniele Caramani. 2nd ed. New York: Oxford University Press.

Kuran, Timur. 1989. "Sparks and Prairie Fires: A Theory of Unanticipated Political Revolution." *Public Choice* 61(1):41–74.

Kurose, James F., and Keith W. Ross. 2013. *Computer Networking: A Top-down Approach*. 6th ed. Upper Saddle River, NJ: Pearson.

Leetaru, Kalev. 2018. "GDELT: Global Data on Events, Location and Tone." http://gdeltproject.org.

Levitsky, Steven, and Lucan A. Way. 2006. "Linkage versus Leverage. Rethinking the International Dimension of Regime Change." *Comparative Politics* 38(4):379–400.

Levitsky, Steven, and Lucan A. Way. 2010. *Competitive Authoritarianism: Hybrid Regimes after the Cold War*. Cambridge: Cambridge University Press.

Lewis, David. 2008. "The Dynamics of Regime Change: Domestic and International Factors in the 'Tulip Revolution.'" *Central Asian Survey* 27(3–4):265–277.

Lichbach, Mark Irving. 1987. "Deterrence or Escalation? The Puzzle of Aggregate Studies of Repression and Dissent." *Journal of Conflict Resolution* 31(2):266–297.

Linz, Juan J. 2000. *Totalitarian and Authoritarian Regimes*. Boulder: Lynne Rienner Publishers.

Lipset, Seymour Martin. 1959. "Some Social Requisites of Democracy: Economic Development and Political Legitimacy." *American Political Science Review* 53(1):69–105.

Litan, Robert E., and Alice M. Rivlin. 2001. "Projecting the Economic Impact of the Internet." *American Economic Review* 91(2):313–317.

Little, Andrew T. 2016. "Communication Technology and Protest." *The Journal of Politics* 78(1):152–166.

Lohmann, Susanne. 1994. "The Dynamics of Informational Cascades: The Monday Demonstrations in Leipzig, East Germany, 1989–91." *World Politics* 47:42–101.

Lorentzen, Peter. 2014. "China's Strategic Censorship." *American Journal of Political Science* 58(2):402–414.

Lotan, Gilad, Erhardt Graeff, Mike Ananny, Devin Gaffney, Ian Pearce, and Danah Boyd. 2011. "The Revolutions Were Tweeted: Information Flows during the 2011 Tunisian and Egyptian Revolutions." *International Journal of Communication* 5:1375–1405.

Lupia, Arthur, and Gisela Sin. 2003. "Which Public Goods Are Endangered? How Evolving Communication Technologies Affect the Logic of Collective Action." *Public Choice* 117(3-4):315–331.

Lynch, Marc. 2011. "After Egypt: The Limits and Promise of Online Challenges to the Authoritarian Arab State." *Perspectives on Politics* 9(2):301–310.

MacKinnon, Rebecca. 2011. "China's 'Networked Authoritarianism'." *Journal of Democracy* 22(2):32–46.

Magaloni, Beatriz. 2006. *Voting for Autocracy: Hegemonic Party Survival and Its Demise in Mexico.* New York: Cambridge University Press.

Marshall, Monty G., Ted R. Gurr, and Keith Jaggers. 2014. "Polity IV Project: Political Regime Characteristics and Transitions, 1800–2014." Available at http://www.systemicpeace.org/.

Maxmind, Inc. 2014. "GeoIP2 Database." Available at http://www.maxmind.com/en/geoip2-databases.

McAdam, Doug, and Dieter Rucht. 1993. "The Cross-national Diffusion of Movement Ideas." *The Annals of the American Academy of Political and Social Science* 528(1):56–74.

McCarthy, John D., and Mayer N. Zald. 1977. "Resource Mobilization and Social Movements: A Partial Theory." *American Journal of Sociology* 82(6):1212–1241.

Meng, Tianguang, Jennifer Pan, and Ping Yang. 2017. "Conditional Receptivity to Citizen Participation: Evidence from a Survey Experiment in China." *Comparative Political Studies* 50(4):399–433.

Merkel, Wolfgang. 2004. "Embedded and Defective Democracies." *Democratization* 11(5):33–58.

Meyer, David S. 2004. "Protest and Political Opportunities." *Annual Review of Sociology* 30(1):125–145.

Mikhaylov, Slava, Michael Laver, and Kenneth Benoit. 2012. "Misclassification in the Human Coding of Party Manifestos." *Political Analysis* 20(1):78–91.

Moore, Will H. 1998. "Repression and Dissent: Substitution, Context, and Timing." *American Journal of Political Science* 42(3):851–873.

Morozov, Evgeny. 2009. "Iran: Downside to the 'Twitter Revolution'." *Dissent* 56(4):10–14.

Morozov, Evgeny. 2011. *The Net Delusion: The Dark Side of Internet Freedom.* Philadelphia: PublicAffairs.

Morris, Aldon. 1981. "Black Southern Student Sit-in Movement: An Analysis of Internal Organization." *American Sociological Review* 46(6):744–767.

Muller, Edward N., and Erich Weede. 1990. "Cross-National Variation in Political Violence: A Rational Action Approach." *Journal of Conflict Resolution* 34(4):624–651.

Myers, Daniel J. 2000. "The Diffusion of Collective Violence: Infectiousness, Susceptibility, and Mass Media Networks." *American Journal of Sociology* 106(1):173–208.

Nam, Taehyun. 2006. "What You Use Matters: Coding Protest Data." *PS: Political Science & Politics* 39(2):281–287.

National Geophysical Data Center. 2014. "DMSP-OLS Nighttime Lights Time Series, Version 4." Electronic resource. Available at http://ngdc.noaa.gov/eog/dmsp/downloadV4composites.html.

Negroponte, Nicholas. 1995. *Being Digital.* New York: Alfred A. Knopf.

Nisbet, Erik C., Elizabeth Stoycheff, and Katy E. Pearce. 2012. "Internet Use and Democratic Demands: A Multinational, Multilevel Model of Internet Use and Citizen Attitudes about Democracy." *Journal of Communication* 62(2):249–265.

Oak Ridge National Laboratory. 2014. "LandScan Global Population Database." Electronic resource. Available at http://www.ornl.gov/landscan/.

Öberg, Magnus, and Margareta Sollenberg. 2011. Gathering Conflict Information Using News Resources. In *Understanding Peace Research: Methods and Challenges*, ed. Kristine Höglund, and Magnus Öberg. New York: Routledge. pp. 47–73.

O'Brien, Sean P. 2010. "Crisis Early Warning and Decision Support: Contemporary Approaches and Thoughts on Future Research." *International Studies Review* 12(1):87–104.

Olson, Mancur. 1965. *The Logic of Collective Action: Public Goods and the Theory of Groups.* Cambridge, MA: Harvard University Press.

OpenNet Initiative. 2009. "Internet Filtering in Saudi Arabia." Online resource. Available at https://opennet.net/research/profiles/saudi-arabia.

Pearlman, Wendy. 2013. "Emotions and the Microfoundations of the Arab Uprisings." *Perspectives on Politics* 11(2):387–409.

Pierskalla, Jan Henryk. 2010. "Protest, Deterrence, and Escalation: The Strategic Calculus of Government Repression." *Journal of Conflict Resolution* 54(1):117–145.

Powell, G. Bingham. 2000. *Elections as Instruments of Democracy: Majoritarian and Proportional Visions.* New Haven, CT: Yale University Press.

Prior, Markus. 2005. "News vs. Entertainment: How Increasing Media Choice Widens Gaps in Political Knowledge and Turnout." *American Journal of Political Science* 49(3):577–592.

Przeworski, Adam, Michael E. Alvarez, José Antonio Cheibub, and Fernando Limongi. 2000. *Democracy and Development. Political Institutions and Well-Being in the World, 1950–1990.* Cambridge: Cambridge University Press.

Putnam, Robert. 1993. *Making Democracy Work.* Princeton, NJ: Princeton University Press.

Radnitz, Scott. 2006. "What Really Happened in Kyrgyzstan?" *Journal of Democracy* 17(2): 132–146.

Raleigh, Clionadh, Andrew Linke, Håvard Hegre, and Joakim Karlsen. 2010. "Introducing ACLED: An Armed Conflict Location and Event Dataset." *Journal of Peace Research* 47(5):651–660.

Rasler, Karen. 1996. "Concessions, Repression, and Political Protest in the Iranian Revolution." *American Sociological Review* 61(1):132–152.

Reuter, Ora John, and Graeme B. Robertson. 2015. "Legislatures, Cooptation, and Social Protest in Contemporary Authoritarian Regimes." *Journal of Politics* 77(1):235–248.

Robertson, Graeme B. 2010. *The Politics of Protest in Hybrid Regimes: Managing Dissent in Postcommunist Russia.* New York: Cambridge University Press.

Rød, Espen Geelmuyden, Carl Henrik Knutsen, and Håvard Hegre. 2017. "The Determinants of Democracy: A Sensitivity Analysis." Working paper, Uppsala University, University of Oslo, Peace Research Institute Oslo.

Rød, Espen Geelmuyden, and Nils B. Weidmann. 2015. "Empowering Activists or Autocrats? The Internet in Authoritarian Regimes." *Journal of Peace Research* 52(3):338–351.

Ruggeri, Andrea, Theodora-Ismene Gizelis, and Han Dorussen. 2012. "Events Data as Bismarck's Sausages? Intercoder Reliability, Coders' Selection, and Data Quality." *International Interactions* 37(1):340–361.

Ruijgrok, Kris. 2017. "From the Web to the Streets: Internet and Protests under Authoritarian Regimes." *Democratization* 24(3):498–520.

Salehyan, Idean, Cullen S. Hendrix, Jesse Hamner, Christina Case, Christopher Linebarger, Emily Stull, and Jennifer Williams. 2012. "Social Conflict in Africa: A New Database." *International Interactions* 38(4):503–511.

Schock, Kurt. 2005. *Unarmed Insurrections: People Power Movements in Nondemocracies.* Minneapolis, MN: University of Minnesota Press.

Schrodt, Philip A. 2001. "Automated Coding of International Event Data Using Sparse Parsing Techniques." Paper presented at the Annual Meeting of the International Studies Association.

Schrodt, Philip A., and Deborah J. Gerner. 1994. "Validity Assessment of a Machine-coded Event Data Set for the Middle East, 1982–1992." *American Journal of Political Science* 38(3): 825–854.

Sears, David O., and Jonathan L. Freedman. 1967. "Selective Exposure to Information: A Critical Review." *Public Opinion Quarterly* 31(2):194–213.

Shirky, Clay. 2008. *Here Comes Everybody: The Power of Organizing without Organizations.* New York: Penguin Group.

Shirky, Clay. 2011. "The Political Power of Social Media." *Foreign Affairs* 90(1):28–41.

Smith, Todd Graham. 2014. "Feeding Unrest: Disentangling the Causal Relationship between Food Price Shocks and Sociopolitical Conflict in Urban Africa." *Journal of Peace Research* 51(6):679–695.

Soule, Sarah A. 1997. "The Student Divestment Movement in the United States and Tactical Diffusion: The Shantytown Protest." *Social Forces* 75(3):855–882.

Starbird, Kate, and Leysia Palen. 2012. (How) Will the Revolution Be Retweeted? Information Diffusion and the 2011 Egyptian Uprising. In *Proceedings of the ACM 2012 Conference on Computer Supported Cooperative Work*, pp. 7–16.

Stein, Elizabeth A. 2017. "Are ICTs Democratizing Dictatorships? New Media and Mass Mobilization." *Social Science Quarterly* 98(3):914–941.

Steinert-Threlkeld, Zachary C. 2017. "Spontaneous Collective Action: Peripheral Mobilization during the Arab Spring." *American Political Science Review* 111(2):379–403.

Sundberg, Ralph, and Erik Melander. 2013. "Introducing the UCDP Georeferenced Event Dataset." *Journal of Peace Research* 50(4):523–532.

Sutton, Jonathan, Charles R. Butcher, and Isak Svensson. 2014. "Explaining Political Jiu-Jitsu: Institution-building and the Outcomes of Regime Violence against Unarmed Protests." *Journal of Peace Research* 51(5):559–573.

Svolik, Milan. 2012. *The Politics of Authoritarian Rule.* New York: Cambridge University Press.

Tarrow, Sidney. 1989a. *Democracy and Disorder: Social Conflict, Political Protest and Democracy in Italy, 1965–1975.* New York: Oxford University Press.

Tarrow, Sidney. 1989b. *Struggle, Politics, and Reform: Collective Action, Social Movements, and Cycles of Protest.* Ithaca, NY: Center for International Studies, Cornell University.

Temirkulov, Azamat. 2008. "Informal Actors and Institutions in Mobilization: The Periphery in the 'Tulip Revolution.'" *Central Asian Survey* 27(3–4):317–335.

Temirkulov, Azamat. 2010. "Kyrgyz 'Revolutions' in 2005 and 2010: Comparative Analysis of Mass Mobilization." *Journal of Nationalism and Ethnicity* 38(5):589–600.

Ten Eyck, Toby A. 2001. "Does Information Mattter? A Research Note on Information Technologies and Political Protest." *The Social Science Journal* 38:147–160.

Teorell, Jan. 2010. *Determinants of Democracy: Explaining Regime Change in the World, 1972–2006.* Cambridge: Cambridge University Press.

Theocharis, Yannis, Will Lowe, Jan W. Van Deth, and Gema García-Albacete. 2015. "Using Twitter to Mobilize Protest Action: Online Mobilization Patterns and Action Repertoires in the Occupy Wall Street, Indignados, and Aganaktismenoi Movements." *Information, Communication & Society* 18(2):202–220.

Tilly, Charles. 1978. *From Mobilization to Revolution.* Reading: Addison-Wesley.

Toft, Monica Duffy, and Yuri M. Zhukov. 2015. "Islamists and Nationalists: Rebel Motivation and Counterinsurgency in Russia's North Caucasus." *American Political Science Review* 109(2):222–238.

Tolbert, Caroline J., and Karen Mossberger. 2006. "The Effects of E-government on Trust and Confidence in Government." *Public Administration Review* 66(3):354–369.

Tollefsen, Andreas Forø, Håvard Strand, and Halvard Buhaug. 2012. "PRIO-GRID: A Unified Spatial Data Structure." *Journal of Peace Research* 49(2):363–374.

Tsai, Lily L. 2007. "Solidary Groups, Informal Accountability, and Local Public Goods Provision in Rural China." *American Political Science Review* 101(2):355–372.

Tucker, Joshua A. 2007. "Enough! Electoral Fraud, Collective Action Problems, and Post-Communist Colored Revolutions." *Perspectives on Politics* 5(3):535–551.

Tucker, Joshua A., Yannis Theocharis, Margaret E. Roberts, and Pablo Barbera. 2017. "From Liberation to Turmoil: Social Media and Democracy." *Journal of Democracy* 28(4):46–59.

Tufekci, Zeynep, and Christopher Wilson. 2012. "Social Media and the Decision to Participate in Political Protest: Observations from Tahrir Square." *Journal of Communication* 62(2): 363–379.

Ulfelder, Jay. 2005. "Contentious Collective Action and the Breakdown of Authoritarian Regimes." *International Political Science Review* 26(3):311–334.

US Agency for International Development (USAID). 2016. "Demographic and Health Surveys." http://dhsprogram.com/.

Varshney, Ashutosh. 2003. "Nationalism, Ethnic Conflict, and Rationality." *Perspectives on Politics* 1(1):85–99.

Walgrave, Stefaan, W. Bennett, Jeroen Van Laer, and Christian Breunig. 2011. "Multiple Engagements and Network Bridging in Contentious Politics: Digital Media Use of Protest Participants." *Mobilization: An International Quarterly* 16(3):325–349.

Wang, Dan J., and Sarah A. Soule. 2016. "Tactical Innovation in Social Movements: The Effects of Peripheral and Multi-issue Protest." *American Sociological Review* 81(3):517–548.

Way, Lucan. 2008. "The Real Causes of the Color Revolutions." *Journal of Democracy* 19(3):55–69.

Weidmann, Nils B. 2009. "Geography as Motivation and Opportunity: Group Concentration and Ethnic Conflict." *Journal of Conflict Resolution* 53(4):526–543.

Weidmann, Nils B. 2015. "Communication, Technology, and Political Conflict: Introduction to the Special Issue." *Journal of Peace Research* 52(3):263–268.

Weidmann, Nils B. 2016. "A Closer Look at Reporting Bias in Conflict Event Data." *American Journal of Political Science* 60(1):206–218.

Weidmann, Nils B., Suso Benitez-Baleato, Philipp Hunziker, Eduard Glatz, and Xenofontas Dimitropoulos. 2016. "Digital Discrimination: Political Bias in Internet Service Provision across Ethnic Groups." *Science* 353(6304):1151–1156.

Weidmann, Nils B., Doreen Kuse, and Kristian Skrede Gleditsch. 2010. "The Geography of the International System: The CShapes Dataset." *International Interactions* 36(1):86–106.

Weidmann, Nils B., and Espen Geelmuyden Rød. 2015. "Making Uncertainty Explicit: Separating Reports and Events in the Coding of Violence and Contention." *Journal of Peace Research* 52(1):125–128.

Weidmann, Nils B., and Sebastian Schutte. 2017. "Using Night Light Emissions for the Prediction of Local Wealth." *Journal of Peace Research* 54(2):125–140.

Weidmann, Nils B., Suso Benitez-Baleato, Philipp Hunziker, Eduard Glatz, and Xenofontas Dimitropoulos. 2016. "Digital Discrimination: Political Bias in Internet Service Provision across Ethnic Groups." *Science* 353(6304):1151–1156.

Winsnes, Eirik. 2014. "Telenor sensurerte internett på ordre fra militæret i Thailand [Telenor censored the Internet on order from the military in Thailand]." *Aftenposten* June 17.

Wolfsfeld, Gadi, Elad Segev, and Tamir Sheafer. 2013. "Social Media and the Arab Spring: Politics Comes First." *International Journal of Press/Politics* 18(2):115–137.

Wright, Robin. 2009. "Iran's Protesters: Phase 2 of Their Feisty Campaign." *Time Magazine* July 27.

Zheng, Yongnian. 2007. *Technological Empowerment: The Internet, State, and Society in China.* Stanford, CA: Stanford University Press.

Index